U.S. Intellectual Property Law and Policy

U.S. Intellectual Property Law and Policy

Edited by
Hugh Hansen
Fordham University School of Law, USA

QUEEN MARY STUDIES IN INTELLECTUAL PROPERTY

Edward Elgar
Cheltenham, UK • Northampton, MA, USA

Published by
Edward Elgar Publishing Limited
Glensanda House
Montpellier Parade
Cheltenham
Glos GL50 1UA
UK

Edward Elgar Publishing, Inc.
136 West Street
Suite 202
Northampton
Massachusetts 01060
USA

A catalogue record for this book is available from the British Library

ISBN–13: 978 1 84542 866 2
ISBN–10: 1 84542 866 8

Printed and bound in Great Britain by MPG Books Ltd, Bodmin, Cornwall

Contents

Introduction

The six essays within this volume identify and address the key principles and policies with regard to the protection of intellectual property in the United States. A comprehensive analysis of the entire body of U.S. intellectual property law would not be possible in a volume of this size. Rather six of the best, if not the best, professors of intellectual property law in the United States have been invited to write essays that illustrate important principles and policies in U.S. law.

The essays collected here illustrate the several themes which are recurrent in many current debates concerning U.S. law and policy on intellectual property law. First, the need for a constant expansion of protectable subject matter is critically analyzed, especially in relation to trademark and patent laws. Secondly, all essays discuss a critical jurisprudential issue: have the legislature and the judiciary taken sufficient consideration of the different economic and constitutional rationales of intellectual property protection when extending the scope of intellectual property protection? Finally, all essays suggest a tentative agenda as to the future direction for both Congress and the courts to adopt in light of the new technological changes which have affected all areas of intellectual property protection equally.

A detailed precis of each essay is set out below.

COPYRIGHT LAW

Professor Jane Ginsburg, in her essay entitled *From Having Copies to Experiencing Works: The Development of an Access Right in U.S. Copyright Law* critically analyzes an important issue under the 1998 Digital Millennium Copyright Act: the right of the copyright owner to control digital access to copyrighted works, and the corollary right of users to the exceptions and limitations to such a right. She notes that, in the digital context, if the copyright owner can control access, it can condition how a user apprehends the work, and whether a user may make any further copies. Access control can at the same time vastly increase the availability of copyrighted works by encouraging online licensing of the viewing or hearing of works and yet constrain the users' ability to convert the 'de-materialized' form to physical copies. The essay questions whether end users in this environment will continue to want their own copies and the consequences of this type of control to the developments in copyright law.

Ginsburg's essay takes as its premise the eventual disappearance of physical copies for some kinds of works. The author stresses that the access right is a crucial right within the 21st century and, moreover, it is part of the copyright regime authorized by the Constitution: the access right does not and should not supplant copyright but should be viewed as being an integral part of copyright. As such, it should serve the policies of copyright that provide economic incentive to creativity and protect the fruits of an author's intellectual labor. Nevertheless, the scope of the access right may need to be modified so as simultaneously to provide strong protection against unauthorized *initial* acquisition of a copy of a protected work, and to allow for circumvention in order to engage in fair uses, once the copy has been lawfully acquired. Interestingly, she suggests that fair use defenses to an access right are not or should not be fully coextensive with fair use defenses to traditional copyright infringement claims. Some traditional defenses may apply, others may not and, importantly, new ones may evolve in the context of experience with digital online distribution. Without further examination as to the appropriate fair use limitation required to rein back the access right, the right may become, Ginsburg warns, an über-copyright.

Professor Pamela Samuelson states that the principal aim of her essay, *Economic and Constitutional Influences on Copyright Law in the United States*, is to acquaint European intellectual property specialists with two interrelated influences – economics and the Constitution – that affect the formation and interpretation of American copyright law. Thus, one perspective of U.S. copyright law is that it has ostensibly moved toward greater conformity with the long-standing norms of European authors' rights jurisdictions. This is especially true if one takes into account the stance of the Supreme Court in the 1991 decision of *Feist Publications, Inc. v. Rural Telephone Service Co.*, the reduction in the role of formalities, the nation's adherence to the Berne Convention, and the cooperation between the United States and the European Union in pushing for higher international standards for intellectual property rights.

Despite these signs of convergence, however, Samuelson's contention is that the copyright law in the United States and the European Union Member States will continue to differ crucially due to two underlying influences on the development and interpretation of U.S. copyright law: the economic basis and the constitutional basis. Thus, the utilitarian rationale for U.S. copyright law manifests itself in the work-made-for-hire doctrine, the fair use doctrine, the scope of protection for computer programs and the narrow scope of moral rights law. The employment of economic thinking in these areas may prefigure even wider uses in the future.

In relation to the constitutional influences, Samuelson notes how Article 1, section 8, clause 8 (the 'Intellectual Property Clause') in the U.S. Constitution imposes an intellectual framework on the thinking of American intellectual property specialists that differs profoundly from the conceptual framework of authors' rights laws. The author notes that Justice O'Connor, in the seminal *Feist* decision, invoked that clause 13 times in her reasoning as to why the 'sweat of the brow' doctrine is an impermissible basis for copyright protection. Copyright law is further molded and influenced by other constitutional provisions such as the First Amendment (on Free Speech), the Supremacy Clause (which forbids the preemption of federal copyright law by state law), and the Eleventh Amendment (which limits the power of federal courts to order state governments to pay damages for infringement of federal intellectual property rights).[1]

Because the Constitution is such a seminal document in the U.S. legal tradition, Samuelson concludes that its influence seems likely to 'abide over time'.

PATENT LAW

In her essay, State Street *or Easy Street: Is Patenting Business Methods Good For Business?*, Professor Rochelle Cooper Dreyfuss critically examines whether the patenting of business methods is good for business, through discussion of Judge Giles S. Rich's 1998 decision in *State Street Bank & Trust Co. v. Signature Financial Group, Inc.* Professor Dreyfuss notes that this is an important decision for two reasons: (1) it simplifies the law on patenting of software; and (2) it reads patent law to encompass protection for business methods. Her essay focuses on the latter part of the decision as it has the potential, Dreyfuss contends, to affect the efficient operation of the United States' marketplace as a whole.

Dreyfuss argues that none of the standard rationales for patent protection support protecting business methods. They do not spur business progress and are, in effect, like patenting nature. She argues that they jeopardize the competitive process itself. Although Judge Rich understood that business method

[1] Florida Prepaid Postsecondary Educ. Expense Bd. v. College Sav. Bank, 527 U.S. 627, 119 S.Ct. 2199 (1999).

patents pose special dangers, he believed, nevertheless, that the patent prerequisites of novelty and nonobviousness (inventiveness)would prevent the patenting of most business methods. Dreyfuss refutes this presumption. For instance, she states, a major limitation of the novelty requirement is that the U.S. Patent and Trademark Office has a difficult time in examining in areas where the birth of the field is not coextensive with the beginning of patenting, i.e., there is a great deal of prior art and practice beyond the reach of the patent examiner. The fact that some business method patents could be held invalid at a later date does not solve the problem because of the *in terrorem* effect of such patents. After considering ways in which to limit the *State Street* decision, Dreyfuss then examines whether such forms of limiting *State Street* would violate TRIPs and concludes that they would not. Her contention is that the best method of limiting *State Street* is to recognize the patents in the computer programs used to implement business methods. She finds that this form of protection does not carry the same danger as business method patents *per se*.

Professor Jay Thomas tackles a completely different yet important issue in his essay, *Discharging the Canons of Claim Construction: Exercises in Interpretation at the United States Court of Appeals for the Federal Circuit*. He posits that the issues of patent eligibility and claim interpretation plague the United States Patent and Trademark Office and the U.S. Court of Appeals for the Federal Circuit, thus diminishing the value of judicial precedent, defeating the expectations of industry, and denying the elusive goal of certainty. Thomas sees in recent years a devolution of patent eligibility principles 'to the extent that our rudderless regime appears ready to appropriate any tangible manifestation of human intelligence', such as mathematical algorithms, mental steps, printed matter and methods of doing business. On the other hand, Thomas notes that the Federal Circuit's jurisprudence with regard to claim interpretation has become increasingly doctrinal, with the court aggressively controlling the reader's encounter with the text of patent claims and erecting more detailed interpretational protocols to augment longstanding canons of claim construction. This strategy has, however, been marked by failures as some canons have been short-lived and others are surrounded by ambiguities of application.

Thomas's essay focuses on the latter 'crisis' in claim interpretation and the Federal Circuit's increasing tendency toward interpretative rulemaking. Although Thomas agrees with the Federal Circuit that a goal of the patent system is consistent interpretation of claims, he criticizes the increasing canonization of claim interpretation protocols and seeks to rationalize new techniques for enhancing textual understanding within the patent community. He begins by reviewing the essential U.S. law governing patent claim construction including the seminal *Markman* and *Warner-Jenkinson* opinions. He then offers a critical assessment of the U.S. experience with proscriptivism in claim interpretation. He concludes that the best hope for clarity in claim construction lies in the 'continued acculturization of patent attorneys towards the reading and writing of texts.' The patent bar, he suggests, provides an ideal community in which administrative rulemaking, training and dialogue could develop shared norms of interpretation. Thomas also calls upon the U.S. courts to unpack the traditional equivalency formula that balances protection to the patentee with notice to competitors for, by inquiring into whether an accused infringer had actual notice of the asserted claims, courts can better assess the scope of protection that should be afforded to those claims.

TRADEMARK LAW

Both the essays on U.S. trademark law and policy analyze the growing concern as to the justificatory basis for the expansion of the protection of trademarks.

Professor Marshall Leaffer, in *Sixty Years of the Lanham Act: The Decline and Demise of Monopoly Phobia*, discusses the dramatic change in attitude towards trademark protection which was at its lowest in the 1930s and the lead-up to the passage of the Lanham Act in 1946, and at its highest in the passage of the federal dilution statute in 1996. Today, Marshall states, the prevailing view is the one that views a strong trademark system, based upon a property rights model, as one that enhances competition and consumer welfare. Trademark law is more than a mere indication of origin. It recognizes that a trademark owner's investment in goodwill in creating a mark should be protected against third party use that would undermine its distinctiveness.

Professor Leaffer looks to three on-going processes that progressively led to these doctrinal and policy changes in the law of trademarks. The first is what he terms 'the new economic learning', demonstrating the competitive benefits of product differentiation and the fundamental role trademarks play in this process as a means of reducing search costs to consumers. The second force has been the way goods are sold in a global marketplace and the phenomenon of a restructured multinational industrial organization. The third force for change is the push toward harmonization of intellectual property worldwide, as manifested in TRIPs. Taken as a whole, he concludes that these three factors have all but dissipated the trademark monopoly phobia and have led to an expanded concept of property rights trademarks. To illustrate the progression of trademark protection, Leaffer concentrates on two substantive areas of trademark law: (1) the relaxation of restraints associated with the assignment and licensing of trademarks; and (2) the expanding scope of the likelihood of confusion doctrine. He concludes that the passage of the Federal Dilution Act reflects the inevitable culmination of a long process whose rationale became ever more persuasive during the first sixty years of the Lanham Act. While Professor Leaffer concludes that the development of greater protection in trademark law is essentially pro-competitive and comports with the new realities in commercial life that exist today, he notes that there remains a persistent skepticism about trademarks prevalent in the academic community.

Professor Graeme Dinwoodie posits a similar thesis in his essay entitled *The Rational Limits Of Trademark Law*. In his view, there have been three areas of expansion within U.S. law that have tested the limits of trademark law: (1) the development of virtual unlimited trademark subject matter; (2) the right to protect against dilution when there is no competition and no likelihood of confusion; and (3) the new protection regime against cybersquatting. Dinwoodie finds that each of these expansions represents ad hoc delineation of trademark holders' rights in response to the latest perceived social or economic threats to brand values. In order to establish rational limits on the scope of protection, however, Dinwoodie argues that trademark law must develop by explicit reference to its basic purposes. Although these purposes are somewhat general in nature, attention to them will ground trademark law in present commercial reality without foreclosing adaptation to future social developments. Since trademark law is 'mercantile' law, it must be shaped and limited by the market forces that it seeks to regulate.

Dinwoodie identifies the classic avoidance of consumer confusion as the appropriate purpose that will be sufficient to serve the legitimate concerns of producers and consumers, especially as this rationale has been implemented in recent years by U.S. courts. Use of avoidance of consumer confusion in 'purposive analysis' to determine the scope of trademark law would offer the possibility of more generous trade dress protection than under the current approach of the Supreme Court; limit the scope of protection more narrowly than Congress has done in the federal dilution statute; and offer a workable vehicle for addressing conflicts between domain names and trademark rights without detailed congressional legislation.

Dinwoodie concludes that this purposive analysis would guide courts in establishing rational limits to trademark law; otherwise, trademark law might simply represent a vehicle for mere rent seeking. As trademark rights come to protect subject matter traditionally protected by other intellectual property regimes such as copyright or patent, the strength of trademark law's claim to regulate such matter in a manner different from those other regimes rests upon the policies of trademark law retaining a distinctive hue. Purposive analysis will ensure that trademark law retains that characteristic coloration.

H.C.H.

Chapter 1

State Street or Easy Street: Is Patenting Business Methods Good For Business?

*Rochelle Cooper Dreyfuss**

American patent law has changed significantly in this half-century. Interestingly, many of these changes have something to do with Judge Giles S. Rich. He was the principal drafter of the Patent Act of 1952[1] and he was one of the first judges to sit on the Court of Appeals for the Federal Circuit, which was established in 1982 to consolidate adjudication of patent appeals.[2] Possibly the longest-sitting federal judge,[3] Rich died in June 1999, not long after he made yet another profound mark on the law of invention: the decision in *State Street Bank & Trust Co. v. Signature Financial Group, Inc.*[4] *State Street* is important for two reasons. It simplifies the law on patenting software and it reads patent law to encompass protection for business methods. Because of the contemporary significance of the computer industry, there will surely be much technical discussion of the first aspect of the opinion, the protection accorded to mathematical algorithms. This paper will, however, mainly examine the second half of the decision, for it has

* Pauline Newman Professor of Law, NYU School of Law. I wish to thank John Peschel and Jessica Litman for comments on earlier drafts, the Filomen D'Agostino and Max E. Greenberg Research Fund of the New York University School of Law for its financial support, and Robert Pfister, NYU Class of '01, for research assistance.

1 The 1952 Patent Act (as amended) can be found at 35 U.S.C. §§ 1–375. All subsequent statutory references are to 35 U.S.C. unless otherwise specified.

2 Pub. L. No. 97–164, 96 Stat. 25. The jurisdiction of the court is set out in 28 U.S.C. § 1295(a).

3 See Jon Thurber, 'Obituaries: Judge Giles Rich; Patent Law Authority', Los Angeles Times, June 14 (1999), at p. 22; Richard A. Oppel, Jr., 'Giles S. Rich, Oldest Active Federal Judge, Dies at 95', N.Y. Times, June 12 (1999), at p. A13, col. 1. Judge Rich was first appointed to the bench in 1956 and remained on active status until the time of his death 43 years later.

4 149 F.3d 1368 (Fed. Cir. 1998), cert. denied, 119 S.Ct. 851 (1999).

the potential to affect not only a single (albeit important) industry, but also the efficient operation of the marketplace as a whole. Imagine, for example, how the airline industry might now be structured if the first company to offer frequent flyer miles had enjoyed the sole right to award them; how differently mergers and acquisitions would be financed (and how rich Michael Milken might have become) if the use of junk bonds had been protected by a patent. *State Street*'s position on business method patenting bears considerable scrutiny indeed.

To be sure, exclusive rights are important devices for encouraging creativity, for they provide innovators with a mechanism for earning returns on their activities. But at the same time, they impose many of the social costs that are standardly associated with monopolies, such as high prices, deadweight losses and misallocation of resources. In general, these effects are balanced by the narrowness of the protection afforded. Patent law draws a dichotomy between ideas and applications, and only the latter are protected. Moreover, the ambit of protection is circumscribed in that patents focus on particular end products or specific processes for producing such products. Despite the range of equivalents also encompassed, it has been rare for an intellectual property right to adhere to an advance so unique that the rights holder dominates the marketplace. In most cases, the availability of near substitutes keeps the practices of the patentee under such tight control that the right of exclusivity falls far short of an economic monopoly.[5] And even if some monopolization does occur, it is short-lived: after the patent term expires, the product or process protected becomes subject to normal market forces.[6]

[5] See, e.g., Howard T. Markey, 'Why Not the Statute', 65 J. Pat. Off. Soc'y 331, 331–32 (1983) (arguing that the term 'monopoly' is a misnomer for patents); Jamesbury Corp. v. Litton Indus. Prod., Inc., 756 F.2d 1556, 1559 (Fed. Cir. 1985) (Nies, C.J.) (holding that it is reversible error to call the patent a monopoly in jury instructions); Schenck, A.G. v. Norton Corp., 713 F.2d 782, 786 n.3 (Fed. Cir. 1983) (Markey, C.J.) ('[i]t is but an obfuscation to refer to a patent as "the patent monopoly" or to describe a patent as an exception to the general rule against monopolies.'); Nickola v. Peterson, 580 F.2d 898, 914 n.25 (6th Cir. 1978) (Markey, C.J.) ('a valid patent never confers a monopoly in the traditional historical, anticompetitive sense') (citation omitted), cert. denied, 440 U.S. 961 (1979). See also Giles S. Rich, 'Are Letters Patent Grants of Monopoly?', 15 W. New. Eng. L. Rev. 239 (1993) (arguing that they do not take anything from the public because they cover only material that is newly invented); U.S. Dep't of Justice, Antitrust Guidelines for the Licensing of Intellectual Property § 2.2 (1995) (patents should not be presumed to confer market power).

[6] New patents endure for 20 years, measured from the date on which the application for protection is filed; some old patents have a life of 17 years from issuance, § 154(a) (2).

In contrast, business methods exist on something of a meta level, one step abstracted from products and their manufacture. Because they deal with the way that transactions in their fields are accomplished, they affect not just products in competition, but also the competitive process itself. By exerting potentially distortive constraints on that process, exclusive rights in business methods undermine the very basis for assuming that patents are not monopolies. Indeed, there are some business methods – frequent flyer programs are one example – that have an especially disruptive effect. They establish relationships (between suppliers and customers, or among customers and products) that are difficult for outsiders to break. In those situations, the impact of the patent could extend well beyond the time when the right expires or is invalidated.

To be sure, Judge Rich understood that business method patents pose special dangers. He believed, however, that other patent prerequisites, such as novelty and nonobviousness (inventiveness),[7] had blocked business method patenting in the past; he also thought that these requirements would prevent the patenting of most business methods in the future.[8] Given that frequent flyer miles are not too different from the trading stamps that were ubiquitous to the supermarkets of the 1960s,[9] and that there were junk bonds long before Michael Milken convinced the financial community that they were legitimate investment vehicles, there is intuitive appeal to his argument.

Nonetheless, there are significant reasons to discount its force. First, a judge's inability to imagine new business methods does not tell us very much because the developments that meet the requirements of patent law are precisely those that cannot be foreseen easily. Second, this sort of analysis merely changes the time frame in which the problem arises. Thus, supermarket trading stamps probably *do* anticipate frequent flyer miles, but so what? Had a patent on a method of procuring consumer loyalty through coupon awards been patented in its time, it too would have disrupted an industry. Third, the Patent and Trademark Office (PTO) has a notoriously difficult time examining in areas where the birth of the field is not coextensive with the advent of patenting, for in those cases there is a great deal of prior art and practice beyond the reach of the examiner corps. Thus, courts need to tread carefully when bringing new subject matter into the

[7] §§ 102 & 103.

[8] See *State Street*, 149 F.3d at 1375–76. See also Judge Newman's dissenting opinion in In re Schrader, 22 F.3d 290, 297–98 (Fed. Cir. 1994), on which Judge Rich relied, *State Street*, 149 F.3d at 1375 n.10.

[9] Cf. Blue Chip Stamps v. Manor Drug Stores, 421 U.S. 723 (1975) (addressing securities problems arising from the merger of trading stamp companies pursuant to an antitrust consent decree).

ambit of protection. Indeed, the business method patents that have issued to date demonstrate the problem, for many arguably encompass well-known methods.

Finally, and most important, by focusing the discussion on questions like novelty, the court managed to obscure the real issue, which is whether there is a good justification for extending patents to business methods. In fact, the failure to offer such a rationale is consistent with other contemporary developments in intellectual property law, such as the increased protection now afforded to celebrities' enterprises through expanding rights of publicity and to trademark owners through federal adoption of anti-dilution law.[10] However, the absence of a justification is problematic. It raises a question about whether there is a real need to impose the costs of exclusivity on the public. Without a theory of harm, determining the scope of infringement is impossible. And if the only reason for creating exclusivity is to provide a way for someone to make more money, then protection becomes a one-way ratchet – once it adheres, it can only expand.

This paper takes the position that patenting business methods is different enough from other forms of patenting to warrant careful consideration of its value. After describing *State Street* and the limitations suggested by Judge Rich and others, I examine the possible rationales for recognizing business method patents. I conclude that none of the standard theories support exclusive rights in this area, and that the benefits of protection are far outweighed by the costs. I end with a look at how business method patenting could be controlled, and at whether taking steps to deny protection to business methods would violate the United States' obligations under the TRIPS Agreement.[11]

I. *STATE STREET BANK & TRUST CO. v. SIGNATURE FINANCIAL GROUP, INC.*

The invention at issue in *State Street* is a data processing system (Hub and Spoke®), which keeps track of individual mutual fund investments ('spokes')

[10] Publicity remains a state law claim, although there is a federal initiative afoot; dilution is now recognized as a federal tort in § 43(c) of the Lanham Act, 15 U.S.C. § 1125(c). See generally, Rochelle Cooper Dreyfuss, 'We are Symbols and Inhabit Symbols, So Should We Be Paying Rent? Deconstructing the Lanham Act and Rights of Publicity', 20 Colum.-VLA J. L. & Arts 123 (1996).

[11] Agreement on Trade-Related Aspects of Intellectual Property Rights, Apr. 15, 1994, Marrakesh Agreement Establishing the World Trade Organization, Annex 1C, 33 I.L.M. 1197 (1994) [hereinafter the TRIPS Agreement].

that have been pooled into a single portfolio (a 'hub'). Pooling allows each spoke to capture economies of scale and tax advantages. Each spoke's value can be easily calculated – its share of the total assets, taking into account the fluctuation in the hub's investments as well as the individual spoke's percentage ownership. The patent, U.S. Pat. No. 5,193,056 (the 056) entitled 'Data Processing System for Hub and Spoke Financial Services Configuration', issued in 1993. By the time of the suit, it had been assigned by its inventor, R. Todd Boes, to Signature Financial.

After issuance, State Street, which is in the same financial services business as Signature, attempted to negotiate a license to utilize the system. When these negotiations broke down, State Street filed an action against Signature for a declaration of patent invalidity. In the district court, Judge Saris granted summary judgment in State Street's favor. Reasoning that the patent basically covered a mathematical algorithm that did not effectuate any sort of physical transformation, she found that the claims were not statutory subject matter within § 101 of the Act, as defined through the so-called *Freeman-Walter-Abele* trilogy of cases and their progeny, as well as the relevant PTO guidelines.[12] Further, because the claims were drafted in means language,[13] Judge Saris viewed the patent as drawn

[12] Id. at 513–14. See In re Freeman, 573 F.2d 1237 (C.C.P.A. 1978); In re Walter, 618 F.2d 758 (C.C.P.A. 1980); In re Abele, 684 F.2d 902 (C.C.P.A. 1982); In re Alappat, 33 F.3d 1526 (Fed. Cir. 1994); and Arrhythmia Research Technology, Inc. v. Corazonix Corp., 958 F.2d 1053, 1060 (Fed. Cir. 1992). The PTO examination guidelines can be found at the PTO's home page, http://www.uspto.gov.

[13] The patent contains six claims, of which only the first is independent. As reproduced in the district court opinion, State Street Bank and Trust Co. v. Signature Financial Group, Inc., 927 F. Supp. 502, 508–09 (D. Mass. 1996), it reads as follows:

(1) A data processing system for managing a financial services configuration of a portfolio established as a partnership, each partner being one of a plurality of funds, comprising:
(a) computer processor means for processing data;
(b) storage means for storing data on a storage medium;
(c) first means for initializing the storage medium;
(d) second means for processing data regarding assets in the portfolio and each of the funds from a previous day and data regarding increases or decreases in each of the funds, assets and for allocating the percentage share that each fund holds in the portfolio;
(e) third means for processing data regarding daily incremental income, expenses, and net realized gain or loss for the portfolio and for allocating such data among each fund;

cont./

to a process – a method of doing business – and held that, 'as established by a series of older cases, business methods are unpatentable abstract ideas'.[14] She concluded her analysis as follows:

> If Signature's invention were patentable, any financial institution desirous of implementing a multi-tiered funding complex modeled on a Hub and Spoke configuration would be required to seek Signature's permission before embarking on such a project. This is so because the '056 Patent is claimed sufficiently broadly to foreclose virtually any computer-implemented accounting method necessary to manage this type of financial structure. Indeed, during licensing negotiations, Signature informed State Street that any data processing system designed to perform book accounting for a multi-tiered fund based on a partnership portfolio configuration would infringe the '056 Patent . . .
>
> In effect, the '056 Patent grants Signature a monopoly on its idea of a multi-tiered partnership portfolio investment structure; patenting an accounting system necessary to carry on a certain type of business is tantamount to a patent on the business itself. Because such abstract ideas are not patentable, either as methods of doing business or as mathematical algorithms, the '056 Patent must fail.[15]

The Federal Circuit reversed. After pointing out that this patent should be analyzed as directed to a machine because the means language was supported by the structure in the written description (but noting that the characterization does not matter in any event),[16] Judge Rich proceeded to eradicate a century of statutory gloss. First, he did away with the physical transformation limitation Judge Saris saw in prior cases, stating instead that any transformation of data that produces a useful, concrete and tangible result is patentable. In this case, the final share price calculated for each spoke qualified because it was recorded and relied upon by regulatory authorities and traders.[17] Next, Judge Rich attacked the notion that business methods have long been considered unpatentable. Noting

cont./

(f) fourth means for processing data regarding daily net unrealized gain or loss for the portfolio and for allocating such data among each fund; and

(g) fifth means for processing data regarding aggregate year-end income, expenses, and capital gain or loss for the portfolio and each of the funds.

14 927 F. Supp. at 516 (citing Loew's Drive-In Theatres, Inc. v. Park-In Theatres, Inc., 174 F.2d 547, 552 (1st Cir.), cert. denied, 338 U.S. 822 (1949); Hotel Security Checking Co. v. Lorraine Co., 160 F. 467, 469 (2d Cir. 1908)).

15 Id.

16 149 F.3d at 1371–72.

17 Id. at 1373.

that prior cases citing this principle could all be explained on other grounds – for lack of novelty or nonobviousness, or because the patent claimed an algorithm that was analyzed under the now-rejected physical transformation test – he held that business method claims should be treated, just like other process claims are treated, as subject matter qualifying for patent protection.[18]

State Street is a welcome decision in certain respects. Most patent lawyers would agree that the computer cases on which Judge Saris relied were confusing. Even with the additional wisdom provided by subsequent opinions, the outcomes of *Freeman-Walter-Abele* analyses were unpredictable. If software innovations are to be eligible for patent protection, then streamlining the analysis and examining these applications with the same tools utilized for other inventions makes sense. Thus, if algorithms are principles of nature – and reasonable minds can differ on this point[19] – then the first part of the case is correct; algorithms should be treated as other rules of nature are handled. The rule itself is not considered patentable, but applications are.

At the same time, however, there is substantial reason to be concerned with the second part of the opinion. The point Judge Saris made in the quotation reproduced above is an important one: recognizing the validity of the Signature patent may be tantamount to giving Signature a monopoly to this field. If pooling mutual funds, while getting special tax treatment and achieving economies of scale, turns out to be an extraordinarily useful vehicle for holding investments in the stock market – and especially if the software covered by the patent is, as some suspect, the only way to efficiently execute calculations required by the law of partnership taxation[20] – then the patent could allow Signature to dominate the financial servicing business. Worryingly, Signature could assume that position even if it is not as good at providing financial services as are its competitors.[21] To the extent that the economy turns on the effective matching of investment funds and business needs, giving Signature this preferred position

[18] Id. at 1375–77.

[19] See, e.g., Rochelle Cooper Dreyfuss & Roberta Rosenthal Kwall, *Intellectual Property* 610 (2d ed. 2004).

[20] Leo I. Raskind, 'The Bad Business of Business Method Patents', 10 Ford. Intell'l Prop'y Media & Entertainment L.J. 57 (1999), points out that Boes patterned the program on the examples provided by Treasury Department in the regulations accompanying the partnership taxation rules, Treas. Reg. § 1.704; 26 U.S.C.§§ 701–06.

[21] The issue, of course, will be whether the cost of Signature's investment mistakes will exceed the advantages accruing from the patented method.

could negatively impact on the market for money.[22] Yet Judge Rich dismissed Judge Saris's concern with the comment, '[a]ssuming the above statement to be correct, it has nothing to do with whether what is claimed is statutory subject matter'.[23]

The basis for this statement is difficult to discern. As the drafter of the Act he was interpreting, Judge Rich could be expected to show a keen interest in implementing the statutory text. Thus, it is understandable that he would believe it 'improper to read limitation into § 101 on the subject matter that may be patented where the legislative history indicates that Congress clearly did not intend such limitations'.[24] But notwithstanding this observation, Judge Rich also acknowledged that the Supreme Court has identified whole categories of unpatentable subject matter – laws of nature, natural phenomena and abstract ideas.[25] These are no more mentioned in § 101 of the Patent Act than is an exception for business methods.[26] Significantly, they are outside the scope of patenting for much the same reason that Judge Saris gave for excluding business methods. They too are valuable advances and it would be useful to have a legal device to encourage their discovery. But they are not patentable because the

[22] For another example, see Patent No. 5,905,974 ('Automated Auction Protocol Processor'), which involves interactive matching technology, bringing together multiple buyers and sellers in a single transaction. The patent was issued just as several exchanges announced plans to market bonds in this way. An infringement action was filed soon after issuance. Cf. Paul A. Beck, 'State Street Bank Causes Shock Waves in Banking and Financial Industry', 147-JAN Pittsburgh Legal J. 7 (1999) (suggesting that since over 1000 patents in the finance area have already issued, bankers and financiers are going to need to pay close attention to infringement issues).

[23] 149 F.3d at 1377. See also AT&T Corp. v. Excel Communications, Inc., 172 F.3d 1352 (Fed. Cir. 1999) (finding a billing method patentable).

[24] 149 F.3d at 1377.

[25] Id. at 1373, citing Diamond v. Diehr, 450 U.S. 175, 185 (1981).

[26] To see the omission, it is useful to contrast § 101with the 17 U.S.C. § 102, the analogous provision of the Copyright Act. Subsection (b) provides:

> In no case does copyright protection for an original work of authorship extend to any idea, procedure, process, system, method of operation, concept, principle, or discovery, regardless of the form in which it is described, explained, illustrated, or embodied in such work.

Another illuminating comparison is to Art. 52(a) of the European Patent Convention, Convention on the Grant of European Patents, as amended by the Decision of the Administrative Council of European Patent Organizations of December 21, 1978, reprinted in 13 I.L.M. 268, which specifically exempts 'discoveries, scientific theories and mathematical methods'.

patent would be too disruptive. Principles, nature and ideas are at the apex of the knowledge pyramid; every application flows from them. If a discovery at the apex could be privately owned, innovation in the fields of that discovery would be substantially impeded.[27] The common law has, accordingly, read into § 101 limits that are not in the text: certain categories of discovery – those that control other discoveries, that are at a meta level of inventiveness – cannot be patented because the benefits of spurring their advance through patenting are outweighed by the costs that exclusivity imposes.

Perhaps the reason Judge Rich ignored the nonstatutory nature of the exceptions for discoveries about nature, yet required statutory guidance before he was willing to exempt business methods, is that he thought the former exemptions were also wrong – that the Supreme Court should not have read limits on patenting nature into the expansive language of § 101. But that position – the notion that meta-natural principles are patentable – would effectuate such a complete shift in the way that all of intellectual property law has been administered, it is impossible to think Judge Rich would present the case for it so obliquely. More likely, he simply did not equate the concern over business methods with the problem of patenting nature. After all, all patents are distortionary in the sense that the exclusive right to make, use, sell, offer to sell and import a particular invention gives every patentee an advantage over his or her competitors. Seeing the problem of business methods as different in kind – or as on a different level – can be difficult.

There is, however, an interesting parallel where this point may be somewhat easier to discern. Thus, there has been considerable debate in the last few years on whether sports moves should be patentable. Games are patentable,[28] sporting equipment is patentable,[29] training methods are patentable,[30] and human maneuvers[31] are patentable. It is, therefore, not much of a stretch to argue that a new grip for delivering a baseball to home plate, a new position for

27 See, e.g., the discussion in Gottschalk v Benson, 409 U.S. 63, 67–71 (1972).

28 See, e.g., Alpex Computer Corp. v. Nintendo Co. Ltd., 102 F.3d 1214 (Fed. Cir. 1996) (home video game system); Patent No. 5,816,819 ('Zodiac Game and Method of Play').

29 See, e.g., Patent No. 5,772,540 ('Racket for Tennis or the Like Game'); Patent No. 5,827,167 ('Three-Piece Wound Golf Ball').

30 See, e.g., Patent No. 5,639,243 ('Training Apparatus Method for Training an Athlete, and Method for Producing a Training Device'), which is patented by the famed pitcher Nolan Ryan.

31 See, e.g., Patent No. 5,498,162 ('A Method for Demonstrating a Lifting Technique').

performing the high jump,[32] or a new type of golf swing[33] should also be eligible for protection.[34] Nonetheless, many who have considered the idea of patenting sports moves reject it.[35] Sporting events are, in essence, comparisons – they identify which team or athlete is the best. But these events can provide true measures of ability only when each participant is tested under the same conditions. Thus, while it may be possible for someone outside a game to own rights in the equipment or even in the game itself, those who are inside the event cannot be put into that privileged position. They would be too likely to refuse to license their competitors freely. Since the integrity of the event quite literally requires a level playing field, the intuition that patents in moves are inappropriate to sport is virtually unavoidable.

The same can be said for business methods. They too set the conditions under which products and manufacturing processes are compared. Thus, just as sporting events identify the best athlete and team, market competition determines the best use for particular resources. And just as patenting sports moves presents problems that are different in kind from other patents touching the sporting industry, patents on business methods are different in kind from patents on the products and processes that are used in business. Now, in organized sports, the reality is that patent protection is not much of a problem. Sporting events have

[32] Lest the argument be made that no sports moves are novel enough for protection, it is worth noting that when Dick Fosbury first high jumped on his back – producing the 'Fosbury flop' – it revolutionized the high jump, see Jeffrey A. Smith, 'It's Your Move – No It's Not! The Application of Patent Law to Sports Moves', 70 U. Colo. L. Rev. 1051, 1071–72 (1999), who also cites as inventive enough to patent Candy Cumming's curve ball, Chris Evert's two-handed back-hand tennis swing, and Pete Gogolak's soccer-style football kick., id. at 1087 n.139.

[33] Cf. Patent No. 5,616,089 ('Method of Putting').

[34] The first to discuss intellectual property protection for sport moves in print was probably Robert M. Kunstadt, F. Scott Kieff & Robert G. Kramer, 'Are Sports Moves Next In IP Law?', Nat'l L.J., May 20, 1996, at C2. Several others have recently jumped into the fray, see, e.g., Smith, supra note 32; Carl A. Kukkonen, 'Be a Good Sport and Refrain From Using My Patented Putt: Intellectual Property Protection for Sports Related Movements', 80 J. Pat. Off. Soc'y 808 (1998); Wm. Tucker Griffith & Ekaterina Godeeva, 'Beyond the Perfect Score: Protecting Routine-Oriented Athletic Performance with Copyright Law', 30 Conn. L. Rev. 675 (1998).

[35] See, e.g., Smith, supra note 32; John R. Thomas, 'The Patenting of the Liberal Professions', 40 B.C. L. Rev. 1139, 1181 (1999).

organizers and the organizers have the power to ban particular products;[36] they can use that same authority to bar the use of patented moves (or products) unless the patentee grants licenses on a reasonable basis to all participants. But in capitalist systems, markets are guided by unseen hands. Consequently, reacting to market failure with compulsory licenses is not so easy.[37] If a level playing field in business is considered a necessity, then a way to limit the reach of *State Street* is essential.

II. LIMITING *STATE STREET*

The first question, then, is whether *State Street*'s rule of law can be limited. This subsection examines the internal constraints posited by the *State Street* court itself; the next two look at limitations suggested by commentators and enacted by Congress.

a. Judge Rich's View

As noted earlier, Judge Rich's own notion was that other conditions of patentability will act as an effective safeguard. In a sense, he is right: there are formidable barriers to receiving patents. They are awarded only to products and processes that are useful,[38] that are new,[39] and that represent such significant advances that the ordinary artisan could not have bridged the gap between prior learning and the subject matter claimed.[40] Moreover, the patent must

[36] See, e.g., Major League Baseball, Official Baseball Rules, Rule 1.10(a), available on the Internet at http://www.majorleaguebaseball.com/u/baseball/mlbcom/headquarters/rules1.htm. (bats must be made of wood (and not of aluminum)). See also Rule 1.17 ('Manufacturers who plan innovative changes in baseball equipment for professional baseball leagues should submit same to the Official Playing Rules Committee prior to production'). Cf. the advertisement at http://www.igadget.com/igadget/pirgolbal.html (golf balls that 'Fly So Far the USGA Wants Them BANNED!').

[37] If nothing else, it might be barred by Art. 31 of the TRIPS Agreement, which limits the availability of compulsory licenses in patents covered by the Agreement. Whether patents on business methods are covered is an issue discussed in the text at notes 123–128, infra.

[38] § 101.

[39] § 102.

[40] § 103.

demonstrate that the patentee was aware (in possession) of the inventive features of the claimed invention[41] and included enough detail to allow ordinary persons in the field to make and practice it.[42] There are, however, several reasons to expect that these requirements will not significantly limit the impact of business method patents.

One consideration is structural. As a normative matter, the requirements for a patent are trans-substantive – they are meant to be interpreted in the same way in every case, no matter what the underlying invention is about.[43] In fact, however, applying these rules is not always a simple matter, and the field to which an invention pertains can play a significant role in determining how the requirements are understood. For example, although usefulness is presumed in most fields, the utility of an invention intended to serve as human therapy receives considerable attention from the PTO, possibly because of the negative connotations associated with the term 'patent medicine'.[44] Likewise, the inventiveness required for a chemical patent is colored by the strong relationship between the structure of elements and molecules and their chemical action: without a special sub-rule on the predictability of the found activity, few chemical compositions could be patented.[45] That kind of relaxed standard, when applied to biotechnology, has in turn arguably been responsible for the evolution of rather strict claiming and enablement rules.[46] Similar results can be expected for business

[41] § 112, ¶2.

[42] § 112, ¶1.

[43] See, e.g., Wilson Sporting Goods Co. v. David Geoffrey & Associates, 904 F.2d 677 (Fed. Cir. 1990) (the doctrine of equivalents is to be interpreted the same way in all fields). The term used in text comes from civil procedure, where it is applied to court rules, which are the same no matter what the field of the dispute.

[44] See, e.g., U.S. Patent and Trademark Office, Utility Examination Guidelines, 60 Fed. Reg. 36263 (July 14, 1995).

[45] See, e.g., the history of chemical nonobviousness traced in In re Dillon, 919 F.2d 688 (Fed. Cir. 1990). See also Robert P. Merges and John F. Duffy, 'Patent Law and Policy: Cases and Materials' 806–808 (3d ed. 2002).

[46] See, e.g., Genentech, Inc. v. Novo Nordisk A/S, 108 F.3d 1361 (Fed. Cir. 1997) (arguing, in essence, that if inventions are considered patentable because of the unpredictability in the field, then the enablement standard must take unpredictability into account. See also Fiers v. Sugano, 984 F.2d 1164 (Fed. Cir. 1993) (description). The scope of patent protection is similarly affected by specific facts about the field of the invention, see Thomas & Betts Corp. v. Litton Systems, Inc., 720 F.2d 1572 (Fed. Cir., 1983) ('while a pioneer invention is entitled to a broad range application of the doctrine of equivalents, an invention representing only a modest advance over the prior art is given a more restricted (narrower range) application of the doctrine').

methods: once it is unequivocally decided that this is an area appropriate for patenting, the rules on what counts as novel, nonobvious and adequately described will be shaped in a way that assures that business methods will receive protection. Indeed, it is difficult to argue that things should be otherwise. If the patent system is construed as intended to encourage and reward innovation in business methods, then interpreting the requirements for protection in a manner that effectively bars patenting would be inappropriate.

A second problem with Judge Rich's limit is conceptual. There is little inherent content to terms like novelty and nonobviousness or their sub-rules. Whether an advance meets these requirements can depend on how the invention is perceived. Consider, for example, the fate of three cases argued on the same day and decided together: *Graham v. John Deere Co.*, *Calmar, Inc. v. Cook Chemical Co.*,[47] and *United States v. Adams*.[48] All involved devices based on known elements, and in each case, the question was whether the development was sufficiently inventive. In the first two, the Supreme Court said no; in the third, yes. It is so difficult to pinpoint the distinction between these cases that the following two explanations for the outcomes have been suggested. The first goes to the way the cases were argued. *Adams* concerned a battery, and counsel for the patentee used an embodiment of the invention to keep a light bulb illuminated during the entire oral argument; the other advocates did not provide such a concrete way to appreciate the inventions at issue (a plough and a spray can). The other explanation concerns the conceits of the bench: *Deere* and *Calmar* involved mechanicals, where every man likes to think he is an expert,[49] but *Adams* involved a battery, and even judges know to keep their hands off electricity. To be sure, these explanations are offered somewhat facetiously. But given the difficulty in drawing the line between new and old or inventive and obvious, it is quite likely that, at the very least, business methods that utilize computers will survive, no matter how little they differ from the way the same business was conducted prior to computerization. The 'black box' of the programmed equipment is likely to function like the electric battery, giving courts a focus for finding novelty and inventiveness.[50] And if it becomes clear that this feature can

[47] These cases were decided together, Graham v. John Deere Co., 383 U.S. 1 (1966).

[48] 383 U.S. 39 (1966).

[49] This is something American television audiences will recognize as the Tim Allen syndrome, named for a comedian known for hurting himself with tools.

[50] See, e.g., Diamond v. Diehr, 450 U.S. 175 (1981), upholding a patent on a method of curing rubber that used well-established equations and measuring devices, but used a computer for doing needed calculations. The case was decided on subject matter grounds, but the Court betrayed no concern that the process lacked inventiveness.

make the case, patent lawyers will be sure to include a computer in every method claimed.[51]

The final factor is practical. Examination is strictly *ex parte*. Although the PTO requires disclosure of material that reflects on novelty and nonobviousness, the applicant need reveal only 'information known to that individual to be material to patentability'.[52] This duty is mainly enforced through infringement actions. At that point – when inequitable conduct is raised as a defense to enforcement – the issue will be whether there was an *intent* to deceive; simple failure to disclose is not a bar to enforcing a patent.[53] Accordingly, the integrity of the examination system relies heavily on material the examiners find themselves. What is readily available to them is the PTO library, which mostly consists of information that, at the time it is gathered, 'aid[s] the officers in the discharge of their duties',[54] including 'publications in all fields of applied technology' and 'publications of many important scientific and technical societies', as well as foreign and domestic patents.[55] The upshot is that until a field becomes the subject of patenting, little information about it will be collected. Despite the fact that individuals have been finding new business methods for centuries, the longstanding objection to business method patents means that examiners have little information at hand with which to supplement representations made by the applicant. Thus, it is likely that many patents will issue on known business methods.

Indeed, experience shows this to be the case. Although the number of applications for business method patents soared after *State Street* was decided,[56] the Federal Circuit's review of business method patenting came about because the PTO had been allowing patents on computer-implemented business methods

[51] See also note 65, infra, on the relationship between narrow construction and obviousness determinations.

[52] 37 C.F.R. 1.56. The duty to disclose is based on § 115 (applicant must swear he believes himself to be the true inventor).

[53] To sustain a defense of inequitable conduct, the infringer must show that the information withheld is material and that it was an intent to deceive, see, e.g., Kingsdown Medical Consultants, Ltd. v. Hollister, Inc., 863 F.2d 867 (Fed. Cir. 1988), cert. denied, 490 U.S. 1067 (1989).

[54] § 8.

[55] U.S. Patent and Trademark Office, Manual of Patent Examining Procedure (MPEP) § 901.06.

[56] See, e.g., '"Boom" in Business Method Patent Filings Has Followed the "State Street" Ruling, PTO Says', 57 Pat., Trademark, & Copyright J. 115 (Dec. 10, 1998).

ever since computer-related inventions generally started receiving protection.[57] Thus, there is a substantial record available for inspection. It does not make for assuring reading, for many of the methods on which patents have been awarded involve familiar activities. Every commentator has a favorite example. Professor Jay Thomas notes a method for running a remodeling business that comprises cataloging ideas, presenting the ideas to a client, allowing the client to select an idea, and then preparing a visual image of the selection.[58] Francisc Keeley-Domokos cites a method for debiting customers' money accounts for purchases.[59] My own is an architectural scheme for eliminating hallways by placing the staircases on the outside of buildings.[60] But the patent most observers have focused on is the one issued to Jay Walker on a system that allows buyers to post firm offers on purchases. (Priceline uses it to match travelers with airline tickets and hotel rooms.[61]) It inspired the following comment from a reader of *Forbes* Magazine:

> Cool! Jay Walker has apparently patented the 'business method' known as a Dutch auction – a method by which the U.S. Treasury sells hundreds of billions of dollars' worth of securities each year.[62]

As worrisome are statistics compiled by Gregory Aharonian on the quality of examination. He has counted the number of references, other than patents, that are cited in issued patents. He finds that, on average, only three such references

[57] See, e.g., Paine, Webber, Jackson & Curtis, Inc. v. Merrill Lynch, Pierce, Fenner & Smith, Inc., 564 F.Supp. 1358, 1369 (D. Del. 1983) (upholding a patent on a computerized system of combining a package of popular financial services). For a study of the precise chronology, see Thomas, supra note 35.

[58] Thomas, supra note 35, at 1162, citing Patent No. 5,668,736.

[59] Patent No. 5,724,424, Francisc Marius Keeley-Domokos, State Street Bank & Trust Co. v. Signature Financial Group, Inc., 14 Berkeley Tech. L.J. 153, 172 n.96 (1996).

[60] U.S. Patent No. 5,761,857 ('Lot Configuration and Building Position and Method for Residential Housing') (issued June 6, 1998).

[61] U.S. Patent No. 5,794,207 ('Method and Apparatus for a Cryptographically Assisted Commercial Network System Designed to Facilitate Buyer-Drive Conditional Purchased Offers') (issued Aug. 11, 1998), see, e.g., John Kasden, 'Obviousness and New Technologies' [GW Symposium]; Wendy R. Leibowitz, 'Patents and E-Business', Nat'l L.J., June 14, 1999, A 19, col. 1; Josh McHugh, 'Barbed Wire on the Internet', Forbes, May 17, 1999, p. 183; Dyan Machan, 'An Edison for a New Age? Jay Walker Becomes an Instant Millionaire', Forbes, May 17, 1999, at p. 178.

[62] Byron L. Winn, 'Readers Say', Forbes, May 31, 1999, at p. 18. Of course, whether Uncle Sam is infringing depends on the scope of protection afforded.

are included in software-implemented business concept patents.[63] Since most business knowledge is not found in patents, the PTO's reliance on so few pieces of nonpatent prior art is indicative of the trouble that lies ahead, and of the futility of believing in novelty and nonobviousness as significant safeguards, at least as an initial matter.

Now, it must be admitted that the situation may not turn out quite so bleak. The patents allowed so far were issued while the Federal Circuit was considering 'first generation' business method cases – answering the question of whether these methods constitute the subject matter of protection. Second generation decisions, on issues involving the other requirements for patent protection, may send the PTO the message that better examination is imperative.[64] And even if these decisions do not dim the PTO's enthusiasm for allowing these patents, third generation cases – on what constitutes infringement – will surely limit their reach in significant ways.[65] Moreover, since the Internet now allows potential challengers to gather patent-defeating prior art expeditiously, the worst of the patents may be cheap to eliminate after they become public knowledge.[66]

[63] Gregory Aharonian, Internet Patent News Service, June 23, 1999, available from srctran@world.std.com and patent-news@world.std.com. Aharonian is the publisher of this service. In addition, he is the Principal of Source Translation and Optimization, which maintains a database of software and hardware prior art and conducts searches in the fields of computer, telecommunication, electronic and bio-technologies. There was only one nonpatent prior art reference cited for Patent No. 5,905,974, described in note 22 supra.

[64] See, e.g., AT&T Corp. v. Excel Communications, Inc., 52 USPQ 2d 1865 (D. Del., Oct 25, 1999), holding the patent on a billing method invalid for anticipation and obviousness, based on a similar billing method utilized by MCI Friends & Family. Significantly, however, this opinion was subsequently reversed, 172 F. 3d 1352 (Fed. Cir. 1999). This was the patent at issue in the first business method case that the Federal Circuit decided after *State Street*, see note 23 supra. But cf. Dickinson v. Zurko, 527 U.S. 150 (1999), holding that at least some decisions of the PTO are entitled to more deference than they have formerly been accorded.

[65] See, e.g., Wang Laboratories, Inc. v. America Online, Inc., 197 F.3d 1377 (Fed. Cir. 1999), holding that AOL's 'favorite places' feature, which utilizes bitmapping protocols, does not infringe Wang's character-based system. Note, however, that narrow claims construction is a two-edged sword. It will reduce the scope of what is considered infringing, but it will also narrow the availability of prior art for anticipation and obviousness purposes.

[66] See, e.g., http://www.w3.org/1999/04/P3P-PatentBackground.html, found from the home page of the World Wide Web Consortium (W3C), www.w3.org. Concerned

But even these steps will not fully cure the problem. Patents have *in terrorem* effects. Even if it appears likely that a patent could be held invalid or narrowed during adjudication, rivals may refrain from practicing the invention because of the high cost of litigation. Thus, even if patent lawyers know that the United States Treasury is not infringing on Walker's business method patent, there are drawbacks to allowing the public – including the rather sophisticated readers of *Forbes* Magazine – to think that Dutch auctions are now private property. Why invest in a business where litigation is likely when there are other places to put one's money?

In addition, even an invalid patent can have significant impact, particularly during the time that a new industry is emerging. An example is a patent on a method for conducting electronic commerce. Such a patent creates important advantages, such as a superior ability to attract investors. These advantages will confer a degree of immunity during the shake-out period that is sure to come, when many start-up Internet companies merge, get acquired or go under. True, the patent may later be held invalid or construed narrowly. But by that time, the result may not matter: the advantage of exclusivity (and the disadvantage of being closed out of the method) will have largely been realized.

Successful challenge is likewise not much help in fields where there are lock-in problems (that is, where the cost of switching products is nontrivial) or where network effects are prevalent (that is, in fields where the value of a product rises as the number of adopters increases). After all, once a patented business method locks in users or creates a substantial network, then new entrants face an uphill battle. That battle will be no less difficult if the patent is later invalidated or held unenforceable.

Consider, for example, Amazon.com's '1-click' technology, which is patented and subject to litigation.[67] The system permits customers to enter their billing and shipping data on their first visit to the site. When they return, they are greeted by name, given suggestions for purchases based on their previous activity at the site, and then, when they are ready to check out, they can do so with a single click – no information given before needs to be re-entered. One advantage to the system is that fewer Amazon.com customers leave the site without purchasing the materials they selected (this is apparently a major problem at other

about a patent that it believes will interfere with its use of P3P, a privacy protection protocol, W3C is advertising as follows:

WANTED: When did you first see a technology like this? . . . W3C is looking for information concerning any systems that predate the Intermind patent . . .

[67] Amazon.com, Inc. v. Barnesandnoble.com, Inc., 239 F.3d 1343 (Fed. Cir. 2001).

sites[68]). More significantly, the system locks in customers because they know that visiting a rival site will take more time and be less informative. Thus, the existence of the patent (and the preliminary injunction preventing others from infringing it) is important because it helps Amazon.com build a strong customer base. Even when the patient is eventually held invalid (or narrowed), lock-in will likely already have occurred. If so, then the patent will no longer be needed to give Amazon.com a competitive advantage.

Similar remarks can be made about technology like the instant messenger service of America OnLine (AOL), which allows users to exchange messages with other subscribers instantaneously (that is, in real time). Once a user convinces his or her friends to join this system, the user is unlikely to switch to a system run by one of AOL's rivals. At that point – after AOL's subscribership becomes significant – it becomes irrelevant whether AOL has a proprietary right in the service; its rivals will not be able to compete effectively because their networks will not be as large – and therefore not as valuable – as AOL's.[69]

Significantly, many of the methods for conducting electronic business have these sorts of network and lock-in effects. Since e-entrepreneurs value this so-called 'stickiness',[70] it is not unlikely that many business methods will be developed (and then patented) precisely *because* they network or lock in customers. If that is so, then invalid patents are especially worrisome. Their residual effects could result in inefficiencies in the product market, and that could happen without the patentee ever having made *any* inventive contribution.

b. Commentators' Views

Several commentators offer other ways of limiting *State Street*. Thus, Jay Thomas suggests a narrowing interpretation. It comes from his observation that the discussion in *State Street* on business methods is pure dictum: 'the claims of the patent were not directed to methods at all, but to computer hardware

[68] See Saul Hansell, 'As Patents Multiply, Web Sites Find Lawsuits are a Click Away', N.Y. Times, Dec. 11, 1999, at A1.

[69] Cf. Leslie Helm, 'AOL Aligns with Apple in Instant Messaging Venture Technology', Los Angeles Times, July 30, 1999, at p.3; Saul Hansell, 'In Cyberspace, Rivals Skirmish over Messaging', N.Y. Times, July 24, 1999, at A1, col. 1 (describing America Online's use of its copyrights and trademarks to reserve its instant messaging service to its own network of subscribers).

[70] See Denise Casuro, 'Digital Commerce, the Battle over Instant Messaging', N.Y. Times, Aug. 2, 1999, at p.C4, col. 5.

programmed to perform certain calculations'.[71] Presumably, the idea here (to which we will return[72]) is that just as sporting equipment might be patentable without encountering the problems associated with patenting sports moves, business machines could be considered patentable without incurring the costs that would be imposed by business method patents.

Unfortunately, it seems unlikely that classifying the second holding in *State Street* as dictum will stem the tide. That the comment is dictum reflects more on its legitimacy than on the predictability of its application to future cases. Judges reach out to decide issues not properly before them precisely because they *want* to send messages to the bar. The message here is that the court is no longer interested in hearing business method defenses to enforcement actions. Accordingly, it is not at all surprising that in an opinion subsequent to *State Street*, the Federal Circuit upheld the patent on a methodology for billing telephone subscribers – an invention that can also be classified as a business method.[73]

Another idea was voiced by Rinaldo Del Gallo. Writing before the Federal Circuit's decision in *State Street,* he proposed focusing on the existence of 'an inventive physical nexus'.[74] Since his view of a physical nexus includes the material manifestation exhibited by a computer program,[75] this distinction survives Judge Rich's rejection of the physical transformation requirement of *Freeman-Walter-Abele* and its progeny. A physical nexus requirement also accords well with a test proposed in Judge Newman's dissenting opinion in *In re Schrader*, on which Judge Rich heavily relied.[76] In her view, 'the patent system is directed to tangible things and procedures'.[77] She thought the patent at issue in *Schrader*, on a method of combining items for auctioning, was invalid, but for lack of novelty and inventiveness, not because it was drawn to nonstatutory matter. The advantage of Del Gallo's analysis is that many business methods, such as raising money with junk bonds or a frequent flyer program, might be found unpatentable.

But even if Del Gallo is right (and many commentators seem to assume so, for most of the discussion of *State Street* has centered on computer-implemented

[71] Thomas, supra note 35, at 1160.

[72] See text at p. 29 infra.

[73] AT & T Corp. v. Excel Comm'ns, Inc., 172 F.3d 1352 (Fed. Cir. 1999).

[74] Rinaldo Del Gallo, III, 'Are "Methods of Doing Business" Finally Out of Business as a Statutory Rejection?', 38 IDEA: J. L. & Tech. 403, 407 (1998).

[75] Id. at 429.

[76] In re Schrader, 22 F.3d 290, 296–99 (Fed. Cir. 1994) (Newman, J. dissenting), cited at 149 F.3d at 1375.

[77] 22 F.3d at 298.

methods[78]), his limitation does not go far enough. Indeed, there may be substantially less there than it seems. One problem is that every invention involves (or, with clever lawyering, can be made to involve) something that is physical. Junk bonds are embodied on pieces of paper and bookkeeping entries; frequent flyer miles are reported to customers by surface mail; the precursor to frequent flyer programs required stamps, stamp books and gift catalogues. Now, courts could limit the materials that could be construed to meet the physical nexus requirement by reviving the 'printed matter' doctrine, which demanded a functional relationship between the invention and its physical manifestation.[79] However, that doctrine proved extraordinarily difficult to apply fairly; it is unlikely to be quickly resurrected. And even if *State Street* is read as limited to computer-implemented techniques, that too can be relatively easily arranged, if not by the inventor, then by his or her patent attorney.[80] Moreover, the computer-implemented business patents are precisely the ones to be most worried about. They include the methods that create enduring advantages in electronic commerce and they are often associated with network effects and lock-in.

Thomas has also suggested another way to look at business methods. He reconceptualizes *State Street* as permitting the 'liberal professions' to patent their techniques. That is, he too disputes the notion that the case is limited to computer-implemented methodologies, arguing that it could be interpreted to approve of patents not only on sports moves but also on medical techniques, or even legal strategies. To Thomas, the extension of patenting to professional activities is reason enough to cap *State Street*'s reach.[81] He would do it legislatively, by limiting patent rights to what the Patent Clause of the Constitution refers to as 'useful Arts',[82] and which, he maintains, we now call 'technology'. He would, therefore, fashion an 'industrial application standard' that would look to the following features:

[78] But see Thomas, supra note 35. Congress also appears to understand *State Street* as applying to all sorts of business methods, see, e.g., 145 Cong. Rec. H12798-01, H12805 (daily ed. Nov. 18, 1999) (statement of Rep. Coble).

[79] See, e.g., Cincinnati Traction Co. v. Pope, 210 F. 443 (6th Cir. 1913) (finding '"time limit" transfer tickets' a functional implementation of the idea of allowing customers to transfer trains all morning or all afternoon at low cost).

[80] See, e.g., Keeley-Domokos, supra note 59, at 153 (suggesting a patent on a method for skipping class that involves a computerized method for determining which classes can be safely avoided).

[81] See Thomas, supra note 35, at 1175–79.

[82] U.S. Const. Art. I, § 8 (giving Congress power to 'Promote the Progress of ... useful Arts' with exclusive rights for inventors).

> production or transformation of artifacts; interaction with the external environment; systematic manipulation of physical forces; and focus upon design.[83]

Once again, there may be less to this limiting technique than meets the eye: even the invention at issue in *State Street* could fulfill Thomas's requirements, depending on what is meant by 'industrial' and 'artifacts' and 'forces'. The firms dealing with investments certainly believe themselves to be in the securities *industry*, the program manipulates value – *artifacts* of the economic *forces* that determine prices. Thomas argues for a 'refined sense of that set of actions and objects that we might judge as technological in character',[84] but he does not provide enough guidance on what this means to create predictable rules. He also gives insufficient support for his notion that 'useful Arts' means 'technology' (as he defines it). He does not even seem to believe it himself. If he did, there would be no need for legislation to overrule *State Street*: an attempt to extend patent law beyond the reach of the Patent Clause is not constitutional.[85]

c. *Congressional Limits*

Since *State Street* is, in fact, a statutory case, the legislature can modify it at will. Indeed, Congress has already made a modest foray in this direction by addressing the problem of patents issuing on known business methods. Under the new 'first inventor defense', known in foreign patent law as a prior user right, there is a defense to infringement in favor of any person who:

> acting in good faith, actually reduce the subject matter [of a business method patent] to practice at least one year before the effective filing date of such patent, and commercially used the subject matter before the effective filing date of such patent.[86]

In order to prevent the first inventor from competing away all patent profits, the defense can be asserted only by the party who established the defense and it can only be used with respect to the specific subject matter claimed.[87] How well this defense works in practice remains to be seen. What can be said now, however, is that it does not go far enough. It will create effective competition only in

[83] Thomas, supra note 35, at 1180.

[84] Id. at 1170.

[85] Cf. Feist Publications, Inc. v. Rural Telephone Services Co., 499 U.S. 340 (1991) (Congress cannot constitutionally extend copyright to fact works).

[86] § 273(b) (1).

[87] § 273(b) (6) & (b) (3) (C).

situations where someone was making substantial use of the method before the time of the patent application.

More important, this amendment may be counterproductive. By providing legislative recognition of business method patents, the provision could make it more difficult for future courts – particularly the Supreme Court – to deal with problems like lock-in and network effects, by eliminating the defense altogether or limiting it in other ways. Further, under prior law, it could be argued that the activity of a 'first inventor' functioned as a reference for anticipation and obviousness purposes. The theory – admittedly controversial – was that § 102(g)'s reference to an invention 'made in this country by another who had not abandoned, suppressed or concealed it' turned commercialized inventions into prior art.[88] Thus, there was good reason to believe that many business method patents would eventually be found invalid. The first inventor defense does not, in fact, rule out this argument (it states only that a patent should not be held invalid 'solely because a defense is raised or established under this section'[89]). However, it does weaken the argument. Section 102(g) is basically a priority rule. The motive for also reading it as a prior art provision is that this interpretation protects the reliance interests of those who choose not to patent discoveries they are using. With a first inventor defense, there is less reason to construe § 102(g) this way.[90]

III. JUSTIFYING *STATE STREET*

There is a more fundamental problem with all of these proposed limits on *State Street*: none provides a justification for recognizing patents in the areas each limitation would preserve, and none explains why patents are not needed in the fields the limitation would exclude. In a sense, the lack of attention to this matter is not surprising, as most contemporary intellectual property developments proceed in exactly the same way. The most recent example is database protection. Fact-based works have traditionally been considered to fall largely outside the purview of copyright. However, in 1996, the countries of the European

[88] See § 102(g); Dunlop Holdings, Ltd. v. Ram Golf Corp., 524 F.2d 33 (7th Cir. 1975); In re Bass, 474 F.2d 1276 (CCPA 1973); Pierre Jean Hubert, 'The Prior User Right of H.R. 400: A Careful Balancing of Competing Interests', 14 Santa Clara Computer & High Tech. L.J. 189, 193 (1998).

[89] § 273(b) (9).

[90] See, e.g., H.R. Rep. 106–287, 106th Cong., 1st Sess. (1999).

Union were directed to revise their copyright laws to protect those elements of databases that are literary or artistic enough to meet the requirements of copyright, and to enact *sui generis* legislation to protect the rest.[91] Ever since, the United States Congress has been busy drafting legislation to follow suit.[92] Database legislation may make sense for Europe, where 'information crunching' is not a well-developed business. Exclusive rights in databases will arguably provide just the sort of jump-start that this industry needs. But the same is not necessarily true in the United States. In the United States, data collection is a robust industry. It relies on contractual obligations to capture a return on the investment it takes to create databases,[93] and for all anyone knows, the industry may even be benefiting from the cost reductions associated with the free availability of the information that escapes contractual bonds. Yet, lawmakers do not seem to be questioning the need for database protection, or to have determined whether the costs of enforcing it will outweigh its benefits. The only justification given is to meet whatever reciprocity requirements Europe might impose.[94] But even the need for reciprocity is questionable, as American compilers seem to be managing quite nicely without protection in Europe.

The same dynamic has been operative in other intellectual property areas. Rights of publicity were created and later expanded without regard to whether there is any good public policy reason to give celebrities the power to prevent others from using their names, images, nicknames and the like.[95] The Copyright Office and PTO are busily working out ways to use copyright law to protect Internet publishers, even though the reduced cost of distributing information in cyberspace is so low that it is difficult to see why copyright principles are fully applicable.[96] The tort of misappropriation, which once protected only against

[91] Directive No. 96/9/EC on the legal protection of databases, 1996 O.J. (L 77) 20. See generally, W.R. Cornish, 'European Community Directive on Database Protection', 21 Colum.-VLA J.L. & Arts 1 (1996).

[92] See, e.g., H.R. 354, 106th Cong., 1st Sess. (1999).

[93] See, e.g., ProCD, Inc. v. Zeidenberg, 86 F.3d 1447 (7th Cir. 1996).

[94] See Jane C. Ginsburg, 'Copyright, Common Law, and Sui Generis Protection of Databases in the United States and Abroad', 66 U. Cin. L. Rev. 151 (1997).

[95] See Diane Leenheer Zimmerman, 'Who Put The Right in The Right of Publicity?', 9 DePaul-LCA J. Art & Ent. L. 35 (1998).

[96] See, e.g., Information Infrastructure Task Force, Intellectual Property and the National Information Infrastructure: The Report of the Working Group on Intellectual Property Rights (1995), available at http://www.uspto.gov. For a critique, see Carol M. Rose, 'The Several Futures of Property: Of Cyberspace And Folk Tales, Emission Trades And Ecosystems', 83 Minn. L. Rev. 129, 153–55 (1998).

destructive competition, can now be used without a need to show any competitive harm whatsoever.[97] Trade secrecy law was designed to protect positive information from unauthorized use;[98] it has been stretched to protect negative information – that is, the 'discovery' of failed experiments – and 'inevitable' use.[99] Of a piece with these developments is the TRIPS Agreement, which requires even the least developed of countries to recognize and enforce intellectual property laws.[100] In all of the Uruguay Round negotiations, no one seems to have considered whether there is benefit in protecting intellectual property in countries whose citizenry cannot afford to pay for it.[101]

What has happened? The answer may go something like this: as information products have begun to constitute a larger portion of the developed countries' production base, their value has become very clear. Those who previously gave information away began to understand what it was they were losing. Accordingly, they began to demand law structured to convert what was consumer surplus into producer surplus. Why courts and legislatures have gone along with these demands is somewhat harder to fathom. One possibility is that courts and legislatures think they are actually *creating* value when they turn it into something producers can capture. Consumers are not a well-organized interest group, so they do not have the resources to draw lawmakers' attention to the benefits of free (or low cost) information products. In contrast, information producers have become excellent lobbyists and litigants: their interests are

[97] Compare Int'l News Serv. v. Assoc. Press, 248 U.S. 215 (1918) (permitting one news service to prevent a rival from using its stories) with Chicago Board of Trade v. Dow Jones & Co., Inc., 98 Ill.2d 109 (1983) (permitting the publisher of the Dow Jones Industrial Average (DJIA) to enjoin the sale of a basket of market securities made up of the stocks used in computing DJIA).

[98] See, e.g., Unif. Trade Secrets Act (amended 1985), 14 U.L.A. 437 (1990).

[99] See, e.g., Novell, Inc. v. Timpanogos Research Group, Inc., 46 U.S.P.Q. 2d 1197, 1217 (D. Utah 1998) (protecting negative information). Cf. Pepsico, Inc. v. Redmond, 54 F.3d 1262 (7th Cir. 1995) (enforcing a confidentiality agreement against inevitable disclosure). See generally, Rochelle Cooper Dreyfuss, 'Trade Secrets: How Well Should We Be Allowed to Hide Them: The Economic Espionage Act of 1996', 9 Ford. Int'l Prop'y, Media & Entertainment L. J. 1 (1998).

[100] TRIPS Agreement Art. 1. Transition rules give less developed countries time to comply, see Arts. 65 & 66, but in the end all must enact and enforce intellectual property law.

[101] See Rochelle C. Dreyfuss and Andreas F. Lowenfeld, 'Two Achievements of the Uruguay Round: Putting TRIPS and Dispute Settlement Together', 37 Va. J. Int'l L. 275 (1997).

always put on the table very clearly. Lawmakers are, in effect, made to see producer value as arising from nowhere, rather than from the pockets of consumers. As important, it may appear to legislators and to courts that there is some sort of moral imperative to give to those who create value, a right to capture it.[102]

What it is crucial to understand, however, is that this leap – from value to right – represents a monumental shift in the jurisprudence of property protection. While it is probably true that rights in real property were recognized before there was a strong theoretical understanding of their justification, it is also the case that there is no shortage of theory now. Real property rights avert the tragedy of the commons; they give particular individuals incentive to husband, encouraging them to put the property under their care to its highest and best use.[103] Outside the intellectual property arena, recognition of a new property rights still seems to be accompanied by this or other form of justification. Whether it be fishing, water or spectrum rights; transferable development or pollution rights, commodification has proceeded only when there are reasons – conservation, resource management, and such – for creating a property rule and making a market.[104] These justifications are more than a philosophical nicety. They play an important role in shaping the law, for they create the foundation on which constraints are built. These constraints prevent the costs of exclusivity from growing to the point where they outweigh the advantages of protection.

Consider, for example, trademark law. It too has been the subject of unchecked growth: from the tort of passing off, which required a showing that a competitor was misleading purchasers about the source of goods,[105] it expanded such that a merchant could win a case merely by demonstrating that the competitor was making a confusingly similar use of the merchant's trademark (at first always a coined word, later any word, symbol or device that could serve to distinguish the merchant's goods from others[106]). After that, the law exploded; courts and legislatures strove to make sure that every value in a mark, including the value over and above the communicative value, could be captured

102 See Rochelle Cooper Dreyfuss, 'Expressive Genericity: Trademarks as Language in the Pepsi Generation', 65 Notre Dame L. Rev. 397 (1990).

103 See Garrett Hardin, 'The Tragedy of the Commons', 162 Sci. 1243, 1244 (1968); H. Scott Gordon, 'The Economic Theory of a Common-Property Resource: The Fishery', 62 J. Pol. Econ. 124, 134 (1954) (giving an earlier version of the theory of the tragedy of the commons).

104 See generally, Rose, supra note 96.

105 See, e.g., American Washboard Co. v. Saginaw Mfg, 103 F. 281 (6th Cir. 1900).

106 See, e.g., Coca-Cola Company v. Koke Company of America, 254 U.S. 143 (1920).

by trademark holders rather than by consumers.[107] Thus, use of marks on non-similar goods is now routinely enjoined;[108] there is federal legislation that prevents the use of a mark in a way that might mislead or falsely imply association, sponsorship or approval of the owner;[109] and most recently, Congress added language to protect against the 'dilution of the distinctive quality of [famous] marks'.[110]

As a result of these developments, it is now nearly impossible to know just when trademark infringement has occurred. What does it mean for a consumer to be misled, or falsely informed about sponsorship?[111] Does it count as infringement if what the consumer is confused about is not the producer of the goods, or the quality of the goods, but rather, the details of trademark law?[112] Trademark owners frequently license their marks to businesses unrelated to their core activity: if that does not dilute a mark, what does?[113] Once there was a justification for trademark law. Providing merchants with an unambiguous way to communicate with consumers gave them the incentive to market products consumers would – and could – purchase repeatedly. That justification produced a reference point for determining what constitutes legally cognizable harm: marketplace confusion about source or origin. When stripped of justification, the reference point was also lost. Every word, symbol or device that someone puts

107 An example may be helpful. Under early law, anyone could put the symbol of a sports team on a cap or tee shirt. Consumers bought these items to express loyalty to the team, and not because they thought the team warranted the quality of the item. Since there was no consumer confusion, the trademark holder had no right of action. The consumer, in other words, did not pay for the expressive value of the mark. Expansion of trademark protection to cover noncompetitive harm, even in the absence of confusion as to source, now makes the unauthorized use of a team logo infringement, see, e.g., University of Georgia Athletic Ass'n v. Laite, 756 F.2d 1535 (11th Cir. 1985). The result is that teams now charge for the privilege of using their logos – and consumer surplus has been converted into producer surplus.

108 See, e.g., Polaroid Corp. v. Polarad Elecs. Corp., 287 F.2d 492 (2d Cir.), cert. denied, 368 U.S. 820 (1961).

109 See § 43(a) of the Lanham Act, 17 U.S.C. § 1125(a).

110 Id. at § 43(c), § 1125(c).

111 See, e.g., Ferrari S.p.A. v. Roberts, 944 F.2d 1235 (6th Cir. 1991) (sale of $8500 kit to make a cheap car look like a Miami Spyder held to be infringement, even though customers clearly knew what they were buying).

112 See, e.g., WCVB-TV v. Boston Athletic Ass'n, 926 F.2d 42, 45 (1st Cir. 1991) (holding that it is not enough to show that consumers are confused about the need, under trademark law, for a license to utilize a particular marketing device).

113 See Dreyfuss & Kwall, supra note 19, at 121–22.

on goods or connects with services is now potentially the seed of a lawsuit. Ironically, even established trademark holders are finding themselves on the wrong side of some of these new rights of action.[114]

The same applies to arguments about patent rights for business methods. If Del Gallo had offered a reason for protecting only those business methods associated with a physical manifestation, then perhaps his thesis would be more persuasive. We might understand why it would be worth the risk of incurring the high social cost of business method patents. As important, we would then have a basis for recognizing which concrete manifestations count as a physical nexus. The same is true for Thomas's notion of excluding the liberal professions from the ambit of protection. After all, there is plenty of room to criticize professions like law and medicine – costs are rising, the poor are cut off, insurance is inadequate. Yet Thomas offers no reason for rejecting the use of patents to spur innovations in these fields. Had he explained what it is about certain professions that makes them unlikely to benefit from patents, we might better appreciate his technological and industrial-application distinctions. And, of course, this criticism can be equally applied to Judge Rich. Expanding patent protection to a long-existing field requires more than an incantation of fidelity to congressional intent. Business method innovations occurred without business method patents. It was, therefore, incumbent upon him to explain why protection is suddenly desirable. We might then also know exactly which business methods qualify.

Of course, Judge Rich's failure to provide a theory does not mean that no justification is possible. This is not the place to give a full account of the rationales available for intellectual property protection.[115] It is sufficient for these purposes to observe that as a matter of American constitutional law, moral arguments play no role; justification must take a purely utilitarian form. That is, in allowing – but not requiring – Congress to protect the work of authors and inventors, by limiting protection to a specified time period, and by constraining Congress to offer protection only for the purpose of promoting progress, the Patent

114 See, e.g., Star Markets, Ltd. v. Texaco, Inc., 950 F.Supp. 1030 (D.Haw. 1996) (Texaco's use of red star trademark challenged by Hawaii grocery store). Cf. Ringling Bros.-Barnum & Bailey Combined Shows, Inc. v. Utah Div. of Travel Development, 170 F.3d 449 (4th Cir. 1999) (challenging the state of Utah's slogan, the 'Greatest Snow on Earth'). Both these challenges lost, but not until after Texaco and Utah paid the expenses of lawsuits.

115 For a fuller discussion, see, e.g., Rochelle Cooper Dreyfuss, 'Intellectual Property Law', in *Fundamentals of American Law* 507 (Alan B. Morrison, ed. 1996); Edmund Kitch, 'The Nature and Function of the Patent System', 20 J.L. & Econ. 265 (1977).

Clause of the Constitution, in essence, rejects natural rights- or morality-based arguments, such as theories of just deserts. Instead, exclusivity is permissible only when it is Congress's judgment that the result will be to advance the frontiers of knowledge.

In making this judgment, Congress has focused on two problems: free riders and adequate disclosure. The free rider rationale mainly supports protection for products, which are usually relatively easy to reverse engineer. The problem here is that after a competitor uses an embodiment to determine its inventive features, figures out how to reproduce these features and enters the field, the innovator loses the ability to set the price. Instead, the rival can compete price down to production cost, the innovator may not earn enough to recoup development expenses, and it is likely that he or she will be unable to garner a return high enough to encourage others to enter the innovation business. Patents cure the problem by assuring inventors that they will enjoy exclusive rights, which will persist irrespective of reverse engineering or independent invention, and will last long enough to capture both costs and profits.

The second rationale is typically the more important one for processes. Because processes can usually be practiced in secret, the innovator can expect to enjoy substantial lead time. If this 'first mover advantage' is enough to allow the innovator to earn profits sufficient to compensate and reward development, free riders will not be a problem. They will not appear soon enough to reduce the incentive to invent. What can be a problem, however, is that the innovator winds up with too much lead time. If the invention does not leak into the public domain, returns can come to greatly exceed those necessary to encourage innovation. More troubling, during the period of extended *de facto* exclusivity, the knowledge base will grow very slowly because others will not know enough to build on the process's inventive features or apply them to new fields. Indeed, resources may be wasted as others invest their time and effort rediscovering something that was already within the sphere of human knowledge. Keeping the secret also entails social loss: employees are bound to agreements that limit their mobility, factories are defended against intruders, competitors are monitored to make sure they are not misappropriating the secret. Secret uses can also pose safety, health and environmental risks. Patent protection avoids these costs. In exchange for sure exclusivity for a period of years, the invention is disclosed – revealed in a manner that permits others to utilize the ideas during the patent period, scrutinize the impact of the usage and enjoy unfettered access when the patent expires.

But broad as these rationales are, neither appears to furnish significant support for protecting business methods. Businesses are conducted in public, making them easily reverse engineered. Since there is no need to induce disclosure, the rationale explaining patents on most processes is not applicable. But even though the public nature of the use raises the possibility of copying, the free rider rationale is also inapposite, for business competition does not have the same bite as product competition. For products, lead time is always somewhat truncated in that the first mover must use some of it to educate consumers about the product and its use. In some cases, the first mover may also need government approval before the product can be marketed at all. In contrast, business methods can be taught to employees in private; the moment when they are revealed is the moment when they start earning returns.[116]

But even in the absence of these effects, business method developers do not usually require patents to earn adequate returns. The inventor of a very significant advance will recoup costs and capture significant profits before rivals appear. Moreover, it is the very nature of sticky methods, methods that produce lock-in and networks, to forestall effective competition. Finally, it is not always the case that business methods can be quickly copied effectively. A recent study of benchmarking – the practice of investigating rivals' methodologies – suggests why this might be.[117] First, employees often resist adopting new methods, especially if they involve more work, do not confer personal benefits or imply that their old routines were inferior. Second, business methods are often tied to social structures within a firm, such as compensation schemes, lines of reporting or supervising policies. It can be difficult to identify all of the changes that need to be made to implement a particular new methodology effectively. Third, no business copies another's methods unless there is someone in the firm who advocates doing so. But in many firms, there is little upside potential and significant downside risk to being, in essence, the firm copyist.

The rivalry between Amazon.com and Barnes & Noble (or, Barnesandnoble.com) corroborates these points.[118] Amazon's method of selling books through the Internet looks easy to imitate. Yet Barnes & Noble, despite extensive

[116] It is not even clear that the price of a company's initial public offering is strongly tied to its patent portfolio. To the extent IPOs are not tied to patents, stock profits also compensate for the cost of innovation.

[117] See Claudia H. Deutsch, 'Competitors Can Teach You a Lot, but the Lessons Can Hurt: The Many Obstacles to Benchmarking', N.Y. Times, July 18, 1999, Sec. 3, p. 4, col. 1.

[118] See, e.g., Leslie Kaufman, 'Not All Hit It Rich in the Internet Gold Rush', N.Y. Times, July 20, 1999, at A1, col. 4; Sholnn Freeman, 'In Internet Spinoffs, Where Should the Riches Fall?', N.Y. Times, July 18, 1999, at Sec. 3, p. 9, col. 2; Jnan R. Dash, 'The Saga of Dell & Amazon.com', Computers Today, June 30, 1999, p. 61.

experience in the bookstore business, despite strong ties to publishers, and despite its unauthorized use of Amazon.com's 1-click technology, did not easily become an effective competitor. Perhaps Barnes & Noble's maintenance of regular book stores means it cannot realize one of the biggest advantages of Internet selling – the ability to keep inventories small; maybe Amazon.com's employees are more motivated by stock options than are Barnes & Noble's. In any event, it is far from clear that Amazon.com needs exclusivity to maintain superiority over this rival.

In the final analysis, the late, great economist Joseph Schumpeter was right: competition and the threat of competition are the main engines of innovation.[119] Absent special problems, such as free riders and inadequate disclosure, there is no reason to incur the costs of exclusivity; the desired goal – progress – will occur anyway. This is a conclusion that the Federal Circuit can be forgiven for missing because its specialized docket can make the tools of patent law appear far more salient to economic progress than they actually are. But given the special costs associated with business method patenting, the legal system as a whole cannot afford to ignore the implications of this lesson.

IV. ESCAPING *STATE STREET*: REEXAMINING LIMITS IN LIGHT OF JUSTIFICATIONS

So far, I have made two arguments. In Part I, I demonstrated that the cost of business method patents is high. Patenting them is like patenting nature. The downstream effects are so substantial that *State Street* is arguably wrong on this ground alone. In Part III, I showed that the benefits of business patenting are low, and that a separate problem with *State Street* is that there is no justification sounding in traditional rationales for intellectual property protection that supports it. But even if neither of these two arguments is fully correct, it can also be maintained that the ratio of costs to benefits is certainly such that patenting business methods must be viewed with deep suspicion. The final issue is what can reasonably be done about the Federal Circuit's approval of business method patents.

[119] Joseph A. Schumpeter, *Capitalism, Socialism, and Democracy* 81–86 (1947). In this connection, it is worth noting that the rivalry between Barnesandnoble.com and Amazon.com has produced many innovations in e-commerce, see 'Associated Press, Barnesandnoble.com Starts Music Store', N.Y. Times, July 8, 1999, at Sec. C, p. 4, col. 1; Saul Hansell, 'Amazon.com Gets Into Two New Businesses', N.Y. Times, July 13, 1999, at Sec. C., p. 1, col. 5.

In fact, *State Street* is not the law's first brush with excessive intellectual property protection. In the past, the Supreme Court usually managed to fix over-extended protection by finding a constitutional problem. Thus, the limited authorization given Congress to enact patent and copyright law was held insufficient to support protection for fact works or intrastate trademarks.[120] If it is thought that business methods are indeed akin to principles of nature, then it can be expected that the Supreme Court will eventually move to overrule the business method aspect of the *State Street* case, for protecting methods would then be considered beyond the scope of the Patent Clause. This kind of constitutional fix is not, however, possible if the Court thinks that the only problem with business method patents is that they are unwise: either superfluous or insufficiently beneficial to outweigh their cost. Congress is not required to tailor its intellectual property legislation so carefully that it applies only to the particular fields (or innovations) where exclusive rights are needed to encourage innovation. To meet constitutional muster, it is enough that the system as a whole promotes progress.

Still, there is room for judicial action on the part of courts who are convinced that *State Street* is a misstep. The opening lies in a key omission in the opinion – the Federal Circuit's failure, in the second part of the case, to consider the implications of its first holding. Business method patents were largely sought by the industry not so much because there was a felt need for more protection of business methods, but rather because the case law and guidelines on software patents taught that programs were not protectable unless they were part of a machine or a step in a larger process.[121] To meet that requirement for computer programs used in commerce, attorneys structured applications as drawn to methods – business methods. Now that *State Street* has made clear that software programs are patentable subject matter, that kind of framing is no longer necessary. Programs could then be claimed in their own right, examined for the utility, novelty and inventiveness of the code, and held to be infringed only when the code, or equivalents of it, are used without authorization.

120 Feist Publications, Inc. v. Rural Telephone Services Co., 499 U.S. 340 (1991); The Trademark Cases, 100 U.S. 82, 93–94 (1879). See also Bonito Boats, Inc. v. Thunder Craft Boats, Inc., 489 U.S. 141 (1989); Sears, Roebuck & Co. v. Stiffel Co., 376 U.S. 225 (1964); Compco Corp. v. Day-Brite Lighting, Inc., 376 U.S. 234 (1964); Lear, Inc. v. Adkins, 395 U.S. 653 (1969); Brulotte v. Thys Co., 379 U.S. 29 (1964) (preempting state attempts to create exclusive rights in non-federally protected works).

121 See, e.g., Diamond v. Diehr, 450 U.S. 175 (1981); Arrhythmia Research Technology, Inc. v. Corazonix Corp., 958 F.2d 1053, 1060 (Fed. Cir. 1992).

This result could be accomplished rather easily by, for example, endorsing (indeed, expanding on) Thomas's observation that the business method part of *State Street* was dictum. It would have many salutary effects. Patents for programs can be easily justified on both of the standard theories. That is, since programs can sometimes be utilized in secret, a mechanism is actually needed to ensure their timely disclosure. And since programs can also sometimes be copied quickly, protection from free riders is likewise desirable. If patents were issued on programs rather than methods, their quality would improve. Applications drawn to programs would focus examiners and judges on whether the code meets the conditions of patentability; the 'light bulb' effect we saw in connection with *Adams* and *John Deere* would abate because the glamour of computerizing a business method would not act as a distraction. And once it became clear that it is the program itself that is being analyzed for patentability, law would develop on when a program is patentable over the noncomputerized method of accomplishing the same task. For example, since the program in *State Street* was conceived (at least in part) to execute calculations required by partnership taxation laws,[122] perhaps the Internal Revenue Code and related Treasury Regulations should be considered prior art. Admittedly, there is also a quality problem in connection with programs in that computer programming is also an art that developed before patenting became common. Thus, the PTO has quite a way to go in collecting references and appointing knowledgeable examiners in the computer field. At the same time, however, that is a problem that has long been recognized and key steps are being, and have already been, taken to correct it.

Limiting *State Street*-type patents to the software utilized in the method would also make important differences in scope and impact. It would become apparent to ordinary members of the business community that known business methods can be practiced even after a patent on a computer program automating the method has issued. It would also become clear that it is not the idea of computerizing the method that is protected, and that programmers are free to write other programs that implement the same business method. That development would, in turn, provoke the development of law on what constitutes an equivalent of a particular subroutine or code fragment. Most important, once it is the case that business methods, including computerized methods, are free to be copied, the potential for detrimentally affecting marketplace competition will be averted.

[122] See note 20, supra.

V. TRIPPING ON *STATE STREET*

One last issue needs to be considered, and that is whether circumventing *State Street* in this way, or in the ways suggested by other commentators, violates Article 27 of the TRIPS Agreement, which requires every member of the World Trade Organization (WTO) to make patents 'available . . . without discrimination as to . . . the field of technology'.[123] The argument is that once a court announces that a particular field is within the ambit of patent protection, then the Agreement prohibits a court or a legislature from later acting to exclude it.[124]

It seems unlikely, however, that a dispute resolution panel convened pursuant to the Agreement will see things this way. If this view were accepted, it would turn the TRIPS Agreement into a one-way ratchet – a broadening interpretation by any WTO member would expand protection but no member could ever narrow protection. Indeed, any member could unilaterally add to the obligations of all others by simply announcing that a particular field was within the ambit of patent law. Given the care with which the subject matter of the TRIPS Agreement – as well as related treaties – has been negotiated, this result would be anomalous.[125]

In the past I have argued that the reference in Art. 3(2) of the Understanding of Dispute Settlement (DSU) to the use of 'customary rules of interpretation of public international law'[126] means that obligations under the Agreement are to be interpreted in light of the domestic laws of the members as they existed when

[123] TRIPS, Art. 27(1).

[124] See, e.g., John R. Thomas, 'Of Text, Technique, And The Tangible: Drafting Patent Claims Around Patent Rules', 17 J. Marshall J. Computer & Info. L. 219, 276 n.41 (1998); Beata Gocyk-Farberm, 'Medical Procedures: A Search For a Compromise Between Ethics And Economics', 18 Cardozo L. Rev. 1527 (1997). But see Gerald J. Mossinghoff, 'Remedies Under Patents on Medical and Surgical Procedures', 78 J. Pat. & Trademark Off. Soc'y 789, 796 (1996) (noting that this limit may be allowable under Art. 30).

[125] See, e.g., Pamela Samuelson, 'The U.S. Digital Agenda at WIPO', 37 Va. J. Int'l L. 369 (1997); Neil W. Netanel, 'Comment: The Next Round: The Impact of the WIPO Copyright Treaty on Trips Dispute Settlement', 37 Va. J. Int'l L. 441 (1997).

[126] Understanding on Rules and Procedures Governing the Settlement of Disputes, Art.3(2), Apr. 15, 1994, Marrakesh Agreement Establishing the World Trade Organization, Annex 2, Legal Instruments – Results of the Uruguay Round, 33 I.L.M. 112 (1994) [hereinafter DSU].

the TRIPS Agreement entered into force.[127] That principle should be used to determine whether business methodology is a 'field of technology' for purposes of Art. 27. According to Thomas, it is clear that neither Europe nor Japan have been protecting business methods. Now, it is true that Judge Rich claimed that United States patent law has never barred business method patents, and that prior cases could all be explained on other grounds. However, the fact of the matter is that prior to the TRIPS Agreement, American case law typically recited, as black letter law, that business methods are ineligible for patent protection.[128] Judge Rich's interpretation of the law was, in other words, artful. He used a technique that judges frequently employ to maintain the illusion of stability in the law, while at the same time shaping it to meet their perceptions of new needs. But however helpful this technique is to the development of the common law, it is not appropriate to treaty interpretation. Those negotiating international agreements cannot be expected to parse member nations' laws and read beyond express language to divine true meaning. Accordingly, if the United States wants others to recognize patents in business methods, it will be required to enter into negotiations to explicitly add that field to the obligations required by the TRIPS Agreement. Until the United States succeeds in that task, all nations – including the United States – have the freedom to choose to deny patents to business methods.

CONCLUSION

Even accomplished judges make occasional mistakes. Judge Rich made one in *State Street*. Patenting business methods is risky business and risky for business.

[127] See Dreyfuss and Lowenfeld, supra note 101, at 289 (comparing Articles 31 and 32 of the Vienna Convention on the Law of Treaties, opened for signature May 23, 1969, Arts. 31–32, 8 I.L.M. 679 (1969), which list preparatory work of a treaty and the circumstances of its conclusion as 'supplementary means of interpretation', with Restatement (Third) of the Foreign Relations Law of the United States § 325 and Comment *e* (1986), which, reflecting the American practice, is more receptive to using negotiating history and other surrounding circumstances as aids to interpretation of international agreements).

[128] See, e.g., In re Chatfield, 545 F.2d 152 (C.C.P.A. 1976); In re Patton, 127 F.2d 324, 327 (C.C.P.A. 1942); Hotel Security Checking Co. v. Lorraine Co., 160 F. 467 (2d Cir. 1908); Ex Parte Murray, 9 U.S.P.Q. 2d 1819, 1820 (Bd Pat App. Inter. 1988). But cf. In re Wait, 73 F.2d 982, 983 (C.C.P.A. 1934) (conceding that some business methods might present patentable novelty).

As the several encounters between Microsoft and government antitrust regulators demonstrate,[129] business methods create their own anticompetitive problems; they do not need help from patent law. To the contrary, business method patents can only further impair the proper functioning of markets and lead to the misallocation of resources. These high costs would be worthwhile if business method patents significantly spurred business progress. But it is difficult to believe that this is the case. Rather, business methods are their own reward; the more important they are, the stickier they are, the more they earn; those who develop new methods do not tend to encounter the free rider problems that patents are designed to solve. And since business methods are conducted in public, there is likewise no need for patent law to promote disclosure.

Judge Rich was also wrong in viewing the question of whether business methods – a field of longstanding inventiveness – should be the subject of patenting as equivalent to the question of whether technologies in a new field should be patentable. Experience to date shows why these two questions are very different. When patents develop coextensively with a new field, the PTO keeps current with the growing knowledge base; when a field comes into the patent fold later, there is a strong possibility that many patents will issue on knowledge that is already known. This is not to say that legislative approval should be necessary before a new field can be considered patentable subject matter – waiting for approval would deter investment in promising new areas. But I do mean to argue for a presumption against judicial extending of patent protection to existing fields. That presumption could be overcome with a credible theory of why the benefits of patenting will outweigh costs. In the absence of such a theory, leaving the issue to the legislature has an important advantage: the legislature may, simultaneous with expanding the Patent Act, provide the PTO with the resources it needs to catch up.

What makes a brilliant judge is not the absence of mistakes; it is the capacity to see error and correct it. Unfortunately, Judge Rich is no longer able to take that step. But the direction that he left in *State Street* on patenting software does offer a way out of the problems created by the business method portion of his opinion. Recognizing patent rights in the programs used to implement business methods does not carry the same danger as patents in the methods. Software patents are justifiable on standard grounds; most important, the PTO is well on its way to improving the quality of the process for examining them.

129 See, e.g., Justice Department Files Antitrust Suit Against Microsoft For Unlawfully Monopolizing Computer Software Markets, DOJ 98-223, 1998 WL 249358, May 18, 1998; U.S. v. Microsoft Corp., 147 F.3d 935 (D.C. Cir. 1998); United States v. Microsoft, 59 Fed Reg 42,845 (1994); 1995–2 CCH Trade Cases ¶ 71,096.

More generally, there is a real need for policy makers to reconsider the advantages of a strong public domain. Even the most cursory examination of the discourse in real property law reveals renewed interest in protecting existing public resources and in reviving conceptions of the 'commons'.[130] Intangible property is by its nature public and there is irony in the eagerness with which law is moving to privatize it.

POSTSCRIPT

I have been given the opportunity to add a short postscript to my article on *State Street* to consider recent developments. There have been too many to chronicle individually, but a few are worth noting.

First, as to business methods themselves. The paper suggested that the quality of these patents would be a major problem because, in part, the Patent and Trademark Office lacked the resources to examine applications properly. That has now changed. The PTO has worked hard to improve its operations. Among other things, it now maintains a special business methods website, provides extensive training to examiners, and it has upgraded its resources and enhanced its review of office actions.[131] The result has been a significant increase in the rejection rate of applications drawn to business methods.[132]

Nonetheless, high numbers of business method patents continue to issue. One can only speculate about the extent to which these patents fueled investment in risky Internet business models, ultimately contributing to the bursting of the dot.com bubble. Certainly, these patents are producing palpable negative effects. New businesses must investigate – and then negotiate – a thicket of rights before they can begin to operate.[133] There is also something of an arms race going on. As Mark Lemley notes:

> many patentees engage in 'defensive patenting,' obtaining patents to stake their claim to an area of technology in hopes of preventing other companies from suing

[130] See, e.g., Robert C. Ellickson, 'New Institutions for Old Neighborhoods', 48 Duke L.J. 75 (1998).

[131] See http://www.uspto.gov/web/menu/pbmethod/.

[132] See Jason Krause, 'Patent Changes Pending: Proposed New Strategy for Federal Office Gets Mixed Reviews', 1 No. 43 A.B.A. J. E-Report 6 ABA Journal E-Report (November 8, 2002) (citing statistics offered by Commissioner Rogan).

[133] See, e.g., Interview with Professor Richard J. Gilbert, 16-SUM Antitrust 15 (2002).

them. Indeed, there is anecdotal evidence that at least among high-technology and start-up companies, the primary purpose of patents is defensive.[134]

Internet patents in particular have created a new set of international jurisprudential issues, stemming from cases in which parts of a claimed patented business method are practiced outside the territory in which the right is registered. These cases raise not only patent interpretation problems, but also jurisdiction, choice of law and enforceability issues.[135]

My original piece also suggested that the decision in *State Street* was part of a larger trend, which accepts the notion that all of the social surplus generated by an intellectual product should belong to the rights holder. That idea can be discerned in many of the current developments in intellectual property law, from limitations on defenses in patent law,[136] to copyright term extension,[137] to special protections against the use of trademarks in cyberspace;[138] it has also worked its way into the popular literature.[139]

However, there are some recent signs of abatement. The Internet file sharing cases (*Napster* and *Grokster*)[140] have made the public aware of the ways in which intellectual property rights can be used to block attractive business models.

134 Mark A. Lemley, 'Intellectual Property Rights and Standard-setting Organizations', 90 Cal. L. Rev. 1889, 1949 n. 249 (2002). See also Mark A. Lemley, 'Reconceiving Patents in the Age of Venture Capital', 4 J. Small & Emerging Bus. L. 137, 143 (2000) ('One of the major reasons that companies get patents is that they're afraid that their competitors have them, and they don't want to be the only one left who doesn't have the ability to play in this game').

135 See, e.g., NTP, Inc. v. Research In Motion, Ltd., 418 F.3d 1282 (Fed. Cir. 2005) (placement of Blackberry relay components in Canada does not avoid infringement liability in the United States). Cf., e.g., Menashe Business Mercantile Ltd. v. William Hill Organization Ltd, [2002] EWCA Civ 1702, [2003] 1 All E.R. 279 (November 30, 2002) (use in England of a gaming system hosted on a computer located in the Netherlands Antilles was held to infringe a U.K. patent). See generally, Michael S. Conner and Frank W. Leak, Jr., 'Challenges of Business Method Patent Enforcement-Extraterritoriality', 10 Computer & Internet Law 1 (2002).

136 See, e.g., Madey v. Duke University, 307 F.3d 1351 (Fed. Cir. 2002) (rejecting the notion that university research is exempt from patent infringement).

137 See Eldred v. Ashcroft, 123 S.Ct. 769 (2003) (upholding the constitutionality of the Copyright Term Extension Act of 1998, 17 U.S.C. § 302(a)).

138 See, e.g., 15 U.S.C. § 1125(d) (the 'Anticybersquatting Consumer Protection Act').

139 See, e.g., Kevin G. Rivette and David Kline, *Rembrandts in the Attic* (2002).

140 A&M Records, Inc. v. Napster, Inc., 284 F.3d 1091 (9th Cir. 2002) and Metro-Goldwyn-Mayer Studios, Inc. v. Grokster, Ltd., 125 S. Ct. 2764 (2005).

A forming coalition of activists is beginning to advocate protection to the intellectual public domain analogous to the protection the environmental movement has created for the physical public domain.[141] Arguably, even the United States Supreme Court has begun to listen. It has just taken a case challenging the patentability of what might be called a medical business method: a diagnostic test used to detect a form of vitamin B deficiency.[142] While its decision on whether this test constitutes patentable subject matter remains to be seen, it is significant that in another recent case, the Court interpreted federal trademark law on dilution[143] surprisingly narrowly, to require a trademark holder seeking injunctive relief to show actual evidence that nonconfusing use of its mark lessens the capacity of the mark to identify and distinguish goods.[144]

In emphasizing that mental association is not enough to create dilution, Justice Stevens reminds us that the scope of an intellectual property right should be measured by the justification that supported the right's reaction. It is to be hoped that this principle will receive broad application in the future.

[141] See James Boyle, 'A Politics of Intellectual Property: Environmentalism For The Net?', 47 Duke L.J. 87 (1997).

[142] Laboratory Corp. v. Metabolite Laboratories, Inc., 126 S. Ct. 543 (2005).

[143] 15 U.S.C. § 1125(c).

[144] Moseley v. V Secret Catalogue, Inc., 537 U.S. 418 (2003).

Chapter 2

From Having Copies to Experiencing Works: The Development of an Access Right in U.S. Copyright Law

*Jane C. Ginsburg**

ABSTRACT

This essay addresses the copyright law's response to new forms of distribution of copyrighted works through the establishment of a right to control digital access to copyrighted works. This right is set out in § 1201 of the 1998 Digital Millennium Copyright Act. When the exploitation of works shifts from having copies to directly experiencing the content of the work, the author's ability to control access becomes crucial. Indeed, in the digital environment, without an access right, it is difficult to see how authors can maintain the 'exclusive Right' to their 'Writings' that the U.S. Constitution authorizes Congress to 'secure'. Even if Congress may qualify the right's exclusivity by imposing a variety of compulsory licenses, or outright exemptions, it is one thing to introduce specific and narrow gaps in coverage, quite another to devise (or to allow to persist) a system that pervasively fails to afford meaningful exclusivity. The latter course would be inconsistent with the constitutional design to secure meaningful rewards and incentives to authors.

Thus, the 'exclusive Right' today is not only a 'copy'-right, but an access right, and the essay explores the implications of that claim. It does not contend that the access right will or should supplant 'copy'-right. On the

* Morton L. Janklow Professor of Literary and Artistic Property Law, Columbia University School of Law. Many thanks to Professors Douglas G. Baird, Graeme Dinwoodie, Jessica Litman, Henry Monaghan, and Kamiel Koelman. Thanks for research assistance to Allison Engel, Columbia Law School class of 2000 and to Carrie Casselman, Columbia Law School class of 2003.

contrary, the claim is that the access right is an integral part of copyright, and therefore should be subject to exceptions and limitations analogous to those that constrain 'copy'-right. Just as a 21st-century copyright regime that did not regulate access would be unrealistic and incomplete, so a regime that limits all availability to works to the copyright owner's terms would undermine the 'progress of Science' that the author's 'exclusive Right' is intended to 'promote'. Without an appropriate fair use or equivalent limitation, the access right under § 1201 becomes more than a necessary and integral component of copyright law. It becomes instead an über-copyright law, rigid as to specified exceptions, and therefore freed of further inquiry into the balance of copyright owner rights and user privileges that the fair use doctrine – and the general structure of copyright law – require.

INTRODUCTION

A radical change looms in the way we apprehend and enjoy works of authorship. For all the transformations in the history of the production and communication of works that technological advances have wrought by making them more plentiful and less expensive, this change is different. From Gutenberg to the photocopier and videotape, prior developments had facilitated, indeed promoted, the acquisition of physical copies of works. At first, only publishers and pirates employed the new copying technologies. Intermediaries controlled the means of making and disseminating copies, because the mechanisms for copying and distributing entire works generally exceeded the financial and technical capacities of end-users. As a result, until now, perhaps the most significant post-printing press technological event for copyright law was the development of mass market audio- and then video-copying devices, because these devices enabled end-users to create physical copies out of previously ephemeral radio and television transmissions. These devices gave consumers the power to 'materialize' copyrighted works that had been made available to the public through means that had previously remained solely within the copyright owner's control. Indeed, U.S. copyright law had long distinguished between public performances, including transmissions, and 'publication', on the ground that only the latter involved a public distribution of copies through which the copyright owner lost control over disposition of the work.[1] Mass market audio and audiovisual recording devices thus began to call into question this long-standing distinction.

[1] For a thorough discussion of the concept of 'publication' in U.S. copyright law, see Estate of Martin Luther King, Jr. v. CBS, 194 F.3d 1211 (11th Cir. 1999).

Digital media made the distinction even more dubious, because any digital transmission received in a computer would effect a copy at least in temporary memory, even if no copy were retained.[2] More important, digital media and communications made it even easier for consumers to create physical copies of any kind of work, whether previously fixed in a hard copy such as CD ROM, or received from a transmission, such as an Internet download. Thus, while digital media in one sense de-materialized copies by instantly, albeit intangibly, converting any work into a series of 1s and 0s available for receipt in RAM, recipients not only could perceive the works fleetingly in 'real' time, but they also held the power to re-materialize them into retention copies, whether printed, engraved on a CD ROM or stored to hard disk.

Now, however, the moment of the freestanding material copy may be passing. The technological balance of control over hard copies, having swung toward empowering end-users, may be reverting to copyright owners. Every act of perception or of materialization of a digital copy requires a prior act of access. And if the copyright owner can control access, she can condition how a user apprehends the work, and whether a user may make any further copy. Access control can at the same time thus vastly increase the availability of copyrighted works in de-materialized form, yet constrain their susceptibility to conversion to physical copies. In the impending era of digital access, we will be able to download anything (at least temporarily), whenever and wherever we want. As a result, we will no longer need hard copies to enjoy the work; indeed, in a world of access conditioned on nonretention of digital copies, we will be able to summon up the work at any time, but we may not be able to have our own copy. Does that mean we will no longer want copies? And, more broadly, what are the consequences of these developments for copyright law?

Until now, a great deal of the enjoyment of works of authorship was possessive and tactile. Many of us liked acquiring works (including unauthorized private copies); we liked having them; and we liked touching them, even if we rarely, if ever, in fact read, viewed or listened to them. None of this matters when we apprehend a work through digital access without retaining a copy. The only reason to access a work in that case, is to read, look at or listen to it immediately. For those whose relationship to works of authorship is businesslike, unsentimental and centered on immediate experience, the decline in hard copies may be liberating. For the more romantically, or at least the more acquisitively, inclined, the reaction may be more desolate. In either event, a shift from hard to evanescent

[2] On the doctrine of RAM copying, see infra, TAN and note 21.

copies recasts copyright law in ways some may find exhilarating and others frightening.

This essay addresses how current U.S. copyright law responds to new forms of distribution of copyrighted works, through the emerging right to control digital access to copyrighted works, as set out in the 1998 Digital Millennium Copyright Act.[3] With respect to the access right, I contend that when the exploitation of works shifts from having copies to directly experiencing the content of the work, the author's ability to control access becomes crucial. More broadly, I suggest that, in the digital environment, the 'exclusive Right' that the U.S. Constitution authorizes Congress to secure to authors[4] is not only a 'copy'-right, but an access right, and I explore the implications of that claim.

I do not contend that the access right will or should *supplant* 'copy'-right. On the contrary, my claim is that the access right is an integral *part* of copyright, and therefore should be subject to exceptions and limitations analogous to those that constrain 'copy'-right. I also acknowledge that there will still be some among us for whom direct experience affords imperfect enjoyment of works of authorship, for whom 'having' may be even more gratifying than 'experiencing'. In that case, however, the 'having' copy may be valued primarily for its physical characteristics rather than for its incorporeal intellectual component. Inexpensive mass market tangible versions may eventually disappear because their primary value is to convey content, not to cherish as an object. Online access may ultimately replace hard copies for content conveyance, but may also, perhaps paradoxically, enhance the appeal of physical originals and fine multiples.

Online but ephemeral ubiquity of the content may make possession of hard copies prized for another reason as well. The 'experiencing' copy can disappear, or be freighted with conditions more restrictive than the limitations either traditional copyright law or practice can place on freestanding hard copies. Just as a 21st-century copyright regime that did not regulate access would be unrealistic and incomplete, so too a regime that assumes, or directs, that *all* forms of exploitation will be intangible may discourage the dissemination of hard copies (or hard copy-able versions), and by limiting all availability to works to the copyright owner's terms, thereby undermine the 'progress of Science' that the Constitution's provision for the author's 'exclusive Right' is intended to promote.

[3] See 17 U.S.C. § 1201.

[4] U.S. Const. art. I, § 8 cl. 8 ('Congress shall have power ... to promote the progress of science and useful arts by securing for limited times to authors and inventors the exclusive right to their respective writings and discoveries').

COPYRIGHT WITHOUT HARD COPIES

It is the near-future. I am jogging along a tropical beach, or traveling across Europe by train, or sitting at my desk at home in New York; wherever I am, I have my palm-sized book reader-audio-video player-satellite cell phone that permits instant access through digital networks to an infinite variety of literary, musical and video works, with payment automatically charged to or debited from my account. At any moment, from any place, I can read, view or listen to any work I want. Moreover, with instant access to audio- and video-streamed works, hard copies need no longer encumber my home or briefcase. On the other hand, instant gratification may not always suffice: sometimes I may wish to annotate my copy, and retain those reflections. No problem: for a slightly higher fee, I am allowed one digital retention copy for note-taking, but I may not further reproduce that copy. Or, for a yet higher fee, I can make a single place-shifting copy to put in a portable player, for the rare times when Internet access fails. And so on.

These kinds of distribution arrangements are likely only when copyright owners are confident that the 'experiencing' copy will not turn into an unauthorized 'having' copy, or worse yet, unauthorized sharing copies.[5] Of course, every 'experiencing' transaction will involve a simple click-on license, whose terms make clear the limits of the end-user's enjoyment.[6] But, for copyright owners, something more, and preferably self-executing, is also needed to deter consumer

[5] S. Rep. No. 105–90, at 8 (1998) (explaining that given 'the ease with which digital works can be copied and distributed worldwide virtually instantaneously, copyright owners will hesitate to make their works readily available on the Internet without reasonable assurance that they would be protected against massive piracy').

[6] The enforceability of these licenses against noncommercial end-users is uncertain. Cf. ProCD v. Zeidenberg, 86 F. 3d 1447 (7th Cir. 1996) (shrink wrap license enforced against commercial user); Maureen O'Rourke, *Progressing Towards a Uniform Commercial Code for Electronic Commerce or Racing Towards Nonconformity?*, 14 Berkeley Tech. L. J. 635 (1999); J.H. Reichman and Johnathan A. Franklin, *Privately Legislated Intellectual Property Rights: Reconciling Freedom of Contract with Public Good Uses of Information*, 147 U. Pa. L. Rev. 875 (1999).

The Uniform Computer Information Transactions Act [UCITA] would validate mass market click-on licenses when the end-user assented to terms that she had the opportunity to view. See arts. 112, 202, 203, 211. UCITA has been enacted in Virginia and Maryland, see Va. Code Ann. § 59.1-501-509.2 (Michie 2001); Md Code Ann., Com. Law I §22 (Supp. 2002).

cheating. Hence the role of technological protection measures, from access barriers to anti-copying controls. Copyright owners nonetheless fear that these measures may prove futile, if no legal impediment exists to offering devices or services designed to circumvent the technological protections.[7] Hence, the provisions of the 1998 Digital Millennium Copyright Act [DMCA] prohibiting both the act of circumventing access controls, and the provision of devices or services designed to circumvent either access or anti-copying controls.[8]

Several commentators have recognized that the DMCA's provisions on circumvention of access protections in effect create a new right under, or perhaps over, copyright: the right to control access to copyrighted works.[9] A notable lack of enthusiasm for this development often characterizes those comments.[10] Some

[7] Anti-circumvention claims filed since enactment of the DMCA suggest that these concerns are warranted. See e.g. *321 Studios v. MGM*, 307 F. Supp. 2d 1085 (N. D. Cal. 2004) (device designed to make 'back-up copies' of DVDs by circumventing access and copy controls held to violate §1201); Universal City Studios, Inc. v. Corley, 273 F.3d 429 (2d Cir. 2001) (affirming a permanent injunction entered against websites posting 'De-CSS' software to neutralize DVD access controls); RealNetworks v. Streambox, 2000 WL 127311 * (W.D. Wash. 2000) (preliminary injunction entered against device converting streamed audio signal from an uncopiable format into a signal that may be copied).

[8] See 17 U.S.C. § 1201(a) (b). See also Directive 2001/29/EC of the European Parliament and of the Council of 22 May 2001 on the Harmonisation of Certain Aspects of Copyright and Related Rights in the Information Society, Official Journal L 167, June 22, 2001, art. 6(2) (prohibiting dissemination of devices designed to circumvent access controls). Compare WIPO Copyright Treaty [WCT], art. 11, obliging member states to protect against 'the circumvention of effective technological measures that are used by authors in connection with the exercise of their rights under this Treaty or the Berne Convention ...'. Neither the WCT nor the Berne Convention clearly articulate a right to control access. But see Jörg Reinbothe & Silke von Lewinski, The WIPO Treaties 1996 43 (2002) (contending that the Berne Convention reproduction right extends to initial entry into computer memory); Sam Ricketson and Jane C. Ginsburg, *International Copyright and Neighbouring Rights: The Berne Convention and Beyond*, ¶¶ 15.14–15.16 (2006) (access controls are within the scope of technological measures that member states must protect).

[9] See e.g. Jane C. Ginsburg, *Copyright Legislation for the 'Digital Millennium'*, 23 Colum.-VLA J. L. & the Arts 137, 140–43, 147–48 (1999); Kamiel J. Koelman, *A Hard Nut to Crack: The Protection of Technological Measures,* 22 EIPR 272, 274–75 (2000).

[10] See e.g. Chris Pennisi, *Anti-Circumvention Law May Circumvent Fairness*, 19 Computer & Internet Lawyer 5, 8 (2002) (arguing that the DMCA 'enables the circumvention of the rights granted to the public in copyright-by-copyright holders'); Julie E. Cohen & Dan L. Burk, *Fair Use Infrastructure for Rights Management*

criticisms express the principle that it is highly undesirable for the law to suppress technology by prohibiting the manufacture and dissemination of anti-circumvention devices.[11] Others object to the increase in copyright owners' power that control of access engenders, and to the consequent shift in the balance of copyright owner/user rights.[12] On the other hand, these commentators generally do not acknowledge that the 'copyright balance' is hardly immutable: the development and distribution of mass market copying devices also shifted the copyright 'balance', in that case away from copyright owners and toward end-users.[13] It is far from apparent why the 'balance' in force from the advent of

Systems, 15 Harv. J.L. & Tech. 41, 50 (2001) (making the observation that '[b]y implementing technical constraints on access to and use of digital information, a copyright owner can effectively supersede the rules of intellectual property law'); Pamela Samuelson, *Intellectual Property and the Digital Economy: Why the Anti-Circumvention Regulations Need to be Revised*, 14 Berkeley Tech. L. J. 519 (1999); Jonathan Band & Taro Issihiki, *The New Anti-Circumvention Provisions in the Copyright Act: A Flawed First Step*, 3 Cyber. Law. 2 (1999).

11 See e.g. Samuelson, *supra* note 10 at 557.

12 See e.g. Pamela Samuelson, *Digital Rights Management [and, or, vs.] the Law*, 4, 41–45 in 46 Comm. ACM, (forthcoming April 2003) (noting the alternative understanding of DRM as 'digital restrictions management', as suggested on the 'words to avoid' list of the Free Software Foundation); Julie E. Cohen, DRM and Privacy, 18 Berkeley Tech. L.J. 575 (2003) (cautioning that DRM technologies have 'the potential to change dramatically the way people experience intellectual goods' and thus raise serious privacy concerns); Julie E. Cohen, *Some Reflections on Copyright Management Systems and Laws Designed to Protect Them,* 12 Berkeley Tech. L. J. 161 (1997); Julie E. Cohen, *A Right to Read Anonymously: A Closer Look at Copyright Management in Cyberspace,* 28 Conn. L. Rev. 981 (1996); Lawrence Lessig, *The Law of the Horse: What Cyberlaw Might Teach*, 113 Harv. L. Rev. 501, 519 (1999). But see June M. Besek, *Anti-Circumvention Laws and Copyright: A Report from the Kernochan Center For Law, Media and the Arts*, 27 Colum. J.L. of the Arts 389 (2004) (for now, appropriate copyright owner–user balance persists); Paul Goldstein, *Fair Use in A Changing World*, 50, J. Copyr. Soc. 133, 146–47 (2003) (concerns about excessive control over digital formats are overstated); Shira Perlmutter, The 'Access Right' in the United States, *in* Adjuncts and Alternative to Copyright: Proceedings of the 2001 ALAI Congress 372 (June M. Besek and Jane C. Ginsburg, eds) (2001) (citing as a primary advantage of access controls a 'maximum range of consumer choice of how to experience a work'); Tom W. Bell, *Fair Use v. Fared Use: The Impact of Automated Rights Management on Copyright's Fair Use Doctrine,* 76 N.C.L. Rev. 557 (1998) (favoring the development of pay-per-view/listen systems).

13 See Trotter Hardy, *Property (and Copyright) in Cyberspace*, 1996 U. Chi. Legal F. 217 (1996).

these devices should be more normative and less contingent than the prior 'balance', or than the now-emerging balance. Before further addressing these concerns, however, it is appropriate first to consider the nature of the access right and its place in U.S. copyright law.

Bases for the Access Right

In the beginning – that is, in the eighteenth and nineteenth centuries – copyright in most countries was divided into two rights: reproduction and public performance.[14] This division reflected the kinds of exploitations to which copyrighted works were then subject: reproduction in copies for public distribution, and performances of works in places open to the public. As time and techniques evolved, the concept of a public performance extended to a growing list of transmissions and re-transmissions, culminating in their coverage in the Berne Convention – the leading multilateral copyright treaty – which became a morass of specific provisions on public communications with or without wires.[15] In 1996, the WIPO Copyright Treaty [WCT] rewove the increasingly disparate strands into a general right of communication to the public, including to a public whose members are separated both in time and in space.[16] As a matter of international norms, the right now extends from live theatrical performances to online delivery of individual songs to individual consumers, thus reflecting the current and future range of exploitations of this kind. As for the reproduction right, with advances in technology, from tape recorders to digital media, domestic U.S. and international copyright law have increasingly recognized that the author's right to authorize, or at least to be compensated for, the making of copies extends not only to one who makes multiple copies for public distribution, but to end-users who make individual copies for private consumption.[17]

[14] See e.g. France, law of Jan. 15, 1791 (public performance right); law of July 21, 1793 (reproduction right); U.K. 8 Anne, ch. 19 (1710) (reproduction right); Dramatic Copyright Act 1833 (public performance right in dramatic works); U.S. Act of May 31, 1790, ch. 15, 1 Stat. 124 (reproduction right); Act of Aug. 18, 1856, ch. 169, 11 Stat. 138 (public performance right in dramatic works).

[15] See Berne Convention, arts. 11, 11bis, 11ter, 14, 14bis(1).

[16] See WIPO Copyright Treaty, art. 8; cf. 17 U.S.C. § 101 (definition of public performance).

[17] See e.g. Germany, Law dealing with copyright and related rights, art. 27(1)–(3) (originally enacted in 1965) (levies for private audio and video taping); France, Code of intellectual property, art. L. 311-1–311-8 (originally enacted in 1985) (same); Spain, Revised law on intellectual property, regularizing, clarifying and harmonizing the

What, then, is or should be the relationship of this evolution to 'access' and its place in the U.S. copyright scheme? First, one might inquire whether 'access' falls within the modern conception of either the right of communication to the public (still called the right of 'public performance' in the U.S.) or the reproduction right. Second, whatever the 'fit' of 'access' with these older formulations, does an access right *belong* in a copyright regime? To answer that question, we must consider what copyright *should* look like in the digital online environment.

By an 'access' right, I mean the right to control the manner in which members of the public apprehend the work. The concept is distinct from reproduction or communication to the public to the extent that I may communicate a copy of my work to the user's hard drive, or the user may purchase a digital copy such as a CD ROM, but the user may not 'open' the work to apprehend (listen to, view) its contents unless the user acquires the 'key' to the work.[18] And the key may vary with the nature and extent of enjoyment of the work. As part of my control over 'access' I may, depending upon the price the user pays, limit listening or viewing by number of plays, by number of computers on which the work may be played, by duration of access, and so on. By contrast, neither traditional reproduction nor public performance rights would have reached much of this conduct. For example, the 'public' performance right does not extend to private enjoyment of a performance that the user generates (as opposed to receives from a transmission), such as by listening to a portable audio disk player.[19] The reproduction right, and its corollary, the distribution right, gave the copyright owner control over the making and dissemination of copies, but once a particular copy was sold, the copyright law did not constrain the purchaser's further disposition of that copy.[20]

Nonetheless, the seeds of an access right can be found in pre-Internet copyright law. For example, the doctrine of RAM copying – which holds that a 'copy'

applicable statutory provisions, art. 25 (originally enacted in 1987) (same); U.S. 1992 Audio Home Recording Act, 17 U.S.C. §§ 1003–07 (levies for digital audio private copying); 2001 Information Society Directive, art. 5, OJEC L167, 22/06/2001 (requiring 'equitable compensation' for private copying, and anticipating the supplanting of digital private copying by technological protections). BMG Music v. Gonzales, 430 F. 32. 888 (7th Cir. 2005) (downloading permanent copies of large quantities of sound recordings held not fair use).

18 See 17 U.S.C. § 1201(a) (3) (B) (definition of technological measure that effectively controls access to a work).

19 See 17 U.S.C. § 101 (definitions of 'performance' and 'perform publicly').

20 See id. §§ 106(3), 109(a) (distribution right; 'first sale' limitation on distribution right).

is made when the work is received in a computer's temporary memory[21] – would cover 'accessing' a work, since apprehending the work through a computer requires making at least a temporary copy. Similarly, in the digital era, extension of the public performance right to cover individual receipt of transmissions approaches an 'access' concept. Indeed, the WCT's articulation of the right of communication to the public covers the 'making available to the public ... in such a way that members of the public may *access* these works from a place and at a time individually chosen by them'.[22] While on its face the definition puts the access choice in the public's, not the copyright owner's hands, the copyright owner's ability to control the terms under which access is made available to the public may be implicit in this formulation.

Even if an 'access' right does not precisely correspond to either of the traditional copyright rights of reproduction or public performance, it does respond

[21] It is by now well established in U.S. copyright law that entry of a work into a computer's random access memory constitutes making a copy – hence the need to exempt certain RAM copies from liability for infringement, see 17 U.S.C. § 117. See Trotter Hardy, *Computer Ram 'Copies': A Hit or a Myth? Historical Perspectives on Caching as a Microcosm of Current Copyright Concerns,* 22 U. Dayton L. Rev. 423, 455 (1997); Michael E. Johnson, *The Uncertain Future of Computer Software: Users' Rights in the Aftermath of* Mai *Systems*, 44 Duke L. J. 327 (1994); Katrine Levin, *Mai v. Peak: Should Loading Operating System Software into RAM Constitute Copyright Infringement?*, 24 Golden Gate U. L. Rev. 649 (1994). But see e.g. Jessica Litman, *The Exclusive Right to Read*, 13 Cardozo Arts & Ent. L. J. 29, 42 (1994) (arguing against doctrine of RAM copying).

The RAM copying doctrine is implicit in E.U. copyright law as well, see Software Directive art. 5 (exempting certain temporary reproductions from liability), Directive 91/250/EC 1991 O.J. (L122) 42. There may be more uncertainty as to whether RAM copying is an international norm. See WCT, Agreed Statement 1 ('The reproduction right, as set out in Article 9 of the Berne Convention, and the exceptions permitted thereunder, fully apply in the digital environment, in particular to the use of works in digital form. It is understood that the storage of a protected work in digital form in an electronic medium constitutes a reproduction within the meaning of Article 9 of the Berne Convention'); Ricketson and Ginsburg, *supra* note 8 at ¶¶ 11.71–11.75 (unclear whether WCT covers RAM copying); Reinbothe & von Lewinski, *supra* note 7, at 43. The ambiguity of the term 'storage' permits arguments that all kinds of copying, including in temporary memory, are covered: see e.g. Dr. Mihaly Ficsor, *Copyright for the Digital Era: The WIPO 'Internet' Treaties*, 21 Colum.-VLA J. L. & the Arts 197 (1997), as well as the contrary, see e.g. Pamela Samuelson, *The U.S. Digital Agenda at WIPO*, 37 Virginia J. Int. L. 369, 390–92 (1997).

[22] WCT, art. 8 (emphasis supplied).

to what is becoming the dominant way in which works are in fact exploited in the digital online environment. After all, there should be nothing sacred about the eighteenth- or nineteenth-century *classifications* of rights under copyright, in a technological world that would have been utterly inconceivable to eighteenth-century minds. By contrast, the *justifications* offered by the Enlightenment-era framers of copyright policy should still guide us. While Madison could not have foreseen the Internet, he clearly believed that the private rights of authors furthered the general public interest in the advancement of learning,[23] and he believed that at a time when printing presses were 'growing much faster even than the population'.[24] As a matter of economic incentive to creativity, as well as the author's right to the fruits of her intellectual labor,[25] copyright should cover the actual exploitation of works of authorship.[26] On that account, one should welcome the access right, new arrival though it might be.[27]

Indeed, without an access right, it is difficult to see how in a digital era authors can maintain the 'exclusive Right' to their 'Writings' that the Constitution authorizes Congress to 'secure'. Even if Congress might qualify the right's

[23] See Federalist 43 ('The public good fully coincides in both cases [patent and copyright] with the claims of individuals').

[24] Michael Warner, *The Letters of the Republic: Publication and the Public Sphere in Eighteenth-Century America* 32 (1990). Significant technological innovations in printing, however, postdated The Federalist. See Helmut Lehmann-Haupt, *The Book in America* 71 (2d ed. 1951) (industrialization of printing begins with the early nineteenth century).

[25] Both these themes can be found in the constitutional copyright clause, in James Madison's brief justification for copyright in Federalist 43, and in other eighteenth-century documents concerning copyright in the U.S., see generally, Jane Ginsburg, *A Tale of Two Copyrights: Literary Property in Revolutionary France and America*, 64 Tulane L. Rev. 991 (1990).

[26] Not everyone would agree with this proposition. Some would contend that, as a purely statutory creation, copyright extends only as far as Congress has provided, and that Congress should not rewrite the copyright laws to increase the statutory grant every time a new mode of exploitation evolves in order to afford copyright owners the full fruits of markets that new technologies have created. See e.g. Jessica Litman, *Reforming Information Law in Copyright's Image*, 22 Dayton L. Rev. 587, 596–98 (1997).

[27] Arguably, the access right was implicit in the reproduction and distribution rights under copyright in the days before mass market copying devices. The copyright owner controlled access by choosing how to make the work available. For a pre-WCT argument for an access right in English copyright law, see Simon Olswang, *Accessright: An Evolutionary Path for Copyright in the Digital Era?* [1995] E.I.P.R. 215.

exclusivity by imposing a variety of compulsory licenses,[28] or outright exemptions,[29] it is surely one thing to introduce specific and narrow limitations in coverage,[30] quite another to design a system that pervasively fails to afford meaningful exclusivity. The latter course would clearly be inconsistent with the constitutional design.

In the past, Congress has usually, albeit not always swiftly or completely, adjusted the contours of copyright protection to correspond to the new technology-driven modes of exploitation. For example, after the advent of cable retransmissions, and after the Supreme Court's rulings that the retransmissions were not a 'performance',[31] the 1976 Copyright Act made clear that the act of performance covered cable retransmissions, although it also imposed a compulsory license regime on much of the activity.[32] In 1995, and again in 1998, Congress established a digital performance right in sound recordings. Before these amendments, sound recording copyright owners neither controlled nor received compensation for transmissions, notably broadcasts, of their works. Exclusion of sound recordings from the public performance right had been justified on the ground that radio broadcasts helped sell copies of sound recordings; no distinct market for transmissions was acknowledged.[33] With the advent of digital transmissions of sound recordings, however, Congress ultimately recognized the importance of a performance right market for sound recordings, a recognition that appears to have evolved from Congress' initial realization that digital transmissions easily become digital private copies. In the digital environment, transmissions no longer advertise or enhance sales, they threaten to

[28] See e.g. 17 U.S.C. §§ 111(d), 115, 118, 119, 122 (compulsory licenses for cable retransmission, phonorecords, public broadcasting, satellite retransmission).

[29] See e.g. id. §§ 107, 108, 110, 121 (exemptions for fair use, library photocopying, certain public performances, reproductions for the blind and disabled).

[30] The fair use exception ranges more broadly, but incorporates limiting doctrines drawn from the constitutional copyright clause, and from the first amendment. See e.g. Rosemont Ents. v. Random House, 366 F.2d 303 (2d Cir. 1966); Paul Goldstein, *Copyright and the First Amendment*, 70 Colum. L. Rev. 983 (1970); Melville B. Nimmer, *Does Copyright Abridge the First Amendment Guarantees of Free Speech and Press?*, 17 U.C.L.A. L. Rev. 1180 (1970).

[31] See Fortnightly Corp. v. United Artists Television, Inc. 392 U.S. 390, 88 S.Ct. 2084 (1968); Teleprompter Corp. v. Columbia Broad. Sys., Inc., 415 U.S. 394, 94 S.Ct. 1129 (1974).

[32] See 17 U.S.C. § 111.

[33] See e.g. Kamesh Nagarajan, *Public Performance Rights in Sound Recordings and the Threat of Digitalization,* 77 J. Pat. & Trademark Off. Soc'y 721, 724–25 (1995).

replace them.[34] The evolution of an access right is consistent with these earlier examples of Congressional response to emerging modes of exploitation of copyrighted works.

As we move to an access-based world of distribution of copyrighted works, a copyright system that neglected access controls would make copyright illusory and in the long run would disserve consumers. Access controls make it possible for authors to offer end-users a variety of distinctly priced options for enjoyment of copyrighted works. Were delivery of works not secured, novel forms of distribution would be discouraged and end-users would continue to be charged for all uses, whatever the level in fact of their consumption. Unauthorized forms of distribution from piracy to peer-to-peer file 'sharing' may fill the gap for some time, but in the long run are likely to depress the market for creating works of authorship.

Exceptions to the Access Right

Even granting that an access right is a Good Thing, is it nonetheless too much of one, at least as implemented by the DMCA? If an access right helps 'secur[e] to Authors ... the exclusive Right to their ... Writings ...', does the DMCA secure the right too effectively, too exclusively? Critics have expressed fear that access controls will foster a digital 'lock up' enabling copyright owners – who will have ceased to make the work available in analog or nonprotected digital formats – to restrict all access to works to their (overreaching) terms.[35] If, indeed, unprotected hard copies or unprotected digital copies disappear, then fair use problems may arise. On the one hand, the 'market failure' genre of fair use should fade away in a world of perfect price discrimination and direct enforcement of copyright through access controls.[36] On the other hand, access controls

[34] For the evolution of the digital performance right in sound recordings, see e.g. Jane Ginsburg, *Copyright Legislation for the 'Digital Millennium'*, 23 Colum.-VLA J. L. & Arts 137, 166–70 (1999); Mark J. Plotkin, *The Times They Are A Changin': The Digital Performance Right in the Sound Recordings Act of 1995 and the Digital Millennium Copyright Act of 1998*, 1 Vand. J. of Ent. L. & Pract. 46 (1999). On Congress response to new copyright-exploiting technology see generally Jane C. Ginsburg, *Copyright and Control over New Technologies of Dissemination*, 101 Colum. L. Rev. 1613 (2001).

See also 17 U.S.C. § 1201(k) (mandating inclusion of anticopying technology in analog video recorders manufactured or distributed after April 28, 2001).

[35] See e.g. sources cited *supra* note 12.

[36] On 'fair use as market failure', see the seminal article of the same title by Wendy Gordon, *Fair Use as Market Failure: A Structural and Economic Analysis of the Betamax Case and its Predecessors*, 82 Colum. L. R. 1600 (1982).

may be a measure too crude to accommodate a variety of noninfringing uses, including reproduction of unprotected information contained within a copyrighted work,[37] and 'transformative' fair uses, in which the second author seeks to create an independent work that comments or otherwise builds on its predecessor.[38]

Since we are here discussing access controls, and not anticopying controls, arguably fair use is not an issue, because fair use normally comes into play only *after* access to the copy has been lawfully obtained. It may be fair use to copy from a protected work; it is not fair use to steal the book in order to copy from it. This epigram, however, may be far too simplistic in the new millennium. The Digital Millennium Copyright Act establishes legal rights against circumvention of technological measures controlling access to a *work*. This is not the same thing as controlling access to a *copy*. The following example illustrates the difference between 'access to a work' and 'access to a copy of a work'. Suppose that I download copyrighted songs or documents from an authorized website. Suppose also that to hear the songs or read the documents, I must register with the copyright owner, accessing the internet from my computer. In turn, the copyright owner communicates a password. A technological measure included in the download recognizes my password and my computer. Thenceforth, when I wish to hear the song or read the document, I must enter my password and listen to or view it on the same computer; I cannot use my downloaded copy of the song or document on another computer.[39]

By making the authorized download, I have acquired lawful access to a *copy* of the work. Section 101 of the U.S. Copyright Act defines 'copies' as 'material

[37] 17 U.S.C. § 102(b) provides that copyright does not 'extend to' the 'ideas' and 'discoveries' (generally understood to mean 'facts') contained within a work of authorship. Extracting facts from a protected work therefore is not copyright infringement. See e.g. Feist Publications, Inc. v. Rural Tel. Serv. Co., 499 U.S. 340 (1991).

[38] On 'transformative use', see e.g. Pierre N. Leval, *Towards a Fair Use Standard,* 103 Harv. L. Rev. 1105 (1990). But see Diane L. Zimmerman, *The More Things Change the Less They Seem 'Transformed': Some Reflections on Fair Use,* 46 J. Copyright Soc'y U.S.A. 251 (1999) (criticizing 'transformative use' analysis).

[39] It also may mean, at least in theory, that I cannot communicate my password to a friend or family member to hear the song or read the document on my computer, since the password protects access to the work, and my disclosure of the password is an act that circumvents a protective measure that had limited access to me. Compare I.M.S. Inquiry v. Berkshire Info. Sys. 307 F. Supp 2d. 521 (SDNY 2004) (unauthorized use of actual password held not to be an act of circumvention) with 321 Studios v. MGM *supra* 307 F. Supp. 22 at 1098 (use of actual key by unauthorized person constitutes circumvention).

objects' in which 'a work' is fixed. The hard drive (or free-standing disk) on which the download was received is a material object. But the physical object 'copy' is distinct from the incorporeal 'work of authorship' that the copy embodies,[40] and I do not access 'the work' until I have entered the password (from the correct computer). Thus, 'access to the work' becomes a repeated operation; each act of hearing the song or reading the document becomes an act of 'access'. When the DMCA bars circumvention of controls on access to the 'work', the law in effect says that I cannot listen to the song or read the document without implicating the copyright owner's access right.

In this light, consider first the implementation of the user right to copy unprotected information, and second, the implementation of a transformative fair use privilege. Regarding the *de facto* protection of information, suppose that the documents I downloaded were substantially composed of public domain information, such as judicial opinions or copyright-expired literary works. § 1201(a) protects technological measures controlling access to a 'work protected under this title'; the provision does not specify how *much* of the work must be 'protected under this title'; nor does it distinguish 'thin copyright' works from more creative endeavors. Accordingly, it appears that, so long as the information provider does not merely encrypt raw public domain documents or unoriginal listings of information, but instead packages the information with copyrightable trappings (such as a new introduction or minimally original reformatting[41]), a copyrighted work will result, however scant the covering. This suggests that the copyrightable fig leaf that a producer affixes to an otherwise unprotectable work could, as a practical matter, obscure the public domain nakedness of the compiled information, and thereby insulate the judicial opinions or copyright-expired poetry from the further access that is a prerequisite to otherwise lawful copying.

Regarding transformative fair use, suppose that I gain lawful access to a song on a pay-per-listen basis, without the right to make a retention copy. Since (for purposes of the hypothetical) I am also a musicologist, I then decide I would like to study the song's harmonic patterns. Unless I have an excellent memory, I will have to pay at least another listening fee and, more likely, a listen-and-copy-once fee in order to examine the music. Exercise of my fair use privilege thus may appear to be more costly in an access-protected world. It seems quite problematic

[40] See 17 U.S.C. §§ 101, 202 (distinguishing the copy from the work).

[41] See e.g. Maljack Productions, Inc. v. UAV Corp., 964 F. Supp. 1416 (C.D. Cal. 1997), aff'd on other grounds sub nom Batjack Prods. v. GoodTimes Home Video Corp., 160 F.3d 1228 (9th Cir. 1998) (panning and scanning).

to require fair users to pay more for the privilege: in theory fair uses come out of the copyright owner's pocket, not the user's.[42]

On the other hand, in an access-protected world, fair use could in fact *cost less overall* than in the hard copy world. Without the price discrimination that access controls permit, all consumers of copyrighted works may now be paying for the fair use privileges of a few: if the work is offered at just one price point, then that price will cover some anticipated level of unauthorized copying.[43] In other words, in the hard copy world, copyright owners are not necessarily subsidizing fair use, other users are. Access controls thus can offer a better deal to consumers who do not seek to make fair uses.

Does this mean that consumers who do wish to make transformative uses would be worse off than in the hard copy world? Perhaps not, because exercising fair use in the hard copy world can carry additional costs. To return to the example of the musicologist, if my first apprehension of the song was over the radio, I would have to endeavor to hear the song more often, rather than enjoying the convenience of hearing it on demand; I thus would incur greater nonmonetary transactions costs. Exercising fair use might also cost me more money than I need spend in an access-controlled environment, since in the hard copy world, I might need to buy a copy of the full recording, at a price presumably higher than a copy-once delivery of just one song.

The real problems arise, not when a would-be noninfringing user must pay for initial access, but primarily when she cannot obtain continued access on reasonable terms. The DMCA anticipates some situations in which continued access to the work should be available, regardless of the copyright owner's goals, and accordingly exempts from the prohibition on circumvention of access controls a narrow and highly specific list of objectives, including reverse engineering and

[42] See e.g. Robert P. Merges, *The End of Friction? Property Rights and Contract in the 'Newtonian' World of On-line Commerce*, 12 Berkeley Tech. L. J. 115 (1997) (fair use is a 'subsidy' from copyright owners to users). Alternatively, one might contend that fair uses, since they fall outside the scope of a copyright owner's rights, were never in the pockets of copyright owners.

[43] For a discussion of the benefits, and problems, of price discrimination in intellectual property systems, see Wendy Gordon, *Intellectual Property as Price Discrimination: Implications for Contract*, 73 Chi.-Kent L. Rev. 1367 (1998) (defending price discrimination when employed by a producer who already has an intellectual property monopoly, such as a copyright, since price discrimination loosens the impact of the monopoly on users; by contrast, price discrimination is not an excuse for *creating* a monopoly in noncopyrightable or nonpatentable subject matter).

encryption research (within the limits set out in the statute).[44] The list, however, is not coextensive with the exceptions to copyright protection set forth with respect to traditional rights under copyright.[45] Another provision of the DMCA, however, states: 'Nothing in this section shall affect rights, remedies, limitations, or defenses applicable to copyright infringement, including fair use, under this title'.[46] Does this provision introduce a fair use defense to circumvention of access controls?

Those courts which have addressed this issue have concluded that the answer is 'no', because the statute makes access circumvention a violation distinct from copyright infringement.[47] Moreover, Congress' direction to the Librarian of Congress to conduct a rulemaking inquiry to determine whether noninfringing users of works 'are likely to be adversely affected by the prohibition' on circumvention of access controls, and, accordingly, to publish classes of works that should be exempted from the prohibition,[48] suggests that § 1201(a) does not otherwise permit a fair use defense.[49] The work is either protected against circumvention of access controls for any purpose other than those explicitly set out

[44] See 17 U.S.C. § 1201 (d)–(j). Most of these exemptions apply only to the act of circumvention. By and large, the prohibition on manufacture and distribution of devices designed to circumvent access controls, under § 1201(a) (2), remains in effect. Only §§ 1201(d) (4), (g) (4) and (j) (4) permit the development or distribution of circumvention devices solely to carry out the circumvention authorized by those sections.

[45] *Compare* id. § 1201(d)–(j) *with* 17 U.S.C. §§ 107–22 (fair use, and other exceptions to reproduction and public performance rights).

[46] Id. § 1201(c) (1).

[47] See Universal City Studios, Inc. v. Reimerdes, 111 F. Supp.2d 294, 324 (SDNY 2000) aff'd sub nom Universal City Studios, Inc. v. Corley, 273 F.3d 429 (2nd Cir. 2001) (dismissing fair use defense on the ground that fair use does not apply to violations of § 1201(a)); U.S. v. Elcom Ltd., 203 F.Supp.2d 1111, 1132 (N.D. Cal. 2002) (noting that although 'Congress could have approached the problem by targeting infringers', it purposefully chose to also target access tools and 'tool sellers'); David Nimmer, *A Riff on Fair Use in the Digital Millennium Copyright Act*, 148 U. Pa. L. Rev. 673, 729 (2000) ('the WIPO Treaties Act adds a wholly separate tort of unauthorized circumvention, to which the fair use defense is inapplicable').Id. § 1203 (authorizing civil action and stating remedies for violation of anti circumvention provisions).

[48] See 17 U.S.C. § 1201(a) (1) (C) (D).

[49] Universal City Studios, Inc. v. Corley, 273 F.3d 429, 443 n.13 (2d Cir. 2001) (legislative history shows Congress intended to preclude fair use defense to sec. 1201(a) access circumvention).

in §§ 1201(d)–(j), or it is exempted; indeterminate defenses, such as the highly contextual fair use privilege, do not fit in this scheme. As the first court to address the availability of a fair use defense to access circumvention determined, if the anti-circumvention provisions lack the user-friendly nuance of the fair use doctrine, Congress intended that result. Having considered the countervailing policy concerns, 'Congress crafted a statute that, so far as the applicability of the fair use defense to Section 1201(a) claims is concerned, is crystal clear. In such circumstances, courts may not undo what Congress has so plainly done by "construing" the words of the statute to accomplish a result that Congress rejected.'[50]

But if the only defenses the statute allows to access circumvention are those set out in the statute's narrowly crafted exceptions, and in the classes of exempted works that the Library of Congress may declare on a triennial basis, and, most importantly, if unprotected copies become scarce, then the risk of overprotection may be realized. Copyright has traditionally been cast as a means to achieve the companion goals of fostering both the 'progress of Science' and free expression; the 'exclusive right' supplies the incentive to speak, while the limitations on exclusive rights, notably the fair use doctrine, ensure that others' speech may productively build on their predecessors'.[51] As the Supreme Court indicated in *Eldred v. Ashcroft*, the limitations the 'traditional contours' of copyright impose suffice; there is no call for further First Amendment overrides.[52] But if fair use does not constrain the ambit of the access right, perhaps some other limiting doctrine must intrude.

This does not mean that defenses to circumvention are or should be fully coextensive with fair use defenses to traditional copyright violations. Rather, circumvention defenses should evolve in the context of digital online distribution; some traditional defenses may remain appropriate, others may not, but new ones may be needed.[53] One appropriate defense may arise in the context of the 'copyrightable fig leaf': when the user seeks to obtain unprotected informa-

[50] See Universal City Studios, Inc. v. Reimerdes, 111 F. Supp.2d at 324, aff'd. sub nom. Universal City Studios v. Corley, *supra* note 49.

[51] See e.g. Harper & Row v. Nation Ents. 471 U.S. 539, 549 (1985) (noting that 'a prohibition of such [fair] use would inhibit subsequent writers from attempting to improve upon prior works and thus ... frustrate the very ends sought to be attained') (citing H. Ball, Law of Copyright and Literary Property 260 (1944)); Eldred v. Ashcroft, 123 S.Ct. 769, 788 (2003) (citing both the idea/expression dichotomy and the fair use defense as 'built-in First Amendment accommodations').

[52] Eldred, 123 S.Ct. at 790.

[53] WCT, Agreed Statement regarding art. 10.

tion rather than to copy the protected work. It should be permissible, once access to a copy of the work has been lawfully obtained, to circumvent any protection attached to the thin copyright veneer in order to access and copy the raw information.[54]

A Fair Access exception for purposes of making a transformative use is, however, more problematic, because in this case the user's claim addresses core copyrighted works. Nonetheless, the user's conduct would be privileged were the work disseminated without access controls. Does the use therefore become less 'fair' when the copyright owner interposes an access control? In fact, fairness may depend on the nature of the access control: what is the copyright owner seeking to prohibit? In theory, access controls are designed to protect a business model based on price discrimination according to intensity of use; they are not intended to prohibit scholarly or critical examination of the works themselves. But that may be the result if the user cannot consult or acquire a fair-usable copy at a reasonable price, or from a source such as a public library. And if hard copies and unprotected digital copies do disappear in a brave new pay-per-access world, then the threat to transformative fair use becomes more than a paranoid fantasy.[55] In fact, works are likely to remain available in traditional hard copies and unprotected digital copies, but this essay takes as its premise the eventual disappearance of those copies for at least some kinds of works. In that event, it may become necessary to modify the scope of the § 1201(a) access right, to continue to provide strong protection against unauthorized *initial* acquisition of a copy of a protected work, but to allow for circumvention in order to engage in fair uses once the copy has been lawfully acquired. In the absence of such a

[54] This approach resembles that of § 1201(f), which permits circumvention of access controls on a lawfully obtained copy in order to 'identify[] and analyz[e]' those elements of the computer program 'necessary to achieve interoperability of an independently created computer program with other programs ...'. See also Sony Corp. of America v. Connectix, 203 F.3d 596 (9th Cir. 2000), *cert denied* 531 U.S. 871 (2000); Sega Ents., Inc. v. Accolade, Inc., 977 F.2d 1510 (9th Cir. 1992).

[55] The potential unavailability of hard copies also threatens future archives: if a work is available only in an access-protected format, and that format becomes obsolete, a record of the work may be lost unless librarians or archivists may circumvent the access control to extract the work for preservation in a more stable and accessible format. The Librarian of Congress has recognized this threat, and has accordingly provided for certain narrow exemptions, from the prohibition on access circumvention. See 68 Fed. Reg. 62011–18 Final Rule, Exemption to Prohibition on Circumvention of Copyright Protection Systems for Access Control Technologies (Oct. 31, 2003).

modification, courts may perceive a First Amendment mandate to craft a lawful use privilege.

The access right is, I would contend, a necessary and integral component of copyright law, despite its formal placement in a separate section of Title 17. But, in a world in which hard copies or unprotected digital copies disappear, without an appropriate lawful use limitation, the access right under § 1201 becomes more than such a component. It becomes instead an über-copyright law, rigid as to specified exceptions, and therefore freed of further inquiry into the balance of copyright owner rights and user privileges that the fair use doctrine – and the constitutional structure of copyright law – require.

Chapter 3

The Rational Limits Of Trademark Law (2000)

*Graeme B. Dinwoodie**

INTRODUCTION

Over the last two decades, the reach of U.S. trademark law has significantly expanded in several different ways. In this essay, I will focus on three expansions that have tested the limits of trademark law: the subject matter potentially protected as trademarks has become virtually unlimited; the scope of rights afforded a trademark owner has been extended to prevent noncompeting uses by others that are not likely to cause consumer confusion but which may dilute the distinctiveness of the trademark owner's mark; and, most recently, trademarks have been reflexively afforded additional protection against conduct known as cybersquatting. After reviewing these three developments, I will suggest that each implicates in its own way a fundamental question about the direction of U.S. trademark law: what is to be the lodestar that will guide trademark law and help establish rational limits on protection?[1] I argue that trademark law must develop by explicit reference to its basic purposes. Although these purposes are somewhat general and more varied in nature than often recognized, attention to them will ground trademark law in present commercial reality without foreclosing adaptation to future social developments. Trademark law is a mercantile law. As such, it is (and must be) both shaped and limited by the market forces that it

* Professor of Law, Chicago-Kent College of Law. Thanks to Mark Janis, Graeme Austin, and Brian Havel for comments on an earlier draft.

1 By this title, I consciously seek to invoke the work of Frank Schechter, whose 1927 Harvard Law Review article *The Rational Basis of Trademark Law* has found substantial vindication in current (i.e. 2000) U.S. attitudes toward the scope of trademark rights. See Frank I. Schechter, *The Rational Basis of Trademark Protection*, 40 Harv. L. Rev. 813 (1927).

seeks to regulate. To be sure, it must not become entirely hostage to market forces; on occasion trademark law will need to recognize and act on its capacity to construct the market. But, even there, trademark law must pay attention to empirical realities (if only to determine when to do more than react to the market). That is, recognizing limits – whether by reacting to, or shaping, market forces – is best achieved through purposive analysis. In the three areas canvassed in this essay, however, the courts and Congress are marking out a different path, involving ad hoc delineation of trademark holders' rights in response to the latest perceived social or economic threats to brand values.

If one seeks to pursue a purposive approach to trademark law, then one must first identify the basic purposes of trademark protection. In this essay, I will reaffirm the classic avoidance of consumer confusion rationale as more than sufficient to serve the legitimate concerns of producers, especially as that rationale has been implemented by U.S. courts in recent years. The basic fairness and utility of this purpose is evidenced, perhaps, by the fact that tying the limits of trademark law to it would draw a balanced and flexible line through the three difficult issues that I discuss. Purposive analysis reflective of the confusion avoidance rationale offers the possibility, dependent upon social and economic developments, of more generous trade dress protection than under the categorical approach recently endorsed by the U.S. Supreme Court. But it would limit the scope of trademark rights more narrowly than Congress has done in the federal dilution statute. And it would offer a workable vehicle for addressing conflicts between domain names and trademark rights without detailed congressional legislation.

But, more important than the specific balance that this purposive approach strikes in particular settings, it would guide the courts in establishing rational limits to trademark law. This is not to say that limits on trademark law might not appropriately emanate from other sources or objectives. But a sense of principled direction is sadly missing from many recent developments. Purposive analysis would ground trademark law in social and market realities; absent that grounding, trademark law may become a vehicle for mere rent seeking. And, as different intellectual property rights converge and trademark rights come to protect subject matter protected by other regimes such as copyright or patent, the strength of trademark law's claim to regulate such matter in a manner different from those other regimes rests upon the policies of trademark law retaining a distinctive hue. Purposive analysis will ensure that trademark law retains that characteristic coloration.

I. THE SUBJECT MATTER OF TRADEMARK PROTECTION: TRADE DRESS AND 'TERTIUM QUIDS'

Recent years have seen an explosion in the number of so-called 'trade dress' infringement cases brought under the federal trademark statute,[2] the Lanham Act.[3] Indeed, all three trademark opinions of the U.S. Supreme Court in the last decade have involved trade dress,[4] and the Court has just agreed to hear another trade dress case next term.[5] The term 'trade dress' is used to refer to source-identifying subject matter other than words or two-dimensional pictorial images; in particular, it commonly refers to the source-identifying aspects of a product's packaging, color or design.[6] Courts in the United States have long protected the packaging of a product under trademark law,[7] and since 1976 the federal courts have also recognized that consumers might identify the source of

[2] For a survey of the volume of product design trade dress litigation in particular over the last decade, see Graeme B. Dinwoodie, *The Death of Ontology: A Teleological Approach to Trademark Law*, 84 Iowa L. Rev. 611, 623 n.58 (1999) (listing number of reported cases annually). See also Jay Dratler, Jr., *Trade Dress Protection For Product Configurations: Is There a Conflict with Patent Policy?*, 24 Am. Intell. Prop. L. Ass'n Q.J. 427, 430–31 (1996) (noting burgeoning trade dress litigation).

[3] 15 U.S.C. §§ 1051–1127 (1994).

[4] See Two Pesos, Inc. v. Taco Cabana, Inc., 505 U.S. 763 (1992); Qualitex Co. v. Jacobsen Products, 514 U.S. 159 (1995); Wal-Mart Stores, Inc. v. Samara Brothers, Inc., 120 S. Ct. 1339 (2000).

[5] See Marketing Displays, Inc. v. Traffix Devices, Inc., 200 F.3d 929 (6th Cir. 1999), *cert. granted*, 120 S. Ct. 2715 (2000).

[6] The term 'trademark' is conventionally reserved for situations where the identifier of a product's source is a word or pictorial symbol, but the significance of this terminology is now slight. See Blau Plumbing, Inc. v. S.O.S. Fix-It, Inc., 781 F.2d 604, 608 (7th Cir. 1986) (concluding that there was 'no substantive difference' between trade dress and trademarks). As discussed more fully below, the Supreme Court's decision in *Two Pesos* supports the suggestion that the terminology is of lesser significance, while the Court's more recent decision in *Wal-Mart Stores* tends to suggest otherwise (at least with respect to trade dress consisting of product design). See *infra* text accompanying notes 39–70.

[7] See e.g. Eastman Kodak Co. v. Royal Pioneer Paper Box Mfg., 197 F. Supp. 132 (E.D. Pa. 1961) (packaging for photographic products); see also George Basch Co. v. Blue Coral, Inc., 968 F.2d 1532 (2d Cir. 1992) (container for metal polish).

a product by its design or configuration.[8] In 1995, the United States Supreme Court resolved a split among the lower courts and held that the mere color of a product could be registered as a trademark.[9] Indeed, in that case, *Qualitex Co. v. Jacobsen Products*,[10] the Court went so far as to comment that, under the statutory definition of 'trademark', anything that is capable of carrying meaning can serve as the subject matter of a trademark.[11]

Although these expansions in trademark subject matter raise more difficult issues for trademark law than according protection to words or two-dimensional images,[12] contemplating possible protection is wholly consistent with the underlying purposes of trademark law. Trademark law protects symbols that identify the source of goods and distinguish those goods from the goods of another producer. If a competitor were able to market its goods under a confusingly similar symbol, consumers could mistakenly purchase the wrong goods, and the producer's investment in the goodwill of the product would be appropriated.[13]

[8] See Truck Equipment Serv. Corp. v. Fruehauf, 536 F.2d 1210 (8th Cir.), *cert. denied*, 429 U.S. 861 (1976) ('*TESCO*') (protecting the appearance of the hopper of a truck); see also Jessica Litman, Note, *The Problem of Functional Features: Trade Dress Infringement Under Section 43(a) of the Lanham Act*, 82 Colum. L. Rev. 77, 83 (1982) (identifying *TESCO* as the first successful product design infringement claim under the Lanham Act).

[9] See Qualitex Co. v. Jacobsen Products, 514 U.S. 159 (1995). Although the Supreme Court has not expressly addressed the issue, it is broadly accepted that other subject matter such as sounds (and perhaps even smells) can serve as trademarks. See *id.* at 162 ('If a shape, a sound, and a fragrance can act as symbols why, one might ask, can a color not do the same?'); see e.g. *In re* Clarke, 17 U.S.P.Q. 2d 1238, 1240 (T.T.A.B. 1990) (scent of thread acted to identify source of thread).

[10] 514 U.S. 159 (1995).

[11] See *id.* at 162.

[12] See Dinwoodie, *supra* note 2, at 624–45. These issues can be addressed by doctrinal vehicles, such as the doctrine of functionality, that are closely tied to competing or additional purposes of trademark, namely not to undermine the patent system and to avoid anticompetitive effects. See *id.* at 684–751.

[13] Two primary justifications have traditionally been offered in support of trademark protection: to 'protect the public so that it may be confident that, in purchasing a product bearing a particular trademark which it favorably knows, it will get the product which it asks for and which it wants to get'; and to ensure that 'where the owner of a trademark has spent energy, time and money in presenting to the public the product, he is protected in his investment from its appropriation by pirates and cheats'. S. Rep. No. 1333, 79th Cong., 2d Sess. 3 (1946). Many limits can also be deduced internally from these justifications. Other limits may reflect additional policy values. See Graeme B. Dinwoodie, Working Paper on file with author.

Trademark protection against confusing simulation thus advances the interests of producers and consumers by protecting the integrity of consumer understanding and the producer's investment in creating goodwill. In turn, trademark protection reduces the customer's costs of shopping and encourages the production of quality products.[14]

If consumers identify a product by its packaging, color or design features, these same concerns are implicated to no less an extent (even though countervailing cencerns related to competition might also be heightened). This purposive analysis of trademark protection undergirds large parts of the opinions in *Qualitex* and *Two Pesos, Inc. v. Taco Cabana, Inc.*[15] It is in part because trade dress can serve the purpose of a trademark, and because the nature of the subject matter is thus irrelevant to the purpose of trademark law, that the Court removed limits on trademark protection derived from the nature or classification of the subject matter.[16] But an essential premise underlying this argument is a mark's distinctiveness, i.e. the claimed mark must represent a feature by which consumers identify and distinguish a product from others. Distinctiveness is central to trademark protection because, without it, no goodwill attaches to the claimed mark and thus no consumers will be confused by others using the same mark. 'A consumer must recognize that a particularly packaged product comes from Source A before she can be confused by a similar package from Source B.'[17]

The distinctiveness of trade dress has thus been one of the principal subjects of the recent Supreme Court case law. It is the rock upon which the expansion of trademark subject matter has been built, both factually and legally. The factual premises have been established by the growing visuality of contemporary society.[18] And in 1992, in *Two Pesos, Inc. v. Taco Cabana, Inc.*,[19] the Court, in the course of upholding trademark protection for the decor and ambiance of a Mexican fast-food restaurant against replication by a competitor, laid the

14 See Qualitex Co. v. Jacobsen Products, 514 U.S. 159, 163–64 (1995).

15 See e.g. *Two Pesos*, 505 U.S. at 773–75; *Qualitex*, 514 U.S. at 163–64.

16 For a fuller explication of the Court's purposive analysis, see Dinwoodie, *supra* note 2, at 645–56.

17 Charles Jacquin Et Cie, Inc. v. Destileria Serralles, Inc., 921 F.2d 467, 472 n.5 (3d Cir. 1990).

18 See generally Mitchell Stephens, *The Rise of the Image, The Fall of the Word* (1998); see also Bernard Stamler, *Mother Jones Returns to Roots With New Look*, N.Y. Times, Aug. 17, 1998, at C7 (reporting views of Jeffrey Klein, founder of Mother Jones magazine, that 'there is an emerging next generation ... but their language is not the same. This generation communicates visually as well as verbally').

19 505 U.S. 763 (1992).

corresponding legal foundation when it approved the assimilation of the principles governing the distinctiveness of verbal trademarks and non-verbal trade dress. In particular, the Court held that the distinctiveness of non-verbal trade dress may (like verbal marks) be established by proof of either inherent distinctiveness or secondary meaning.[20] Prior to *Two Pesos*, the circuit courts were divided on whether trade dress could be inherently distinctive; some, such as the Second Circuit, required evidence of secondary meaning before offering protection to trade dress.[21]

The *Two Pesos* decision was, however, incomplete in two primary respects. First, it failed to address the *means* by which the assimilation of the principles governing the distinctiveness of verbal marks and non-verbal dress was to be effected. Classical distinctiveness analysis[22] was developed to adjudicate the protectability of verbal or pictorial marks, and those modes of analysis proved inadequate when transplanted to trade dress. They were particularly deficient when applied to determine whether a design feature was distinctive. Thus, lower courts struggled with the development and application of tests designed to measure the distinctiveness of trade dress. Some continued to apply the classical (*Abercrombie*) test used with respect to word marks.[23] Others applied different

[20] Secondary meaning exists when consumers over time come to associate the word or dress in question with a single source. See Restatement (Third) of Unfair Competition § 13 cmt. e (1995) ('Secondary meaning exists only if a significant number of prospective purchasers understand the term, when used in connection with a particular kind of good, service, or business, not merely in its lexicographic sense, but also as an indication of association with a particular, even if anonymous, entity').

[21] See Graeme B. Dinwoodie, *Reconceptualizing the Inherent Distinctiveness of Product Design Trade Dress*, 75 North Carolina L. Rev. 471, 488–92 (1997).

[22] Under U.S. law, distinctiveness is measured by locating the mark in one of a spectrum of conceptual categories that 'blend without clear differentiation into one another'. See *id.* at 485. A mark will be regarded as inherently distinctive if it is 'fanciful', 'arbitrary' or 'suggestive' in relation to the goods upon which it is affixed. Marks classified as 'descriptive' of the goods are not inherently distinctive and can be protected only upon proof that they have actually acquired distinctiveness in the minds of consumers. See generally Abercrombie & Fitch Co. v. Hunting World, Inc., 537 F.2d 4, 9 (2d Cir. 1976).

[23] See e.g. Stuart Hall Co. v. Ampad Corp., 51 F.3d 780, 788 (8th Cir. 1995) (applying same doctrinal tests to trade dress and trademarks); Kompan A.S. v. Park Structures, Inc., 890 F. Supp. 1167, 1174 (N.D.N.Y. 1995); see also Sunbeam Prods. v. West Bend Co., 123 F.3d 246, 252 & 260 (5th Cir. 1997) (applying *Abercrombie* to product design despite express recognition of differences between words and designs). This

tests to measure trade dress distinctiveness, such as the so-called *Seabrook* test, which called upon a court to consider whether a shape or packaging feature was 'a common, basic shape or design, whether it [was] unique or unusual in a particular field, or whether it [was] a mere refinement of [a] commonly-adopted and well-known form of ornamentation for a particular class of goods viewed by the public as a dress or ornamentation for the goods.'[24] Finally, some concluded that while existing distinctiveness analysis might helpfully assist in an evaluation of the distinctiveness of product packaging, it was unhelpful in the case of product design,[25] and thus developed different tests depending upon the category – design or packaging – into which the trade dress fell.[26]

This final approach required the courts in question to develop new analytical devices with which to measure the distinctiveness of product design.[27] The tests

approach was supported by some scholars. See e.g. David W. Opderbeck, *Form and Function: Protecting Trade Dress Rights in Product Configurations*, 20 Seton Hall. Legis. J. 1, 38 (1996) (endorsing application of *Abercrombie* to product design); see also Dratler, *supra* note 2, at 488–92 (approving application of *Abercrombie* if conceived of in terms of range of alternative designs).

24 Seabrook Foods, Inc. v. Bar-Well Foods, Ltd., 568 F.2d 1342, 1344 (C.C.P.A. 1977).

25 This difficulty arises for two primary reasons. First, the *Abercrombie* formulation is rooted in notions, such as descriptiveness, that tap into our facility with the meaning of words and are thus less intuitive in the case of non-verbal signs. Second, in product design cases, unlike those involving product packaging or words affixed to products, courts saw no obvious relationship between the mark and the product which comprised the mark, and it is that relationship to which the *Abercrombie* test was directed. See Duraco Prods. v. Joy Plastic Enters., 41 F.3d 1431, 1441 (3d Cir. 1994) ('The very basis for the trademark taxonomy – the descriptive relationship between the mark and the product, along with the degree to which the mark describes the product – is unsuited for application to the product itself'); *id.* at 1434 ('[T]raditional trade dress doctrine does not "fit" a product configuration case because unlike product packaging, a product configuration differs fundamentally from a product's trademark, insofar as it is not a symbol according to which one can relate the signifier (the trademark, or perhaps the packaging) to the signified (the product))'; *id.* at 1440–41 ('Being constitutive of the product itself and thus having no such dialectical relationship to the product, the product's configuration cannot be said to be "suggestive" or "descriptive" of the product, or "arbitrary" or "fanciful" in relation to it').

26 See e.g. Duraco Prods. v. Joy Plastic Enters., 41 F.3d 1431 (3d Cir. 1994); Knitwaves, Inc. v. Lollytogs Ltd., 71 F.3d 996 (2d Cir. 1995).

27 It should also have caused consideration of how to distinguish between packaging and design. See *infra* text accompanying notes 65–67 (discussing *Wal-Mart Stores*).

that they developed[28] were unduly complex and tended to provide lesser trade dress protection for product designs than for packaging.[29] This result was justified in large part by the contention that design features were less likely to act as trademarks for consumers (although, more candidly, might have been supported by countervailing concerns apart from distinctiveness).[30]

The development of separate approaches to different categories of trade dress tied in with the second incomplete aspect of *Two Pesos*. The *extent* of the assimilation announced by the *Two Pesos* court was unclear: did it apply to forms of trade dress other than restaurant decor? In particular, did it apply to product design? Courts developing the new (and stricter) tests for inherent distinctiveness of product designs largely proceeded on the assumption that *Two Pesos* did require the possibility of inherently distinctive product designs.[31] But they also concluded that *Two Pesos* did not foreclose them from developing separate tests that might confine the circumstances in which that legal conclusion would be reached.[32] By either route – blanket denials of inherent distinctiveness or tests that effectively precluded the possibility – a categorical approach that distinguished between packaging and design was being forged.[33]

[28] See e.g. *Duraco*, 41 F.3d at 1434 & 1448–49 (holding that 'to be inherently distinctive, a product feature or a combination or arrangement of features, i.e., a product configuration, for which Lanham Act protection is sought must be (i) unusual and memorable, (ii) conceptually separable from the product, and (iii) likely to serve primarily as a designator of origin of the product').

[29] See Dinwoodie, *supra* note 21, at 553–62 (discussing effects of these tests).

[30] See *Duraco*, 40 F.3d at 1448 ('[A] consumer is substantially more likely to trust a product's packaging rather than its configuration as an indicium of source'); Knitwaves Inc. v. Lollytogs Ltd., 71 F.3d 996, 1007–08 (2d Cir. 1995); see also EFS Mktg. v. Russ Berrie & Co., 76 F.3d 487, 491 (2d Cir. 1996) ('In *Knitwaves*, ... we explained that product-configuration trade dresses are less likely than packaging-configuration dresses to serve the source-identification function that is a prerequisite to Lanham Act protection ... [Consumers] are more likely to be attracted to the product for the product's features, rather than for the source-identifying role the features might play').

[31] See *Duraco*, 40 F.3d at 1445–46 ('[W]e do read *Two Pesos* as giving an imprimatur to finding trade dress in a product configuration to be inherently distinctive under certain narrow circumstances').

[32] See *id.* at 1442.

[33] In part, it might be viewed as the re-establishment of a traditional distinction between packaging and design. See Jerome H. Reichman, *Design Protection And The New Technologies: The United States Experience In A Transnational Perspective*, 19 U. Balt. L. Rev. 6, 87 (1989).

Throughout the 1990s, it was far from clear which approach to trade dress – the purposive or the categorical – would prevail. The Court's subsequent decision in *Qualitex Co. v. Jacobsen Prods.*, in which the Court recognized that a color *per se* could be registered as a product's trademark under the Lanham Act, did not answer this question. The *Qualitex* opinion can be read as expansionist in nature, in that it endorsed the disregard of limits on trademark subject matter; and the Court rejected the formulation of blanket rules of trademark law based upon problems that might occasionally be presented by this new subject matter. But the Court also analogized color to descriptive marks and thus appeared to require secondary meaning as a prerequisite to protection.[34] These mixed signals suggested, perhaps, an unease with extending the assimilationist decision in *Two Pesos* too far. The policy considerations, and exercises in statutory interpretation, that led the *Two Pesos* court to recognize inherently distinctive trade dress, should in theory permit of the same argument with respect to color. And it should do likewise with product design. But *Qualitex* contained hints of caution with respect to color, and some lower courts found room in *Two Pesos* to inject similar restrictions into the protection of product design.

This brief summary of judicial developments does not capture the range of divergent approaches that developed in the lower courts.[35] Courts were pervasively divided, and a congressional effort to resolve the splits in the lower courts, which would have involved legislating a single test (modeled on the *Seabrook* test) for all trade dress, stalled in the face of opposition from constituents of the

[34] The *Qualitex* Court contrasted marks consisting of color *per se* with inherently distinctive marks and compared them with descriptive terms. See *Qualitex*, 514 U.S. at 162–63 (noting that 'a product's color is unlike "fanciful", "arbitrary" or "suggestive" words or designs, which almost automatically tell a customer which brand they refer to'); *id.* (analogizing consumer association with color to descriptive terms, and stating that lack of objection to protection existed with respect to color that has attained secondary meaning); *id.* at 1307 (logic of protecting descriptive marks that have acquired secondary meaning applies also to color *per se*); see also Mana Prods. v. Columbia Cosmetics Mfg., 65 F.3d 1063, 1071 (2d Cir. 1995) ('In light of the Supreme Court's decision in *Qualitex*, color is capable of obtaining trademark status in the same manner [as] a descriptive mark ... by attaining secondary meaning'); Knitwaves, Inc. v. Lollytogs Ltd., 71 F.3d 996, 1008 (2d Cir. 1995) ('[The *Qualitex*] court concluded [that] a product's color is ... eligible for trademark protection only when it acquires secondary meaning ...').

[35] For a fuller analysis, see Dratler, *supra* note 2, at 469–506; Dinwoodie, *supra* note 2, at 656–80.

relevant House sub-committee chair.[36] In March 2000, however, the U.S. Supreme Court answered some of these open questions. In *Wal-Mart Stores, Inc.* v. *Samara Brothers, Inc.*,[37] the Court granted certiorari on the question 'what must be shown to establish that a product's design is inherently distinctive for purposes of Lanham Act trade-dress protection?'[38]

Wal-Mart involved trade dress rights that the plaintiff claimed in the design of a line of children's seersucker clothing. The plaintiff had prevailed before the Second Circuit, where the court had found the design to be inherently distinctive. Although the Court granted certiorari to determine, '*what must be shown* to establish that a product's design is inherently distinctive for purposes of Lanham Act trade-dress protection?', Wal-Mart argued that product designs could be protectable trade dress only if secondary meaning was shown. In a unanimous decision the Court accepted that argument, concluding that while packaging may be inherently distinctive, product design may not.[39] Thus, although the Court endorsed an expansive view of trademark subject matter, it also supported a categorical distinction between packaging (which could be inherently distinctive) and product design (which could not). It thus raised to the surface the ambivalence that underlay *Qualitex*.

That the Court was operating from a different mindset is seen by its interpretive use of Section 2 of the Lanham Act. Section 2 lists the grounds upon which a federal trademark registration may be denied; it makes no reference to trademark subject matter. In *Two Pesos*, the Court interpreted that silence as suggesting no basis upon which to make a distinction between different types of trademark subject matter;[40] eight years later, the Court read that silence as suggesting no barrier to the development of such a distinction.[41] Similarly, although the *Qualitex* court has analogized color to descriptive marks, the court in *Wal-Mart* made explicit that in *Qualitex* 'we held that a color could be protected as a trademark, but only upon a showing of secondary meaning'.[42]

36 See Trade Dress Protection Act, H.R. 3163, 105th Cong. (articulating predictive test for determining distinctiveness of trade dress and listing non-exclusive factors).

37 120 S. Ct. 1339 (2000).

38 See Wal-Mart v. Samara Bros, 120 S. Ct. 308 (1999).

39 The respondent, Samara Brothers, had argued (with some basis but ultimately unsuccessfully) that that question was not encompassed by the certiorari grant.

40 See *Two Pesos*, 505 U.S. at 772–74 (White J.) (finding no textual basis for distinction between trade dress and trademarks either in registration or infringement provisions of statute).

41 See *Wal-Mart Stores, Inc.* 120 S. Ct. at 1343–44.

42 *Id.* at 1344.

What had altered the Court's perspective in eight years? The Court marshaled two primary reasons for requiring secondary meaning for product design protection. First, the Court suggested that product designs do not automatically identify source for consumers in the way that packaging or word marks do.[43] This categorical conclusion probably bears some incidental correlation to present social reality. But there may be circumstances in which it does not, and indeed those circumstances may become more frequent as society becomes more visual and global marketing reduces reliance on linguistic forms of communication.[44] If the Court believed it less likely that consumers would identify a product by its design than by its packaging, it could have adopted a test (like *Seabrook*) that enables courts to ask that very question.[45] Instead, the Court foreclosed individualized scrutiny of its (unsupported) social generalization, by embedding that generalization as a rule of law.

Given the reluctance of the Court in *Qualitex* to develop rules of law based upon blanket assumptions,[46] the thinking that persuaded the Court to entrench an increasingly questionable factual premise as a rule of law is more candidly revealed by the second reason tendered by the Court. The Court feared that broad product design trade dress protection might have anticompetitive effects because design, unlike packaging or words, serves purposes other than source identification.[47] Concern for the potentially anticompetitive effects of trade dress protection is typically reflected in the functionality analysis, whereby a

[43] See *id.*

[44] See Dinwoodie, *supra* note 2, at 639–45. The Internet may change things in ways that are as yet unclear. Thus, while global marketing (facilitated by the Internet) might highlight the use of non-verbal symbols to bridge cultural and linguistic divides, the Internet is still heavily text-dependent. For example, the means of searching the Internet will likely affect the means by which online consumers identify and distinguish products, and the leading search engines are text based. But this facet of the Internet may be changing. See Kelly v. Arriba Software, 77 F.Supp.2d 1116, 1121 (C.D. Cal. 1999) (finding that a 'visual search engine' that copied images in the course of indexing images necessary to fulfill its search engine function was protected by the copyright fair use doctrine), in part, rev'd in part, 336 F. 811 (9th Cir. 2003).

[45] The *Wal-Mart* court's focus on the producer's purpose in selecting the word or design as relevant to distinctiveness fundamentally misunderstands trademark law. See Dinwoodie, *supra* note 21, at 547 (noting that distinctiveness and trademark protection are based upon 'public association, not private aspiration').

[46] See *Qualitex*, 514 U.S. at 168 (rejecting rule prohibiting protection of color *per se* because 'it relie[d] on an occasional problem to justify a blanket prohibition').

[47] See *Wal-Mart Stores, Inc.*, 120 S. Ct. at 1344.

design found to be 'functional' will be unprotected by trademark.[48] Indeed, the *Qualitex* opinion 'elevated the importance of the functionality doctrine by casting it – and not the ontological status of the mark subject matter – as the sentinel of competition'.[49] And, since *Qualitex*, Congress has heightened the efficacy of the functionality doctrine by imposing the burden on that question on a plaintiff where the design is not registered as a trademark.[50]

Despite this, the *Wal-Mart* court viewed the mere possibility of a claim of inherently distinctive product design trade dress as a threat to competition because a rule of law permitting such a claim would 'facilitate plausible threats of suit against new entrants based upon alleged inherent distinctiveness'.[51] The court's fear of such suits stemmed from its lack of confidence that a clear test for the inherent distinctiveness of product design could be devised.[52] At oral argument, and in the briefs submitted to the Court, the possible test upon which most debate centered was the *Seabrook* test.[53] Although Samara argued that application of the classical *Abercombie* trademark test[54] should, under *Two Pesos*, be applied to all trade dress, its more significant argument had been that the *Seabrook* test could provide appropriate guidance in trade dress cases. And the *Seabrook* test was also endorsed by various amici, including the United States government.[55]

The *Seabrook* test does, however, suffer from one conspicuous frailty. Without an overarching test, a mere assessment of 'uniqueness' is irrelevant to trademark law. The justices noted as much at oral argument, as had scholars before them.[56] The *Seabrook* test will only work – but *will* work – if it is viewed in light of the

[48] The doctrine of functionality denies the grant of trade dress rights where protection would significantly hinder competition (because a competitor needs to be able to use the trade dress feature in order to compete effectively) or would undermine the limits of the patent system. See *Qualitex*, 514 U.S. at 165 ('This court ... has explained that "in general terms, a product feature is functional," and cannot serve as a trademark, "if it is essential to the use or purpose of the article or if it affects the cost or quality of the article," that is, if exclusive use of the feature would put competitors at a significant non-reputation related disadvantage').

[49] See Dinwoodie, *supra* note 2, at 655.

[50] See 15 U.S.C. § 1125(a)(3) (West Supp. 1999).

[51] *Wal-Mart Stores, Inc.*, 120 S. Ct. at 1344.

[52] See *id.* at 1344–45.

[53] See *supra* text accompanying note 24.

[54] See *supra* note 22.

[55] See Brief of the United States as Amicus Curiae in Support of the Petitioner, 1999 WL 1045127 at * 8; Transcript of Oral Argument, 2000 WL 72053 at * 19.

[56] See Dinwoodie, *supra* note 2, at 658–59 n.195; Transcript of Oral Argument, 2000 WL 72053 at * 40–43.

overarching inquiry of whether consumers are likely to identify the product in question by its design. Without repeating the explanations I have sketched elsewhere of how this test could be made to work and serve the purposes of trademark law,[57] suffice it to say that the government compounded the weakness of *Seabrook* operating without any such overarching inquiry by refusing at oral argument to answer questions regarding how *Seabrook* would be applied in the case before the Court.[58] The justices reacted adversely to that response at oral argument,[59] and the Court (perhaps understandably) responded in its opinion with a conclusion that the test was 'insufficiently clear to provide the basis for summary disposition of an anticompetitive strike suit'.[60]

Because such arguments regarding the overarching purpose of the *Seabrook* test were not put to the Court,[61] the holding was as much grounded on concern over the anti-competitive effects of uncertain doctrinal tests,[62] as on a firm conviction that a secondary meaning requirement was warranted either by the purposes of trademark law or was rooted in the statutory language.

But this prudentially derived conclusion raised another problem, which the Court acknowledged.[63] *Two Pesos* 'unquestionably established the legal principle

[57] For a fuller explication of how the *Seabrook* test can be used in tandem with an overarching predictive inquiry, see Dinwoodie, *supra* note 21, at 568–602.

[58] See Transcript of Oral Argument, 2000 WL 72053 at * 20.

[59] See *id*. at * 20–21.

[60] *Wal-Mart Stores, Inc.*, 120 S. Ct. at 1345.

[61] During oral argument, some members of the Court appeared to be searching for such guidance (by supplementing the *Seabrook* inquiry with 'additional questions'), but counsel for Samara resisted such efforts out of a concern that any formulation would tend toward a requirement of secondary meaning. See Transcript of Oral Argument, 2000 WL 72053 at * 40–41. But this need not be the case. See Dinwoodie, *supra* note 21, at 568–602.

[62] At oral argument, Justice O'Connor commented that inherent distinctiveness is like obscenity (difficult to define, but 'I know it when I see it'). See Transcript of Oral Argument, 2000 WL 72053 at * 6.

[63] The Court's conclusion also raised the possibility of harm to a producer foreclosed from obtaining immediate trademark protection for its inherently distinctive design, and having to wait instead to prove secondary meaning. But the Court suggested that the availability of a design patent or copyright protection for designs reduced the level of harm that a producer might suffer. See *Wal-Mart Stores*, 120 S. Ct. at 1345. This statement is remarkably oblivious to the deficiencies of copyright and design protection for product designs in the United States. See David Goldenberg, *The Long And Winding Road: A History of The Fight Over Industrial Design Protection In The United States*, 45 J. Copr. Soc'y 21, 22–24 (1997)

that trade dress can be inherently distinctive'.[64] The Court distinguished *Two Pesos*, however, by describing that case as involving 'product packaging' (which the Court implies can be inherently distinctive) 'or else some *tertium quid* that is akin to product packaging and has no bearing on the present case.'[65] And because this categorical distinction between packaging and design would be difficult to define,[66] the Court suggested that in close cases, courts err on the side of classifying trade dress as product design and thus requiring secondary meaning.[67]

The Court believed that this pragmatic approach to the difficulties of drawing a line between design and packaging would be unproblematic because it would occur with lesser frequency than would the dilemma that would otherwise occur, namely seeking to determine the inherent distinctiveness of product design.[68] Yet this statement ignores two likely litigation strategies. Because trade dress is often a composite of features and packaging, to be considered as a whole and not as merely the sum of its parts,[69] litigants will likely seek to include some packaging elements in their claimed trade dress to take advantage of more liberal tests of distinctiveness. In short, this will encourage 'category-shopping', and thus involve a wholly unnecessary use of judicial resources in seeking to

(discussing design patent protection); Shira Perlmutter, *Conceptual Separability And Copyright In The Designs of Useful Articles*, 37 J. Copr. Soc'y 339 (1990) (discussing copyright protection). Indeed, given the inter-relationship of different forms of intellectual property protection for designs, see Reichman, *supra* note 33; it may be that this restriction on trade dress protection may give added impetus to design legislation proposals in the U.S. Congress. See Graeme B. Dinwoodie, *The Integration of Domestic and International Intellectual Property Lawmaking*, 24 Colum.-V.L.A. J. L. & Arts 305 (1999) (discussing study of design legislation ordered by the Digital Millennium Copyright Act).

[64] *Wal-Mart Stores,* 120 S. Ct. at 1345.

[65] *Id.* at 1345.

[66] See Dinwoodie, *supra* note 21, at 573–85.

[67] See *Wal-Mart Stores,* 120 S. Ct. at 1346.

[68] See *id.*

[69] See e.g. American Greetings Corp. v. Dan-Dee Imports, Inc., 807 F.2d 1136, 1141 (3d Cir. 1986) ('Trade dress is a complex composite of features and the law of unfair competition in respect to trade dress requires that all of the features be considered together, not separately'); Paddington Corp. v. Attiki Imports & Distribs., 996 F.2d 577, 584 (2d Cir. 1993) ('One could no more deny protection to a trade dress for using commonly used elements than one could deny protection to a trademark because it consisted of a combination of commonly used letters of the alphabet').

classify the trade dress in question. This would not be new.[70] Moreover, the Court's dicta suggesting that the stricter rule may not apply to packaging or some 'tertium quid' merely invites litigation on whether a claimed trade dress constitutes a 'tertium quid' akin to packaging rather than design. In short, the Court's opinion merely illustrates, rather than solves, the difficulties of categorical classification.

Although the *Wal-Mart* opinion will have a limited effect on current trademark law, because only a small number of product designs can properly be treated as inherently distinctive,[71] it suffers from two important flaws as a means of establishing the limits of trademark law. First, it creates uncertainty by forcing parties to litigate abstract questions of classification that are not relevant to the purposes of trademark law. Second, it entrenches (without any factual support) a generalized assumption of consumer practices as a rule of law. It thus prevents trademark law from fully reflecting changes in consumer behavior. In particular, it ignores shifts in social and economic conditions that, prompted by globalization, have made younger consumers much more visually cognizant. It also ignores the increasing attention of trademark law to the problem of post-sale confusion.[72] The purposive approach, which the Court followed in *Two Pesos* and *Qualitex*, would have avoided both of these problems. If consumers identify a product by a feature, whether packaging or design, the purposes of trademark law support the possibility (subject to countervailing policy

[70] In Fun-Damental Too, Ltd. v. Gemmy Indus. Corp., 111 F.3d 993 (2d Cir. 1997), the plaintiff claimed protection for the trade dress of its product, a novelty bank in the familiar form of a tank toilet. The product was displayed and sold in stores in an open box. The box bore illustrations of the means of operation, but the toilet bowl was covered by clear plastic to prevent customers from placing any object in the bowl while the bank was on display. The defendant's product closely imitated the design of the product, the nature of its packaging and the markings on the box. Judge Mukasey emphasized that the plaintiff's product, 'alone and apart from its packaging' was not at issue in the lawsuit. Rather, the trade dress allegedly infringed was a composite of the product's design and its packaging, and on this basis the district court judge (affirmed by the Second Circuit) followed the approach of the Second Circuit towards packaging claims. See also Fundex, Inc. v. Imperial Toy Corp., 26 U.S.P.Q. 2d 1061 (S.D. Ind. 1992) (applying *Abercrombie* to determine inherent distinctiveness of trade dress comprising composite of product's features and its packaging).

[71] See Dinwoodie, *supra* note 21, at 563–65 (discussing number of designs found to be inherently distinctive after *Two Pesos*).

[72] In the post-sale context, supplementary verbal indicators on packaging or labels may be of less use in distinguishing between two similarly designed products because the packaging or attached labels will often be discarded after purchase.

concerns) of protection against the confusing simulation of that feature.[73] But this analysis can be performed without consideration of whether that feature is a design or packaging feature.

II. SCOPE OF RIGHTS: FEDERAL DILUTION PROTECTION

Classically, trademark rights protected a mark holder only against uses by a rival that caused consumer confusion as to the source of the rival's goods. As the U.S. Supreme Court explained:

> Then what new rights does the trade-mark confer? It does not confer the right to prohibit the use of the word or words. It is not a copyright ... A trade-mark only gives the right to prohibit use of it so far as to protect the owner's goodwill against the sale of another's product as his ... When the mark is used in the way that does not deceive the public, we see too much sanctity in the word as to prevent its being used to tell the truth.[74]

This scope of rights was sufficient both to protect consumers and to prevent the appropriation of the producer's goodwill by a competitor passing off its goods as those of the mark holder. As trademarks came to signify the intangible qualities of a product as well as its source,[75] the scope of rights afforded a trademark holder expanded to protect against misleading suggestions of association or endorsement. Yet, this expansion in the scope of rights was accommodated internally within the likelihood of confusion infringement test.[76] The perceptions of the consumer remained central to, and guided, the inquiry.

[73] The functionality doctrine identifies countervailing objectives that might require moderation of the producer's trademark rights. But where a design is functional, see *supra* note 48, balancing these conflicting objectives should be done in full awareness that denial of any trademark protection undermines full effectuation of the consumer avoidance purpose of trademark protection. See Dinwoodie, *supra* note 2, at 729–38.

[74] Prestonettes, Inc. v. Coty, 264 U.S. 359, 368 (1924).

[75] See Nicholas S. Economides, *The Economics of Trademarks*, 78 Trademark Rep. 523, 527 (1988) ('By the beginning of the twentieth century trademarks were understood not to be useful in identifying the source, but rather as identifying a quality standard').

[76] In 1962, Congress amended section 32 of the Lanham Act, Pub. L. No. 87–772, 76 Stat. 769, evincing 'a clear purpose to outlaw the use of trademarks which are likely to cause confusion, mistake or deception of any kind, not merely of purchasers nor simply as to source of origin'. Syntex Labs. v. Norwich Pharmacal, Co., 437 F.2d

In 1995, Congress enacted the Federal Trademark Dilution Act.[77] This Act provides that the owner of a famous mark is entitled to enjoin another person's commercial use in commerce of that mark if such use causes dilution of the distinctive quality of the mark, regardless of the presence or absence of: (a) competition between the owner of the famous mark and the other party, or (b) likelihood of confusion, mistake or deception. The enactment of a federal law was intended to provide uniform national protection against dilution; previously, dilution protection had been available in approximately one half of the states.[78] Under state laws in the United States prior to the enactment of the Federal Dilution Act of 1995, dilution causes of action generally rested upon proof of 'blurring' or 'tarnishment'. The federal statute, although not explicit, has been interpreted as targeting similar acts.[79]

Dilution protection is aimed at the harm (the 'whittling away' of the distinctiveness of a mark) that might occur to the producer from the use of the mark

566, 568 (2d Cir. 1971). Section 32 of the Lanham Act, 15 U.S.C. § 1114, imposes liability upon 'any person who, without the consent of the registrant, uses ... the registered mark in connection with the sale, offering for sale, distribution, or advertising of any goods or services in connection with which such use is likely to cause confusion', but no longer limits actionable confusion to source confusion. See also 15 U.S.C. § 1125(a)(1)(A) (imposing liability upon any person who, 'on or in connection with any goods or services, uses any word, term, symbol, or device, or false designation of origin, false or misleading description of fact, or false and misleading representation of fact, which is likely to cause confusion as to the affiliation, connection, or association of such person with another person, or as to the origin, sponsorship or approval of his or her goods, services, or commercial activities by another person').

[77] See 15 U.S.C. § 1125(c).

[78] See H.R. Rep. No. 104–374. at 3–4 (1995). The failure to preempt state laws may thus undermine some of the objectives of the legislation. See New York Stock Exchange, Inc. v. New York, New York Hotel, LLC, 69 F. Supp.2d 479 (S.D.N.Y. 1999) (interpreting federal and New York legislation to be of different scope).

[79] See Ringling Bros.-Barnum & Bailey Combined Shows v. B.E. Windows Corp., 40 U.S.P.Q.2d 1010, 1016 (S.D.N.Y. 1996); see also 141 Cong. Rec. 19310 (daily ed. Dec. 29, 1995) (statement of Sen. Hatch). But see Robert C. Denicola, *Some Thoughts On The Dynamics of Federal Trademark Legislation And The Trademark Dilution Act of 1995*, 59 Law & Contemp. Prob. 75, 88–90 (1996) (explaining legislative evolution of 1995 statute and concluding that it should not extend to tarnishment claims); Miles J. Alexander and Michael K. Heilbronner, *Dilution Under Section 43(c) of the Lanham Act*, 59 Law & Contemp. Prob. 93, 121–25 (1996) (noting that, despite legislative history reference to tarnishment claims, the language of the federal statute may not support tarnishment claim).

on noncompeting or dissimilar products.[80] Under classical infringement analysis, where only confusion as to source was actionable, the dissimilarity of products might easily preclude a finding of trademark infringement. But the expanded confusion avoidance rationale now captures many of these activities and protects the mark in those cases, rendering dilution protection less urgent.

But why should these limits of trademark protection be set by a contemporary confusion rationale rather than dilution protection? Dilution protection moves trademark law away from its basic purpose of mutual consumer and producer protection, and instead focuses solely on protecting the producer.[81] But once untethered from the concept of consumer protection, the parallel concept of producer value imposes no a priori limits on the scope of protection. At what point is protection of the producer too much protection? Which competitive activities that adversely affect the producer (as competitive activities are wont to do) are permissible?

The absence of any rational limits is evidenced by the confused and conclusory nature of judicial opinions applying the dilution law. Recent efforts to explicate a test for blurring, one of the two actionable effects that constitute dilution, illustrate the quandary.[82] Prior to the federal legislation, the most quoted analysis by which courts had assessed the claim of blurring was that offered in Judge Sweet's concurring opinion in *Mead Data Central, Inc. v. Toyota Motor Sales, USA, Inc.*[83] There, in applying the same test under New York law, Judge Sweet suggested six factors that should be considered.[84]

[80] See Milton Handler, *A Personal Note on Trademark and Unfair Competition Law Before the Lanham Act*, 59 Law & Contemp. Probs. 5, 10–11 (1996).

[81] See I.P.Lund Trading ApS v. Kohler Co., 163 F.3d 27, 36 (1st Cir. 1998).

[82] Tarnishment may raise these concerns in even starker relief. See Robert C. Denicola, *Some Thoughts On The Dynamics of Federal Trademark Legislation And The Trademark Dilution Act of 1995*, 59 Law & Contemp. Prob. 75, 85–86 (1996) (noting that while protection against dilution of a mark's distinctiveness is self-limiting, the tarnishment rationale is not so limited). And one can detect similar problems with the concept of a 'famous mark' upon which dilution protection is conditioned. Despite a statutory laundry list of factors for courts to consider in assessing fame, many courts fail to consider the issue, see Lori Krafte, *Judicial Interpretation of The Federal Trademark Dilution Act of 1995*, 66 U. Cin. L. Rev. 659 (1998) and many others have offered tortured interpretations of the condition. See e.g. Nabisco, Inc. v. PF Brands, Inc., 191 F.3d 208 (2d Cir. 1999).

[83] 875 F.2d 1026, 1035 (2d Cir. 1989) (Sweet J., concurring).

[84] The factors are: (1) similarity of the marks; (2) similarity of the products; (3) sophistication of the consumers; (4) predatory intent; (5) renown of the senior mark; and (6) renown of the junior mark. See *id*.

These 'Sweet factors' have been applied by several courts under the federal legislation.[85]

Yet these factors fail to identify or even target a harm other than one grounded in consumer response; the Sweet factors are a minor variant on the likelihood of confusion factors.[86] This has convinced some courts to suggest that the factors need augmentation[87] or wholesale rejection.[88] Yet, the alternative tests that have been formulated are no better. For example, the First Circuit rejected the Sweet factors, but instituted an inquiry instead 'into whether target consumers will perceive the products as essentially the same'.[89] But this test also falls short of clearly identifying a harm other than consumer confusion. Indeed, to the extent that it differs from the confusion-based test for classical trademark infringement, it bears strong resemblance to the test of copyright infringement,[90] raising further concerns of offering de facto copyright protection to certain famous words or designs for which copyright is or may not be available. Such perceived 'end-runs' on the limits of copyright[91] and patent protection[92] have raised the ire of courts in recent years, and threaten the legitimacy of trademark law as an autonomous source of regulation.

Finding a test that is both workable and is targeted at a harm that dilution seeks to redress is difficult because these extended rights have no independent grounding. By linking the scope of protection to the avoidance of consumer confusion, and thus to an identifiable harm, trademark law will possess an internal compass that imposes rational limits (albeit, not the only limits) on its extension. And that compass, in the person of the consumer, will be one that is responsive to social and economic changes, and thus to the harms to which trademark law must address itself.

[85] See e.g. Ringling Bros.-Barnam & Bailey Combined Shows, Inc. v. B.E. Windows Corp., 937 F. Supp. 204, 211–14 (S.D.N.Y. 1996).

[86] See 3 J. Thomas McCarthy, Trademarks and Unfair Competition § 24.94.1.

[87] See Nabisco, Inc. v. PF Brands, Inc., 191 F.3d 208 (2d Cir. 1999).

[88] See I.P.Lund Trading ApS v. Kohler Co., 163 F.3d 27, 33 (1st Cir. 1998).

[89] *Id.*

[90] See Laureyssens v. Idea Group, Inc., 964 F.2d 131 (2d Cir. 1992).

[91] See Jeffrey Milstein, Inc. v. Greger, Lawlor, Roth, Inc., 58 F.3d 27, 32 (2d Cir. 1995) (acknowledging that overextension of trademark law can undermine principles of copyright law); Leigh v. Warner Bros., Civ. No. 497-340, 1998 WL 351878, at *8–9 (S.D. Ga. June 22, 1998) (noting the potential for 'undermining copyright' by offering trade dress protection to a photograph).

[92] See Vornado Air Circulation Sys. v. Duracraft Corp., 58 F.3d 1498 (10th Cir. 1995).

III. TRADEMARKS IN CYBERSPACE: CONFLICTS WITH DOMAIN NAMES

The digital revolution has forced intellectual property law to confront many new and perplexing issues. In the context of trademark law, particular problems have resulted from the interaction of trademark rights and ownership of domain name registrations. The scope of trademark rights is defined by the goods upon which the mark is used (and by the geographic area in which it is used), thus permitting the use of the same term by several mark owners on different goods. For example, the term UNITED is used as a trademark separately by an airline and by a moving company. Domain names are, however, unique; under the current configuration of the Internet and the domain name system, there can only be one United.com.[93]

Thus, in the online environment, conflicts over domain name ownership may arise between two legitimate trademark owners. This has been dealt with, thus far, by the expedient of adopting a first-come-first-served approach to the allocation of domain names.[94] But this liberal approach to the allocation of

[93] In fact, it is owned by United Airlines. See http://www.united.com (visited September 6, 2000).

[94] This expedient may generate other long-term problems. First, it simply avoids the issue of the appropriate owner of the united.com domain name registration. Second, as business models begin to require domain name registration of the term for which traditional trademark protection is sought, the maintenance of appropriate competition might require that we infuse some trademark principles into domain name registration practices. Although full-scale, trademark-like searches would both impose significant transaction costs and impose peculiarly American notions of trademark ownership in words, both of which are substantial downsides to be considered. Some incorporation of the notions of trademark law may be helpful. One might consider, for example, whether it is necessary to exclude certain basic terms from domain name ownership, as does trademark law. Otherwise, such ownership might be too significant a competitive advantage for the domain name owner; certainly, the prices paid for certain domain names would suggest that such possibilities exist. Similarly, although it cuts against the grain of international trademark developments, a delayed 'use' requirement might be imposed to maintain domain name ownership. This would provide a small disincentive to domain name speculation, an activity thus far permitted but which becomes problematic if business models effectively require companion domain name ownership of the term for which trademark registration is sought. Absent any such restrictions on domain name registration, the depletion of domain names might effectively be transferred into the trademark system.

domain names raises other problems. Because a domain name comprising a trademarked term may easily be first registered by someone other than the mark owner, there has been extensive litigation and recent federal legislation regarding the rights that a mark owner has against the owner of a domain name who has no trademark rights in the term.

Some of the defendants in this type of litigation have been competing producers using, in an online environment, marks (as domain names) that were confusingly similar to existing protected marks. Others have been, to use the favored neologism, 'cybersquatters', that is, persons who had registered domain names consisting of well-known trademarks and then sought to extract payment from the mark owner in return for transfer of the domain name registration. Early efforts to address the allegedly infringing use of trademarks as domain names, in either of these categories but particularly the latter, relied heavily upon the federal dilution legislation. They did so because of statements in the legislative history expressing the hope that the dilution legislation would assist in redressing the problem of cybersquatting. But such protection fits uncomfortably within the tendered justification for dilution protection; the courts have thus shoehorned the factual scenario of cybersquatting into the dilution statute.

This judicial reaction is perhaps an understandable attempt by courts to err on the side of protecting intellectual property rights in new technological environments. The same trend can be seen in the early treatment of software under the copyright laws.[95] But it also reveals two other themes, both of which are pertinent to this essay. First, the amorphous, directionless nature of dilution protection permits it to be invoked in an unlimited range of settings. And, second, if trademark protection online is to be rationally limited, it must be constructed upon some principle other than reflexive protection for the property of the mark holder. It must be hitched to something other than the protection of producer value.

Some courts have begun this task.[96] They have done so primarily in the context of classical infringement analysis, tailored to protection of the consumer against an expanded range of actionable confusion. This guiding purpose requires courts to construct a cyber-consumer, by inquiring as to consumer understandings that online shopping, marketing and browsing create. These understandings, which inevitably and appropriately involve the use and meaning

[95] Compare Whelan Assocs. v. Jaslow Dental Labs., 797 F.2d 122 (3d Cir. 1986) with Computer Associates Int'l, Inc. v. Altai, Inc., 982 F.2d 693 (2d Cir. 1992).

[96] See e.g. Avery Dennison Corp. v. Sumpton, 189 F.3d 868 (9th Cir. 1999) dilution; Brookfield Comms., Inc v. West Coast Ent. Corp., 174 F.3d 1036 (9th Cir. 1999).

of domain names, thus will enable a scope of limited trademark rights to be established in the online environment.

In Congress, a different approach is being adopted. Trademark owners have singled out particular contexts, such as cybersquatting, in which their interests are at stake, and have sought property-like protection in those settings. Thus, Congress recently enacted the Anticybersquatting Consumer Protection Act,[97] which creates a new Section 43(d) of the Lanham Act.[98] Section 43(d) now provides a cause of action against anyone who, with bad-faith intent to profit from the goodwill of another's trademark or service marks, 'registers, traffics in, or uses a domain name that is identical to, confusingly similar to, or [in the case of famous marks] dilutive of such trademark'. It is important to recognize first that this legislation addresses only one of the many dilemmas that cyberspace raises for trademark law, and, second, that trademark owners will likely seek additional legislation to address concrete, new categories of behavior.[99] Yet, the

[97] Pub. L. 106–13, Tit. III (1999).

[98] The civil action established under paragraph (1) and the in rem action against the domain name established under paragraph (2) of the new Section 43(d) are in addition to any other civil action or remedy otherwise applicable. Damages and injunctive relief will be available for violations of the new law, see *id.* § 3003, as will statutory damages under a new Section 35(d) of the Lanham Act, which provides that 'in a case involving a violation of section 43(d)(1), the plaintiff may elect, at any time before final judgment is rendered by the trial court, to recover, instead of actual damages and profits, an award of statutory damages in the amount of not less than $1,000 and not more than $100,000 per domain name, as the court considers just'. Section 43(d) applies to all domain names registered before, on or after the date of the enactment of the Act, but damages are not available with respect to the registration, trafficking or use of a domain name that occurs before the date of the enactment of the Act. See Section 3010.

[99] The statute also creates a cause of action in Section 3002(b) intended to offer additional protections for individuals. This provides that 'any person who registers a domain name [on or after December 2, 1999] that consists of the name of another living person, or a name substantially and confusingly similar thereto, without that person's consent, with the specific intent to profit from such name by selling the domain name for financial gain to that person or any third party, shall be liable in a civil action by such person'. See Section 3002(b)(1)(A). However, no cause of action will exist under this separate provision if a registration of such a name is made in good faith and is used in, affiliated with or related to a protected work of authorship, and the person registering the domain name is the copyright owner or licensee of the work, the person intends to sell the domain name in conjunction with the lawful exploitation of the work, and such registration is not prohibited by a contract between the registrant and the named person. This exception only applies to

approach of serially legislating stronger trademark protection with respect to one category of cyber-behavior at a time will always be behind the curve of harmful activities and will be devoid of rational limits that derive from sources other than the practical constraints of political power – a problem of political economy not unique to trademark law, of course. Hewing close to the basic purposes of trademark law, and being guided by the internal compass of protecting the integrity of consumer understandings, would both provide rational limits and afford courts the flexibility to tackle new issues as they arise.

CONCLUSION

In its most recent trademark cases, the Supreme Court has charted an uncertain path for trademark law. That uncertainty stems in part from the Court's own ambivalence about committing to a purposive approach to trademark law. Such an approach, seen in *Two Pesos* and *Qualitex*, may suggest to some only an expansionist vision of trademark protection. And in those two cases, to be sure, the Court favored the position of trademark owners. But purposive analysis, rooted in consumer confusion avoidance, is not inherently expansionist. It will offer broad protection only where the integrity of consumer understanding is severely threatened, and less where that is not so. It can supply a coherence to trademark law that cannot be achieved by judicial or legislative attention to competitive behavior on a category-by-category approach. And it can ensure that trademark law responds flexibly to changing markets. Finally, because the purposes of trademark law are limited in nature, purposive analysis can establish rational limits to trademark law in ways that ad hoc legislative protection of producer value cannot.

POSTSCRIPT

In the time since the preceding essay was written, the courts have been the site for the principal developments of the three issues of trademark law covered in the essay. Some of those judicial decisions have borne out concerns I expressed

causes of action under Section 3002(b) and does not limit other more traditional trademark or other causes of action. If a plaintiff is successful under Section 3002(b), a court may award injunctive relief, including the forfeiture or cancellation of the domain name or the transfer of the domain name to the plaintiff (or, in its discretion, award costs and attorneys fees to the prevailing party).

in 2000 (e.g., trade dress protection and dilution causes of action remain shrouded in uncertainty, lacking direction), while others suggest that my fears were over-stated (e.g., there has been little of the 'category-shopping' I predicted in trade dress litigation). Yet, none of these developments calls into question the basic thesis of the essay: the coherence of modern U.S. trademark law is being undermined by a failure expressly to link its development to its basic purposes. To be sure, in each of its four opinions since 2000, the U.S. Supreme Court has endorsed or articulated limits on the availability or scope of trademark protection. Taken with *Wal-Mart*, this group of 21st-century cases may signal an unease with the unbridled expansion of trademark rights. And, significantly, while some of those limits can be deduced from the internal consumer protection rationale discussed in the 2000 essay, others reflect sources or purposes that might be viewed as external (or often peripheral) to trademark law. Incorporating these broader purposes within trademark analysis remains a crucial task, but one that may fall largely to scholars if the Supreme Court continues to speak only obliquely on its basic approach to trademark policy.

In the context of trade dress, *Wal-Mart* has indeed obliged many courts to address the unduly metaphysical question of whether trade dress is 'product design' or 'product packaging'. However, ready reliance by courts on the Supreme Court's instruction to err, in close cases, toward a 'design' classification has over time made this satellite question less consumptive of judicial resources. Indeed, as predicted, the rule announced in *Wal-Mart* has had little direct effect on the availability of trade dress protection because few designs would under any standard likely be regarded as inherently distinctive. However, taken with the trade dress case handed down by the Court in 2001, *TrafFix Devices, Inc. v. Marketing Displays, Inc.*,[100] it can now be seen as a clear signal to lower courts to rein in product design trade dress protection.

The *TrafFix* Court highlighted the vitality of the functionality doctrine[101] in product design trade dress litigation. The Court's confirmation of what it previously said (in a footnote) in *Inwood* and (in dicta) in *Qualitex*, namely that 'in general terms, a product feature is functional . . . if it is essential to the use or purpose of the article or if it affects the cost or quality of the article,' was hardly radical. However, the Court also disapproved the lower court's reliance on both insubstantial anticompetitive effect and the availability of alternative designs to save the plaintiff from a functionality determination. These holdings (if faithfully followed) might have greatly contracted trade dress protection. But because

100 532 U.S. 23 (2001).

101 See *supra* n. 48.

the Court failed to explain how its test applied absent regard to competition or alternatives – and, more importantly, how its test meshed with the *purposes* of trademark law – lower courts have easily managed to avoid the full effects of the Court's decision.

Likewise, the *TrafFix* Court's other functionality holding – that where trade dress rights were claimed in the design of an article that had previously been the subject of a utility patent since expired, that utility patent is 'strong evidence that the features therein claimed are functional' – has raised more questions than it has answered. And, again, this is because of a failure by the Court to explain the purpose behind the rule it announced. Was this rooted in the competitive advantages of a patented feature or a concern for the integrity of the patent system? A later case, *Dastar Corp. v. Twentieth Century Fox Film Corp.*,[102] in which the Court held that Section 43(a) of the Lanham Act did not prevent the unaccredited copying and distribution of an uncopyrighted public domain work, suggests that the Court may indeed be concerned about the encroachment of trademark law into other areas of intellectual property law. But, as in *TrafFix*, we are left to speculate because the Court strictly rested its opinion on an unsatisfying dissection of the word 'origin' in Section 43(a). The Court's real concerns about the expansion of trademark and unfair competition law are raised only tangentially, teasing but hardly clear.

Just as trade dress law has seen the Supreme Court insisting on limits (however poorly articulated), the Court has since 2000 interpreted the dilution statute in ways that address some of the concerns I expressed about the potentially capacious scope of dilution law. In *Moseley v. V Secret Catalogue, Inc.*,[103] the Court held that a plaintiff seeking relief under Section 43(c) of the Lanham Act must show *actual* rather than a mere *likelihood* of dilution in order to make out a claim. Thus, the dilution protection which I suggested lacked satisfactory theoretical foundation was indeed cut back, but by using a textual interpretation almost certainly inconsistent with legislative intent. As such, it is a limit that is not likely to last; indeed, it is already the subject of congressional efforts to override. Courts and scholars still have not fully explained 'blurring' or 'tarnishment' in other than conclusory or talismanic phrases that offer very little guidance to producers and the public. This continuing gap merely confirms my insistence on grounding protection in consumer confusion.

Change has been most fast-moving (though as yet untouched by the Supreme Court) in the context of trademark law online. Attention has moved beyond the

[102] 539 U.S. 23 (2003).
[103] 537 U.S. 418 (2003).

cybersquatting activities that consumed Congress and the courts in 1998–99 (though a reduced volume of cybersquatting cases remain in the courts). Courts are beginning to grapple with the application of confusion-based doctrines (most notably, initial interest confusion) in the richer array of situations that arise in the online environment. Although these decisions have not yet reached a stage of ideal consistency or equilibrium, the courts are proceeding blessedly free from further congressional intervention.

Because the doctrines that are guiding these courts are, unlike early cybersquatting cases, grounded in consumer protection justifications, there would appear to be sufficient basis for courts to recognize appropriate limits on trademark regulation of banner, keyword and pop-up advertising. Yet, courts may find that although these classic purposes do establish some limits on trademark rights, other limits may also be necessary. In particular, courts might need to recognize that trademark law both reflects and *constructs* the market; on occasion, trademark rules will proactively shape that market by developing new limits on the scope of trademark rights. Some courts are thus restricting the expansion of trademark rights online through rules such as the requirement that the defendant be using 'as a mark'. At present, such rules have lacked a full theoretical justification. But if limits linked to consumer confusion are insufficient (though necessary) to establish an ideal scope of trademark protection, it is incumbent upon scholars to develop those other justifications and to integrate them into a purposive analysis of trademark law.

Chapter 4

Sixty Years of the Lanham Act: The Decline and Demise of Monopoly Phobia

Marshall Leaffer[*]

I. INTRODUCTION: 'THE RATIONAL BASIS OF TRADEMARK PROTECTION' REDISCOVERED

Well over fifty years ago, when the Lanham Act was in its infancy, Beverly Pattishall coined the term 'monopoly phobia' in describing an attitude prevalent at the time.[1] The phobia referred to in his article related to a thirty-year period beginning in the 1930s where judges, formed in the anti-business climate of the Great Depression, expressed a profound skepticism about the justification for trademark rights. This anti-trademark sentiment was shared in the academic community that viewed trademarks as a means for creating monopoly power in favor of the trademark owner. According to this view, the trademark system reinforces irrational consumer demand through artificial product differentiation and erects barriers to entry for other firms that may wish to compete in the product market.[2] As one court declared, '[T]he trademark is endowed with a sales appeal independent of the quality or price of the product to which it is attached; economically irrational elements are introduced into consumer choices; and the trademark owner is insulated from the normal pressures of price and quality competition'.[3] The anti-trademark stance was not limited to the bench. Governmental policy toward trademarks echoed the same outlook, most prominently in the Federal Trade Commission, which contemplated compulsory licensing of trademarks as a measure in eliminating monopoly power in companies

* Distinguished Scholar in Intellectual Property Law and University Fellow, Indiana University School of Law.

1 Beverly W. Pattishall, Trade-Marks and the Monopoly Phobia, 50 Mich. L. Rev. 967 (1950).

2 A.G. Papandreou, The Economic Effect of Trademarks, 44 Cal. L. Rev. 503 (1956).

3 Smith v. Channel, Inc., 402 F.2d 562, 567 (9th Cir. 1968).

which enjoyed ownership of well-known marks.[4] At that time, the FTC promoted governmental intervention in situations where trademarks and brand promotion became a barrier to competition. The heyday of trademark skepticism had played itself out by the end of the 1970s and conclusively ended with the passage in 1996 of Federal Anti-dilution statute.[5] Today, the prevailing view is one that views a strong trademark system, based on a property rights model, as one that enhances competition and consumer welfare.

How and why did this about face occur? The change in attitude from manifest trademark skepticism to a more positive view did not happen overnight but transpired over several decades. The 1996 Act culminated an on-going rethinking about trademark law, one that viewed the function of a trademark beyond its narrow confines as a mere indicator of origin, to one that recognized that the trademark owner's investment in goodwill in creating a famous mark should be protected against third party use that would undermine its distinctiveness. This departure from the traditional confusion model had been anticipated many years before, in a 1927 article by Frank Schechter, entitled 'The Rational Basis of Trademark Protection'.[6] In his elegant and prescient article, Schechter argued that true functions of the trademark are to identify a product as satisfactory and thereby stimulate further purchases by the consuming public.[7] He states that 'To describe a trademark merely as a symbol without recognizing in it an agency for the creation and perpetuation of goodwill, ignores the potent aspect of the nature of a trademark and that phase in most need of protection'.[8] One may ask why it took so long – a half century after the passage of the Lanham Act – for Schechter's 'rational basis of trademark protection' to come to fruition. Here, one can look to three on-going processes that progressively led to doctrinal change in the law of trademarks. The first is what one may term 'the new

[4] See Richard Craswell, Trademarks, Consumer Information, and Barriers to Competition, Office of Policy Planning (January 1979) at 2. Borden Inc. F.T.C. (1978). In addition the FTC also voted to petition the Patent and Trademark Office to cancel the registration of Formica Corporation's 'Formica' trademark, on the grounds that the term had become generic.

[5] Lanham Act section 43(c), 15 U.S.C. section 1125(c). 15 U.S.C. section 1125(a) (1) provides in part: The owner of a famous mark shall be entitled ... to an injunction against another person's commercial use ... of the mark ... if such use causes dilution of the distinctive quality of the mark ...'

[6] 40 Harv. L. Rev. 813 (1926–27), reprinted in 60 Trademark Reporter 334 (1970) (hereinafter Schechter).

[7] 60 Trademark Reporter at 337.

[8] Id.

economic learning', demonstrating the competitive benefits of product differentiation and the fundamental role trademarks play in this process as a means of reducing search costs to the consumer. The second force buttressing the new economic learning has resulted from the marketing environment in the way goods are sold in a global marketplace and a restructured industrial organization. A third force for change is the push toward harmonization of intellectual property worldwide, as manifested in the Trade Related Aspects of Intellectual Property (TRIPS) agreement as part of the World Trade Organization (WTO), of which the United States was a major promoter. Taken as a whole, these three factors have all but completely dissipated the trademark monopoly phobia and have led to an expanded concept of property rights in trademarks.

In this article, I plan to examine the nature of this progressively pro-trademark attitude reflected in current legal doctrine. My position is that these developments are essentially pro-competitive and comport with the new realities in commercial life that exist today. To illustrate the progression from 'monopoly phobia' to 'trademarkphilia', I will concentrate on two substantive areas of trademark law that reveal the basic trends. The substantive issues that I will focus on are the relaxation of restraints associated with the assignment and licensing of trademarks, and the expanding scope of the likelihood of confusion doctrine. In so doing, I have chosen a time frame beginning with the passage of the Lanham Act to the adoption of the federal anti-dilution in 1996, an emblematic fifty-year period. The federal anti-dilution law represents the logical, if not inevitable, outcome of trends already well established in the substantive law of trademarks, which in themselves are a function of the new economic learning, the realities of today's marketplace, and the push toward the international harmonization of norms regarding trademark rights. Despite the significant changes in attitude as represented in the trademark world, there still remains a persistent skepticism about trademarks prevalent in the academic community.

II. LINGERING MONOPOLY PHOBIA: ACADEMIA VERSUS THE RATIONAL BASIS OF TRADEMARK PROTECTION

A. *The 'Propertization' of Trademark Law*

Despite the virtual demise of monopoly phobia in most circles, the skeptical attitude toward trademark law has persisted in the academic legal community. One finds this stance in varying degrees. The first is an attitude that the 'propertization' of trademark rights has abandoned trademark law's primary focus as a mechanism to protect the consumer against deception. Many years ago, Learned

Hand expressed the same sentiment: '[w]e are nearly sure to go astray as soon as we lose sight of the underlying principle that the wrong involved is diverting trade from the first user by misleading customers who mean to deal with him'.[9] In other words we have strayed from the original and fundamental purpose of trademark law: to deter companies from confusing purchasers about the sources of goods or services. Much to the chagrin of these critics, this disassociation with unfair competition law has been replaced by the view that trademarks are a form of property – intellectual property. In moving away from a consumer deception model, the rhetoric of real property directs the way we conceptualize the very different world of 'intellectual property'.[10] This 'property'-based discourse reflects the fundamental changes that have expanded the ambit of trademark protection in an inexorable 'drift' toward the protection of 'trademark rights in gross'.[11]

In many ways, the critics are accurate in showing how the courts had progressively extended the sphere of trademark rights across product boundaries, and relaxed the restraints in the assignment and licensing of trademark rights. Trademark skeptics specifically point to developments, legislative and judicial, that exemplify the push toward a property-based trademark system. Since the enactment of the Lanham Act in 1946, federal registration of a trademark confers national rights even in markets that the registrant might never enter and where the mark has no meaning.[12] Even worse, the intent-to-use provisions of the Lanham Act confer trademark rights on non-existent entities. We have also seen the constant expansion of trademark subject that now covers varieties of trade dress and product configurations, which can even be protected, in some instances, without proof of secondary meaning.[13]

[9] S.C. Johnson & Son v. Johnson, 116 F.2d 427, 429 (2d Cir. 1940); see also Felix Cohen, Transcendental Nonsense and the Functional Approach, 35 Colum. L. Rev. 809, 814–17 (1935).

[10] See Mark A. Lemley, Romantic Authorship and the Rhetoric of Property, 75 Tex. L. Rev. 873 (1997); and Mark A. Lemley, The Modern Lanham Act and the Death of Common Sense, 108 Yale L. J. 1687 (1999); Glynn S. Lunney, Jr. Trademark Monopolies, 48 Emory L. J. 367 (1999).

[11] See e.g. Lisa Johnson, Drifting toward Trademark Rights in Gross, 85 Trademark Rep. 19 (1995).

[12] See Stephen L. Carter, The Trouble With Trademark, 99 Yale L. J. 759 (1990) ('The trouble with the Federal law of trademarks is that it rests on unstated assumptions about how marks are selected and marketed, and, because of its assumptions, it might be granting too much return for too little') at 759; see also Stephen L. Carter, Owning What Doesn't Exist, 13 Harv. J. L. Pub. Policy 99 (1990).

[13] Two Pesos, Inc. v. Taco Cabana, Inc., 505 U.S. 763 (1992).

B. The Creation of Language Exclusivities

Other academic critics have focused on more transcendent problems that may arise in a property-based trademark system. They express alarm at how expansive trademark law, in granting language exclusivities, distorts competition by erecting barriers to entry. The assumption is that the number of pleasing marks is finite and the more the set of attractive marks becomes depleted, the greater the costs imposed on market entrants. This concern is overstated because one finds little empirical evidence that the supply of appropriate trademarks is reaching the exhaustion point; even though the costs of clearing trademarks rights do rise as brands and corresponding trademark registrations proliferate.[14] Moreover, in a trademark system with well-defined property rights, the ownership of the trademark will gravitate to the party whose use it values the most.

To another group of critics the threat posed by a strong property-based trademark system transcends the interests of a competitive marketplace and the purchasing decisions of consumers. Trademarks – particularly famous ones – have become symbols of popular culture. The recent trend in trademark law, that provides trademark owners with greater control over rights in words, misunderstands the evocative significance of trademarks and, pushed too far, risks the suppression of freedom of social, political and artistic speech. Numerous academics have decried the tendency to curb the referential use of trademarks in describing, commenting on social and political phenomena, threatening fundamental First Amendment values.[15] Although I believe this claim is exaggerated, the concern must be taken seriously, albeit largely exaggerated. Certainly trademark law, as well as copyright law for that matter, may restrain certain forms of expressive communication. But one must also take into account

[14] For some indication that trademark clearing costs are rising see Suein L. Hwang, Picking Pithy Names is Getting Trickier as Trademark Applications Proliferate, Wall Street Journal, January 14, 1992, B 1.

[15] See e.g. Rochelle Cooper Dreyfuss, Expressive Genericity: Trademarks as Language in the Pepsi Generation, 65 Notre Dame L. Rev. 397 (1990); Alex Kozinski, Trademarks Unplugged, 68 N.Y.U.L. Rev. 960 (1993); Diane Leenheer Zimmerman, Information as Speech, Information as Goods: Some Thoughts on Marketplaces and the Bill of Rights, 33 Wm. & Mary L. Rev. 665 (1992); New Kids on the Block v. News A. Publ'g, 971 F.2d 302 (9th Cir. 1992) (allowing a newspaper to refer to the band 'New Kids on the Block' in a for-profit telephone poll).

certain ameliorative doctrines in trademark law such as fair use[16] and nominative use of trademarks,[17] not to mention the First Amendment itself.[18]

The basic theme of much of this criticism is nostalgia for some bygone era where trademarks were protected against imitation only to the extent that their use in the market actually identified the goods or services of a particular firm.[19] Based on a 1960s worldview, a purely consumer protection model of trademark has never really existed in a pristine state under modern trademark law. The reasons are clear. A purely consumer deception-based model ignores the other important function of trademarks in a competitive economy, the encouragement of investment in product differentiation, and the role of trademarks in reducing search costs to the consumer.

To encourage this investment, trademarks have always been treated as a property right and one that has always enjoyed the attributes of property. Of course, the trademark owner's right to exclude others from using the mark under certain conditions is predicated on the criteria set forth under the law, but trademarks have also been viewed as property rights whose value represents the goodwill as embodied in the mark. As we will see in the examples I have chosen (assignment and licensing of trademarks, and the likelihood of confusion doctrine), legal doctrine has progressively accentuated the role of trademarks as a property right of the trademark owner.

Before discussing the developments in two substantive areas of trademark law, I would like to examine the marketing and intellectual environment that has led to a more property-based trademark regime. In this regard, the focus should be on three interrelated factors in this evolution of trademark law: first, the way in which goods are marketed in today's world, second 'the new economic learning'

[16] Lanham Act, section 33(b) (4), 15 U.S.C. section 1115(b) (4); Zatarains, Inc. v. Oak Grove Smokehouse, Inc., 698 F.2d 786, 217 U.S.P.Q. 988 (5th Cir. 1983) (holding that third party of 'fish fry' was a fair use of plaintiff's Fish Fry trademark). Oswego, Inc. v. Shell Oil Co., 617 F.2d 1178, 207 U.S.P.Q. 278 (5th Cir. 1980) (defendant's use of 'larvicide' on grain fumigants was a fair non-trademark use in good faith and did not infringe plaintiff's incontestable mark LARVICIDE).

[17] See New Kids on the Block v. News A. Publ'g, 971 F.2d 302 (9th Cir. 1992) (allowing a newspaper to refer the band 'New Kids on the Block' in a for-profit telephone poll).

[18] See L.L.Bean, Inc. v. Drake Publishers, Inc., 811 F.2d 26 (1st Cir.), cert denied, 483 U.S. 1013 (1987) (defendant's risqué parody of merchandiser's catalog was privileged under First Amendment).

[19] Steven L. Carter, The Trouble with Trademark, 99 Yale L.J. (1990); Vincent N. Palladino, The Real Trouble with Trademarks, 81 Trademark Rep. 150 (1991).

and third, the inexorable push for international harmonization in an era of global commerce.

III. TRADEMARKS IN A POSTMODERN WORLD

A. *The New Marketing Environment*

The property model of trademarks reflects the way in which we market products in today's world. Sixty years ago, fewer companies sold products on an international scale. We have for some time existed in a global commercial environment where firms launch massive multi-country marketing of both new and old products. From the 1970s, we have seen a marked trend toward brand extension. In the pre-merchandizing days, when the Lanham Act was passed and conglomerate enterprise was relatively unknown, brand extension was more the exception than the rule. Today, by contrast, a conglomerate enterprise may apply its name to products as diverse as insurance and bread. Companies like Ralph Lauren may append their name not only on clothing but also on dinnerware and luggage, while institutions ranging from sports teams to universities apply their identifying symbols on a dizzying number of products. In this setting, the very notions of trademarks and other indicia of identity have undergone a major re-conceptualization.

This globalization of commerce is one dominant trend accentuated by the digital age. Most obvious here is the impact of electronic commerce and the growth of the Internet as a selling medium, one that transcends national boundaries and bears no physical location on 'Main Street'. On-line commerce, worth some 20 billion dollars in 1999, was predicted to reach 184 billion by 2004.[20] The reach, richness and intricacy of on-line commerce will be felt in ways as yet unanticipated as its speed, capacity and security improve. But its effect is already apparent. More than ever, the reputation of a product or service travels fast these days and can reach foreign markets long before the owner of the mark for the product has actually begun doing business there.[21]

In this world of instant communication, trademarks have become even more fundamental in our commercial lives due to the basic changes taking place in the intensely competitive international markets for consumer goods. As compared with a few decades ago, today's consumer demands variety, quality and constant

[20] A Survey of E-Commerce, The Economist, February 26, 2000 at pp. 5–6.

[21] See Roger Schechter, The Case for Limited Extraterritorial Reach of the Lanham Act, 37 Va. J. Int'l L. 619, 628 (1997).

novelty. To meet these demands, businesses tailor their products to smaller and increasingly heterogeneous niche markets while they search for the least expensive production site to compete in global markets where consumer tastes change quickly and are ever more sophisticated. In this environment, trademarks are the means by which the public is informed of a product's characteristics material to a purchasing decision and which are not observable on the surface of the product.

This ever-increasing refinement of consumer tastes has resulted in the branding of products at one time thought homogeneous. One only has to visit any supermarket to witness the phenomenon. Even though most fruits and vegetables are still sold without a brand name, new breeding techniques and better storage methods have allowed products that taste fresh and last longer. A company has no incentive to provide a better product (at presumably a higher cost) if the credit goes to the market as a whole. Branding constitutes a judicious business decision, fraught with risk. Unless a firm can provide better produce consistently, consumers may eventually hold a brand's name against it. In addition, even if consumers believe in the quality of the product and are willing to pay a premium for it, the premium may not be high enough to cover the extra costs of producing higher quality and establishing a brand name. In this commercial environment, trademarks are instrumental to consumer welfare and to enhance the competitive process.

So much has changed in the production and marketing of consumer goods since the 1970s. How often did companies revamp their product lines in that distant era? Take the example of two heavily advertised products: sneakers and automobiles. How many models in those two products were available twenty-five years ago? Only a handful. Today, by comparison, Nike introduces new sneaker models every six weeks. Peruse any Sunday newspaper supplement and you will find hundreds of models of automobiles for sale.[22]

The drift away from a purely deception-based trademark system is a response to practical marketing needs in modern commerce, which has increasingly become international in scope. In this world of e-commerce the need for certainty and speed in the acquisition of property rights is paramount. When models proliferate and product lines are constantly revamped, relentless pressure is imposed on companies to create a constant flow of new trademarks. Once created and searched for availability, these trademarks must be registered and maintained simultaneously in many jurisdictions. The figures are revealing. The

[22] See Jeff Madrick, Computers: Waiting for Revolution, New York Review of Books, Vol. XLV, No. 5, March 26, 1998 at p. 32.

number of registrations taking place in 1967 was 400,000; by 1992, they totaled 1,200,000: a three fold increase.[23] This number should increase even more sharply in the years to come. Obviously, trademark owners need speed, certainty and efficiency in seeking and maintaining rights both domestically and internationally. The courts have responded to the reality of this fluid environment in recognizing that the trademark originator's intent to expand beyond its original market should be presumed.

B. *The New Economic Learning*

The dominant view among mainstream economists is that a reliable, stable and efficiently structured trademark system is one that reduces search costs to the consumer and facilitates the competitive marketplace. Search costs are reduced to the consumer where brand identity is vibrant and unequivocal. In reducing search costs to the consumer, trademarks allow buyers to make rational purchasing and repurchasing decisions, with speed and assurance, particularly for goods whose qualities are not observable before purchase.[24] A properly ordered trademark system is one that encourages the trademark owner to invest in developing a strong trademark and rewards firms who do so by preventing free riding on the goodwill of the mark. In this way, the law allows the trademark owner to recoup his investment in generating goodwill under the mark and at the same time rewards firms which produce products with desirable qualities. In conjunction with advertising, a trademark is the most effective vehicle for symbolizing the desirable traits embodied in a product. The information created through image differentiation can help consumers select products of high quality and reliability. It also motivates producers to maintain adequate quality standards. The consumer, through repeat purchases, rewards those manufacturers which achieve high quality or cater to special tastes.

Indeed, in today's marketing environment, strong brand identity is all the more necessary as product categories proliferate, competing for the limited attention span of the consumer, bemused by a multitude of product choices. We

23 Arpad Bogsch, Trademarks in 2017: Their Creation and Protection, 82 Trademark Reporter 880, 881 (1992).

24 See generally, William Landes and Richard Posner, Trademark Law: An Economic Perspective, 30 J.L. & Econ. 265 (1987). Trademarks help to solve the problem of consumer ignorance about the quality of a product. When quality is opaque or not apparent on the goods themselves, the consumer can use the trademark as a signal of quality. In this way, trademarks reduce the costs to consumers of searching for a product with specific qualities.

are simply barraged with commercial stimuli. Walk down any supermarket aisle or browse various websites and it is quickly apparent how distinctive marks reduce search costs in such a setting. The reality is that trademarks, particularly in a networked environment, not only compete for market share but also compete for 'mind share' or the attention of the consumer.[25] Moreover, the products we buy today embed more and more intangible information, largely unobservable to the human eye. Trademarks operate as convenient symbolic shorthand that brings this information across to consumers in the most efficient manner. For example, a washing machine might include software that controls the correct temperature, or a microwave may regulate the length of time a certain vegetable is cooked. These intangible and unobservable inputs account for an ever-greater value of products[26] and are determinative in purchasing decisions. Thus, a smoothly operating trademark system, one that encourages strong brand identity, enables the conscientious shopper to make purchasing decisions expeditiously without having to make repeated inquiries about experience, goods susceptible to quality or taste variations.

Trademark critics are troubled by the fact that trademarks themselves often bear little objective information. This concern, however, misunderstands the role that advertising plays even when the advertisement conveys little or no objective information about the product. The new economic learning has demonstrated that advertisements, irrespective of informational content, at least signal to would-be consumers that a product exists and that the originator is sufficiently confident of the product's merits to spend money promoting it. For experience goods – products whose quality can only be ascertained through actual consumption experience rather than pre-purchase inspection – advertisements declare 'try me, you'll like me'. If the consumer finds the product satisfactory, he will repeat his purchase. Thus, the greater the product's superiority, the higher will be the probability of repeat purchases. This will result in an increased stream of continuing profits, and thus the more it pays to advertise. From this, one may conclude that the most highly advertised products are in fact the best buys.

Of course, competitive tradeoffs are involved in the choice of any legal rule, particularly those that establish intellectual property rights. Although trademarks can efficiently convey information about a product's characteristics, they

[25] Dan L. Burk, Trademark Doctrines for a Global Electronic Commerce, 49 S. C. L. Rev. 695 (1998).

[26] Id. citing Frances Cairncross, The Death of Distance: How the Communications Revolution Will Change Our Lives, Harvard Business School Press, 1997.

have a persuasive capacity designed to shift consumer's taste. As a product becomes more differentiated, a firm may face a higher and less elastic demand curve, so that it can charge a higher price and earn greater profits. For example, a heavily promoted brand of bleach, aspirin or canned corn may charge a higher price than many others that are physically identical. But on the whole, in today's world, the competitive benefits of a robust trademark system clearly outweigh its costs.

The previous discussion has focused on the costs and benefits of a trademark system where the consumer obtains no utility directly from the trade symbol itself. But as we all know, not all symbols are equally attractive or desirable. Some have intrinsic value for the person who uses them: whether it's the pleasant design of a Coke can or a catchy name for a cereal, they can influence consumer choice. Other symbols most effectively remind the consumer of the essential features of the particular product. Efficient first-comers will use and register the symbol, and the monopoly thus afforded by the trademark owner can have a direct effect on competition, providing an advantage to the first holder of the symbol. In most cases the advantage will be very small. Most of the value of any trademark will be created by its identification with the product. Any advantage from the monopoly right to use the best symbol will be temporary and small once disappointed consumers refuse to make repeat purchases.

In sum, trademarks enhance the competitive process. Brands can instantly convey a wealth of information about product attributes: that a Volvo is safe, and a Jaguar is sleek. They express ideas about the price and benefits of a product. They transmit information about buyers themselves who may prominently carry a Gucci handbag to signal wealth and good taste, or give a Tiffany bracelet as a Christmas present. Brands facilitate a broader spectrum of goods, aid the consumer in product selection, foster quality control, and ease competitive entry.[27]

C. *Harmonization, Globalization and the Decline of Territoriality*

The critics of more expansive trademark rights often either fail to recognize or are hostile to the international pressures that have forced legal change in U.S. trademark law. Some of these changes, like intent-to-use registration, have

[27] Two Pesos, Inc. v. Taco Cabana, Inc., 505 U.S. 763 (1992) (in holding proof of secondary meaning is not necessary for inherently distinctive trade dress, the Court noted that a contrary holding would impede competitive entry particularly for small startup companies).

materialized from the practical commercial need in a global economy.[28] Other changes, such as the acceptance of a longer term for presumptive abandonment, have taken place as a function of treaty obligations.[29] Whatever the underlying reason for the changes, multilateral efforts in the harmonization of intellectual property law have resulted in the broadening of trademark rights consistent with the rest of the world that confers trademark rights on the basis of registration, not use.

The past five years have witnessed fundamental changes in the world of intellectual property, the centerpiece of which is the TRIPS Agreement,[30] negotiated under the auspices of the Uruguay Round of the GATT. TRIPS reconfirmed, reinterpreted and generally extended the norms of the major treaties, the Paris Union[31] and the Berne Convention. TRIPS has already changed the face of intellectual property law as nation-states modify their laws to comply with the Agreement. These effects have been chiefly noticeable worldwide in a more

[28] See Lanham Act, section 1(b), 15 U.S.C. section 1051(b).

[29] See Lanham Act, section 45, 15 U.S.C. section 1127.

[30] TRIPS trademark provisions are found in section 2 of the Agreement at Articles 16–24. Art.15 provides a definition of trademarks and expressly requires the protection of service marks; it requires a system of publication whereby each trademark is published for opposition, either before it is registered or promptly thereafter. This affords opponents a reasonable opportunity to bring action for opposition or cancellation (15(5)). Under Art. 16, service marks are to be afforded protection as well-known marks as required by Article 6 of the Paris Convention and protection is to be extended to goods and services that have no connection with a registered mark, but whose use would suggest such a relationship and where such use is likely to harm the interests of the registered mark holder. The term of protection for a trademark must exist for no less than seven years, and holders must renew the trademark's registered mark, but whose use would suggest such a relationship (Art. 18). Cancellation of a mark for non-use can occur only after three non-interrupted years, unless valid reasons for non-use exist, such as import or other governmental restrictions (Art. 19).TRIPS bars compulsory licensing for trademarks. It also requires that 'use of trademarks in the course of trade shall not be unjustifiably encumbered by special requirements, such as use with another mark, use in a special form, or use in a manner detrimental to its capability to distinguish goods or services' (Art. 21). Geographical indications identifying a good originating in a member's territory, region or locality must receive protection against use misleading the public or constituting an act of unfair competition (Art. 22). Additional protection is given for geographical indications identifying wine and spirits (Art. 23).

[31] For the Stockholm text of the Paris Convention, see Marshall A. Leaffer, International Treaties on Intellectual Property, 2d Ed., 20–43 (1997).

expansive recognition of trademark subject matter in the law of many countries, including the United States. In addition to the harmonization of basic substantive law, trends show the dismantling of administrative, procedural and technical requirements that so complicate trademark practice for those who embark on an international trademark launch in numerous countries. These harmonizing trends point to the diminishment of territoriality as the organizing principle of trademark and other branches of intellectual property law. This push toward greater harmonization will continue the expansion of property rights in U.S. trademark law as it already has done.

Unlike trademark skeptics, I view the globalization of trademark law (what I call 'the new world of international trademark') favorably. In the near term, I do not envisage developments in this 'new world' as leading to an inevitable progression toward some centralized unification of trademark law. I do believe, however, that we will see a progressive harmonization of trademark law among nations – one that will lead to ever-greater simplification and expediency in the acquisition and protection of trademark rights worldwide. The benefits from this trend toward harmonization will be enjoyed not only by trademark owners but also by consumers whose welfare will be enhanced by these trends.[32]

Trademark skeptics in this country have their counterparts in developing countries that view trademarks as a form of neo-imperialism. Their basic claim is that local consumers are exploited by entrenched brand names that act as insidious vehicles for persuasive advertising, encouraging irrational preferences among the vulnerable and largely illiterate. Indeed, some developing countries have shown hostility to trademarks, viewing them as an obstacle to achieving economic self-sufficiency.[33] This third world trademark monopoly phobia is as ill founded as it is in the developing world counterpart. Local consumers, even illiterate ones, may be defrauded and sometimes even exposed to health risks by counterfeit goods just like anyone else. Like consumers anywhere, those in the developing world look to brand names to guide rational purchasing decisions.

In addition to developing countries, small business interests have criticized the push toward global harmonization. The concern of small business is that technologies facilitate the transborder flow of trademarked images and are perceived as threatening to their interests. Large companies with their permanent legal and administrative staffs have the wherewithal to engage in the worldwide filing of

[32] See generally, Marshall A. Leaffer, The New World of International Trademark Law, 2 Marquette. Intell. Prop. L. Rev. 1 (1998) (hereinafter Leaffer).

[33] See Marshall Leaffer, Protecting United States Intellectual Property Abroad: Toward a New Multilateralism, 76 Iowa Law R. 273, 284 (1991).

trademark applications and to make use of facilitating mechanisms as provided by the Madrid Protocol and Trademark Law Treaty.

This fear is exaggerated. Of course, there will be some instances where large companies may take advantage of their economies of scale and know-how in such matters, whereas local businesses are only beginning to gravitate toward transnational exploitation of their trademarks. Clearly, multinational companies which own the most recognizable marks, and possess the resources to market them, have the most to gain from this new world. Local companies, however, are not excluded from the benefits of an ever-strengthened global trademark system. They are strongly positioned to exploit local tastes and to furnish the kind of warranties and services essential in a particular geographic region. But the real winners in this changing environment are the consumers because a strong trademark system enhances competition. Indeed, without trademark protection, companies would have little reason to provide unique services or goods of consistent quality if free riders could destroy competitive advantage. Although the most sophisticated trademark systems are found in western developed countries, a reliable trademark system benefits consumers in all countries, whatever that country's stage of development may be.

Much to the chagrin of those who advocate limited trademark rights, we can expect even more changes in the direction of more expansive rights and more vigilant enforcement of those rights resulting from practical necessity. Brand name counterfeiting continues to confound trademark owners,[34] and issues such as the treatment of domain names are far from being resolved. Their resolution will entail increased remedies and mechanisms that will protect trademarks against cybersquatters and others who would usurp trademark rights in cyberspace. Trademark law has already undergone profound changes, both multilaterally and regionally, and we can anticipate further changes on these two fronts. Multilaterally, two new treaties that will change the face of trademarks have come to fruition: the Madrid Protocol and the Trademark Law Treaty.[35] The United States has ratified the latter treaty, which streamlines the application process, thereby facilitating transnational trademark registration. The international registration processes will further be strengthened by the eventual U.S. adherence to the Madrid Protocol.

Among the major developments on the regional level, the most significant development is creation of the Community Trademark.[36] These changes,

[34] See e.g. Jean Schemo, The Paraguay Border Town: Almost Anything Goes, New York Times, March 15, 1998, Col. 1 p. 3.

[35] See generally Leaffer, note 32 supra for the texts of these treaties.

[36] Id. for the text of regulation establishing the Community Trademark.

brought about by the ever-increasing globalization of markets, are leading toward the acceptance of universal transnational norms and perhaps, in some distant future, toward the eventual unification of trademark law among nations.

The changing market environment, the new economic learning and increasing globalization have led to major changes in trademark law in the United States. In sections IV and V, I will concentrate on two aspects of trademark law that represent the expansionary development of trademark: the relaxation of rules regarding the assignment and licensing of trademarks, and the expanding contours of the likelihood of confusion doctrine. I have chosen these two areas of trademark because they best reveal the current trends in the field and have been singled out as two negative developments by critics in the increasing 'propertization' of trademark law. As I will show, the changes in these two major areas of trademark law follow naturally from the trends mentioned above. I do not suggest that the changes in theory are hardly manifested in a smooth and consistent manner in the doctrine. Rather, as I hope to show, the process of change is revealed in practical results more than in explicit rulings. Although restraints in assignment and licensing have been progressively relaxed in the case law, the courts still pay tribute to older and stricter conceptions. Likewise, dilution concepts have crept into the likelihood of confusion doctrine, but the courts have not overtly recognized the phenomenon. The untidiness and inconsistency of trademark law represent a progressive recognition that the orthodox view of trademarks as mere indicators of origin ignores the dynamics of today's marketplace and the teachings of the 'new' economics.

IV. RELAXING THE RESTRAINTS ON ASSIGNMENT AND LICENSING OF TRADEMARKS

A. *'Assignments in Gross' and 'Naked Licenses'*

One aspect of trademark law that trademark skeptics have singled out is the increasing tendency of courts to relax the rules concerning the assignment and licensing of trademarks. As embodied in the Lanham Act, the constraints on conveying rights in trademarks are founded on the role of trademarks as symbols of origin and quality. When an assignment does not transfer the goodwill that the mark symbolizes, it is called an 'assignment in gross' and as such may result in the abandonment of the mark.[37] Similarly, a licensor who does not

[37] Section 10 of the Lanham Act provides: 'a registered mark or a mark for which application to register has been filed shall be assignable with the goodwill of the

exercise quality control over his licensee has created a 'naked license' and, like an 'assignment in gross', this may result in an abandonment of rights in the mark.

These two rules are grounded in the view that trademarks function primarily as symbols of origin and quality. The rule against 'assignments in gross' is intended as a means to protect the purchaser from being misled about the source of a product. Similarly, the rule against naked licenses has the same purpose: to keep the consumer from being deceived about the misleading uses of the trademark by licensees who do not assure a uniform quality of the goods they sell under the licensed mark. These two rules are incorporated into the Lanham Act, section 10 (assignments) and section 5 (licenses). As one court stated, 'Unlike patents or copyrights, trademarks are not separate property rights. They are integral and inseparable elements of the goodwill of the business or services to which they pertain'.[38]

Despite these traditional limits on the unfettered alienability of trademarks, the courts have treated these longstanding limitations on the assignment and licensing of trademarks with increasing indulgence. To trademark skeptics, this development is yet another indication that property rights in trademarks are becoming increasingly absolute, eroding the underlying consumer deception policy of trademark law. In reality, the permissive trend in trademark law in relaxing the requirements of the sale and licensing of trademarks is a practical response to traditional legal doctrines that are inherently illogical, and do not comport with today's marketing environment. These two rules emanate from an era where companies marketed their own goods and were largely focused on domestic markets.

B. The Assignment in Gross Doctrine: Form, Substance and Inconsistencies

A well-known axiom of trademark law states that property in a trademark does not exist except as a right applicable to an established business or trade with which the mark is associated.[39] This principle is embodied in section 10 of the Lanham Act that specifically requires a transfer with the 'goodwill of the business or that part of the business ... symbolized by the mark'.[40] A sale of a

business in which the mark is used, or that part of the goodwill of the business connected with the use of and symbolized by the mark.'

[38] VISA, U.S.A., Inc. v. Birmingham Trust Nat. Bank, 696 F.2d 1371, 1375 (1982).

[39] United Drug Co. v Thereodore Retanus Co., 248 U.S. 90, 97 (1918).

[40] Lanham Act section 10, 15 U.S.C. section 1060.

mark separated from its goodwill is called an 'assignment in gross' and cannot validly transfer rights in a mark. When the assignee uses the mark on a different product or service, a different business and a different goodwill, the continuity of that which the mark symbolized is broken. Use of the mark by the assignee for a different goodwill and different product may result in a fraud on the purchasing public, who assume that the mark signified the same values.[41] Based on the guarantee theory of trademark law, the assignment in gross doctrine is said to provide assurance to the public that a mark represents a legal guaranty of quality.

In practice, however, doctrine is largely ignored, existing as it does in a state where form over substance reigns. The parties to a contract for an assignment normally indicate in the document that the mark was assigned together with the goodwill of the business symbolized by the mark. The existence of a contract purporting to transfer goodwill is not conclusive on the issue,[42] but courts have tended to accept these recitations as a matter of course. The question is: why has this erosion of the doctrine taken place?

1. *The Transfer of Goodwill*

Despite its surface appeal, on deeper scrutiny the rule regarding assignment in gross suffers from internal inconsistency and practical irrelevancy as a result of the continued adherence to obsolete common law doctrine. If the trademark owner is blocked from making the sale, it can accomplish the same result by reducing the quality of its own brand. One can search the case law in vain to find a single instance where a trademark owner has lost its mark due to its changes in the quality of its goods. In addition to its basic inconsistency, assignment in gross doctrine overstates the threat arising from the sale of a trademark without the goodwill of the business. It presumes that the subsequent assignee will produce an inferior good. It is just as possible that the assignee would produce an equally good or even superior product at the same price. In reality, the likelihood of a subsequent owner producing an inferior good is slim because it is not in the assignee's interest to do so. In other words, the doctrine does not take into account the market checks on the trademark owner's selling a mark for deceptive use by the assignee of the mark. Once consumers become aware to the fact

[41] Syntex Laboratories v. Norwich Pharmacal Co., 315 F. Supp. 45 (S.D.N.Y. 1970), aff'd 437 F.2d 566 (2d Cir. 1971). Universal Studios, Inc. v. Nintendo Co., Ltd., 578 F. Supp. 911(S.D.N.Y. 1983) (holding invalid the separate transfer of the King Kong mark by its owner when all of the business associated with the mark had been developed by a third party movie studio).

[42] Haymaker Sports, Inc. v. Turian, 581 F.2d 257 (CCPA 1978).

of inferior quality, both the trademark owner and assignee will lose reputation and lose business. Most businesses know the value of the trademark they have bought and as rational actors would engage in activity to increase their market share. Thus, except in cases where the assignee of a trademark is planning to leave the market, after making a quick profit in selling the inferior good, there appears little rationale for the assignment in gross doctrine.[43]

Through years of inconsistent application, the assignment in gross doctrine has become ever more unclear in its basic terms. The case law has not articulated a clear standard to determine in all cases when a transfer of goodwill has occurred. In its simplest expression, goodwill in the assignment context has come to mean that the assignee's use of the mark maintains continuity with the assignor's use of the mark. The courts, however, are split on whether transfer of assets is required to maintain this continuity. Some courts require a transfer of assets. In this regard, both tangible assets, such as a plant and equipment, and non-tangible assets, including a secret formula, trained personnel, customer lists[44] or continuity of management, may suffice in transferring goodwill.[45]

Other courts have declared assignments valid without the transfer of any assets if the assignee's product is substantially similar to that of the assignor.[46] Under this view an assignment in gross occurs only if a substantial change in the nature and quality of the goods under the assigned mark has transpired.[47] Here, the ultimate question is whether the assignee's continued use of the mark deceives the public. Courts have shown varying toleration of changes in the nature of goods in connection with the assignee's use of the mark. Occasionally, relatively minor differences are sufficient to raise the issue of customer deception.[48] Thus in the

[43] This point is forcefully made in William M. Landes and Richard A. Posner, Trademark Law: An Economic Perspective, 30 J. Law and Econ. 265, 286 (1987).

[44] Re Roman Cleanser Co. 802 F.2d 207 (6th Cir 1984).

[45] Marshak v. Green, 746 F.2d 927, 930 (2d Cir 1984).

[46] Visa, U.S.A., Inc. v. Birmingham Trust Nat. Bank, 696 F.2d 1371 (Fed. Cir. 1982). Defiance Button Machine Co. v. C & C Metal Products, 759 F.2d 1053, 1059 (2d Cir) cert denied, 474 U.S. 844 (1985). Sterling Brewers, Inc. v. Schnley Industries, Inc. 441 F.2d 675 (CCPA 1971).

[47] Clark & Freeman Corp. v. Heartland Co. Ltd., 811 F. Supp. 137 (S.D.N.Y. 1993).

[48] Clark & Freeman Corp. v. Heartland Co. Ltd., 811 F. Supp. 137 (S.D.N.Y. 1993) (assignor's use of mark on woman's boots was substantially different from men's boots and constituted an assignment in gross); Warner Lambert Pharm. Co. v. General Foods Corp., 164 U.S.P.Q. 532 (TTAB 1970) (assignor's mineral-vitamin pharmaceutical was not similar enough to assignee's anti-caries preparation in chewable tablet and capsule form to establish a transfer of goodwill).

oft-cited *Pepsico v. Grappette*[49] the court found that the assignor's cola-flavored syrup and the assignee's pepper-flavored syrup were sufficiently different to prevent a transfer of goodwill and thus invalidate the assignment.

The artificiality of the assignment in gross doctrine is particularly revealed when trademarks are used as a security for a loan.[50] As valuable business assets, trademarks are often used as collateral on a loan. Having to transfer the goodwill associated with the mark runs at cross-purposes with this need. For example, suppose A has a valuable trademark for a hair care product sold through beauty shops and wishes to offer it as collateral for a loan to acquire assets for its expanding business. Bank B accepts the trademark as collateral for the loan. If A defaults on the loan, B acquires ownership of the mark. The problem arises because B is not in the hair care business and the situation is complicated if A wishes to stay in that business. B will try to sell the mark to the highest bidder, but what does it own if A has not also conveyed the goodwill associated with the business? Under the traditional rule, B owns nothing unless the goodwill of the business is transferred along with the mark.

Clearly, a strict application of the assignment in gross doctrine would increase the costs to a borrower who would wish to avoid putting up the goodwill of the business in case of default. Alternatively, creditors wish to know with certainty that they can expeditiously dispose of the mark for sale to the highest bidder. Absent such assurance, owners of valuable marks would see their borrowing power reduced if the goodwill were not sold along with the business. Ideally, transfers of trademark rights should be liberated from such formalities and should be assignable without restriction. As argued above, market discipline renders the assignment in gross doctrine largely irrelevant. The United States should consider following the trend in most countries of the world that have eliminated the requirement that trademarks be conveyed with the goodwill of the business.[51]

[49] 416 F.2d 285, 288 (8th Cir. 1969).

[50] See Allison Sell McDade, Generally, Trading In Trademarks – Why the Anti-Assignment in Gross Doctrine Should Be Abolished When Trademarks are Used as Collateral, 77 Tex. L. Rev. 465 (1998).

[51] The U.S. is one of the few countries in the world that requires the transfer of the goodwill or business assets of the business in assigning trademarks. Susan Barbieri Montgomery & Richard J. Taylor, Key Issues in World Wide Trademark Transfers: Law and Practice at 22 (5th ed. 1998).

2. *Valid and Invalid Assignments and Their Effect*

Not only is the case law in disarray over a key concept such as the transfer of goodwill, it is also hopelessly confused over the legal effect of an assignment in gross. Some courts hold that assignment in gross results in an abandonment of the mark. This means that the assignor has assigned the mark to another with no intention to resume use.[52] If such is the case, the continuity of use in the mark is broken. Because the goodwill has not been transferred with the mark, the assignee can no longer rely on the transferor's priority date.[53] By contrast, some courts have indicated that assignment in gross renders the assignee unable to establish any rights in the trademark at all. Generally, this harsh result has been rejected. When, however, the assignee has deceived the public by using the mark on substantially different goods and a serious case of public fraud has occurred, the courts may apply the equitable doctrine of 'unclean hands'. Here, the assignee may be prevented from asserting trademark rights at all.

The courts have progressively moderated the harsher contours of the assignment in gross doctrine. In the long term, the uncertainty may be resolved by the TRIPS agreement, which specifies that the owner of a registered trademark shall have the right to assign it with or without the transfer of business to which the trademark belongs.[54] Whatever the ultimate future of the assignment in gross doctrine, the current trends suggest that it will continue in name but diminish in importance. The United States' position is not followed in other countries, in which the prevailing rule is that trademarks may be assigned without goodwill in the business. No country in Europe requires that a mark be transferred with its underlying goodwill. Eventually the doctrine may be explicitly abrogated.

[52] 416 F.2d 285 (8th Cir.) Hy-Cross Hatchery, Inc. v. Osborne, 303 F.2d 947 (8th Cir. 1962); L'il Red Barn, Inc. v. Li'l Red Barn, System, Inc., 322 F.Supp. 98 (N.D. Ind. 1970) (7th Cir. 1972) (Assignor's on-going use following transfer precludes abandonment).

[53] Suppose A assigns the mark to B without goodwill in 1980. Here, an 'assignment in gross' has occurred and, as such, the assignee acquires no rights in the mark. The principal result is that the assignee loses the assignor's priority in the use of the mark and must rely on his own priority. Thus, if a third party's use predates the assignee's use of the mark (for example in 1975), the third party will succeed to its ownership rather than the assignee. On the other hand, if no third party use predates B's 1980 priority, B will simply acquire rights to the mark with the latter priority date. From a practical standpoint, the assignment in gross is irrelevant so long as no third party use has occurred.

[54] TRIPS Art. 21.

C. *Licensing of Trademarks: Source as Quality Control*

During the last 60 years, changes in marketing methods and technology have changed our attitudes toward trademarks. At one time, companies themselves distributed their products under their trademark. Consequently, the public generally expected that the company was the physical source of the product: that the product emanated from the trademark owner. As such, the licensing and franchising of trademarks seemed to run contrary to this source theory of trademark rights. If trademarks represented physical source, the licensing and franchising of trademarks conflicted with what was considered the policy justification of trademark protection.[55] But changing methods in the distribution of products leading to an increasingly impersonal rapport between the producer and consumer altered fundamental notions about the role of trademarks in a market economy.

Under a quality theory of trademarks, the trademark owner is permitted to authorize others to sell a product or service under the mark, so long as the trademark owner exercises quality control over the sale. In this way, the quality theory of trademarks reflects the reality of consumer decision-making. Most consumers do not really care who made the product; they are simply interested in the quality of the goods they are purchasing. The mark functions as an efficient means of recall, reminding the consumer of past satisfaction with the product, and offering the promise of future satisfaction.

In this sense, the quality control theory of trademarks does not supplant the source identification role of trademarks; it modifies and expands. It simply means that the trademark owner no longer has to be the physical origin of the goods but can be the quality-assuring source of the product. The source theory has been broadened to include not only the manufacturing source but also the source of standards and specifications of the goods bearing the mark.[56] A trademark, however, guarantees nothing except that the marked goods emanate from a single controlling source, not that they adhere to previous quality standards. As we will see, the restraints on the licensing of trademarks, however, are based on a misguided notion of trademarks as warranties. As such, they suffer from

[55] Macmahon Pharmacal Co. v. Denver Chemical Mfg. Co., 113 Fed. 468 (8th Cir. 1901); see Alfred M. Marks, Trademark Licensing – toward a More Flexible Standard, 78 TMR 641 (1988).

[56] 2 Stephen P. Ladas, Patents Trademarks and Related Rights, Ch. 30, section 620, p.1128 (1975).

inconsistency, do not comport with the realities of modern marketing and are rarely enforced in present practice.

1. *The Status of Trademark Licensing: Section 5 of the Lanham Act*

Licensing was first specifically authorized under federal law in the Lanham Act of 1946, subject to quality control of the licensor. Section 5 of the Lanham Act provides:

> Where a registered mark or a mark sought to be registered is or may be used legitimately by related companies, such use shall inure to the benefit of the registrant or applicant for registration, and such use shall not affect the validity of such mark or of its registration, provided such mark is not used in such manner as to deceive the public.[57]

Under the Lanham Act, a 'related company'[58] refers to any person who legitimately controls or is controlled by the registrant or applicant for registration in respect to the nature and quality of the goods or services in connection with which the mark is used. [59] A failure to control the licensee's goods falls within the definition of abandonment as a course of conduct of the registrant, including acts of omission as well as commission, which causes the mark to lose its significance as an indication of origin'.[60]

Even though the courts appear willing to find sufficient quality control procedures and are reluctant to find naked licenses, a totally uncontrolled or naked licensing program can result in the loss of trademark rights by abandonment. The statutory authority for this is section 45 of the Lanham Act, providing that a mark can be abandoned if acts of the trademark owner cause the mark to lose its 'significance as a mark'. This differs from abandonment through non-use because a trademark owner who engages in uncontrolled licensing does not necessarily intend to abandon the mark. The result of either form of abandonment can be the same. Uncontrolled licensing can cause a break in the continuity of

[57] Lanham Act section 5, 15 U.S.C. section 1055.

[58] See Ronald B. Coolley, Related Company: The Required Relationship in Trademark Licensing, 77 Trademark Rep. 299, 304 (1987) (tracing the related company concept in the common law); the Coca Cola Company was the pioneer in developing the quality function of trademarks in the licensing arrangements between itself and its bottlers, justified by its supervision and control exercised over them: see Coca-Cola Company v. J.G. Butler & Sons, 229 Fed. 224 (E.D. Ark. 1916).

[59] Lanham Act section 45, 15 U.S.C. section 1127.

[60] Lanham Act section 45, 15 U.S.C. section 1127.

use and the trademark necessary to prove its priority over third party use.[61] In addition, the trademark owner may be estopped in enforcing its rights.[62]

2. Naked Licenses and the Quality Control Requirement[63]

The quality control requirement has become the vehicle by which the guarantee function of trademarks is effectuated.[64] Should a licensor fail to ensure quality control, the license is 'naked' and invalid. The naked license doctrine suffers from some of the same defects as the related assignment in gross doctrine discussed above. Much of the problem relates to the lack of clarity given to the critical terms. The Lanham Act defines neither 'quality' nor 'control' and it has been left to the courts to interpret and apply the requirement. This lack of statutory guidance has led to some inconsistency in the nature and amount of control necessary to satisfy the requirements of the Lanham Act. Overall, the courts have judged each situation case by case. In essence, no absolute rule may be articulated because the quality control is based on consumer expectations. As such, it should vary with the expectations of the consumer in a certain marketing context that varies from product to product. Thus, a consumer will probably expect less in the exercise of quality control for a poster than he would for a computer or a medicine. Unfortunately, the case law has not articulated this principled view of the quality control requirement.

In addition to the lack of clarity in certain basic terms, the cases are inconsistent in specifying what constitutes quality control. Some cases indicate that a contractual right of quality control is sufficient to support a trademark licensing agreement while others require actual control.[65] The amount of actual control varies with each license, from close, hands-on scrutiny to complete reliance on the contractual obligations of the licensee to honor the licensing agreement. Total reliance on the licensee need not be fatal. Such reliance, if reasonable

[61] Heaton Enterprises of Nevada, Inc. v. Lang, 7 USPQ2d 1842 (TTAB 1988); First Interstate Bankcorp v. Stenquist, 16 USPQ 2d 1704 (ND Cal. 1990).

[62] Haymaker Sports, Inc. v. Turian, 581 F.2d 257 (CCPA 1978).

[63] William M. Borchard and Richard M. Osman, Trademark Licensing and Quality Control, 70 Trademark Rep. 99 101(1980); Sidney A. Diamond, Requirements of a Trademark Licensing Program, 17 Bus. Lawyer 295 (1962); Ronald B. Coolley, Related Company: The Required Relationship in Trademark Licensing, 77 Trademark Rep. (1987).

[64] Dawn Donut Co. v. Hart's Food Stores, 267 F.2d 358 (2d Cir. 1959).

[65] Wolfies Restaurant, Inc., v. Lincoln Restaurant Corp., 143 USPQ 310 (N.Y. Sup. Ct. 1964) (license of tradename WOLFIES for restaurant services).

under the circumstances and particularly if few consumer complaints occur, will provide a positive indication that the licensee has maintained quality control. Moreover, the quality control requirement can be fulfilled by supervision or testing conducted by third parties, such as testing agencies[66] or sub-licensees.[67] A review of the case law reveals that the courts have never provided a workable quality control standard.

As in the case for assignments, prime importance is given to the formal written document, in this instance, the written contract setting forth a quality control program. So much so that one gets the impression that mere form is the most important ingredient in establishing a valid agreement, despite certain case law stating that a mere paper agreement specifying quality control procedures is not in itself sufficient.[68] Generally, most parties begin with a well-drafted agreement containing the appropriate quality control provisions. Typically, trademark licensing agreements contain provisions that the licensee's use inures to the benefit of the licensor and that failure to comply with the conditions of the license results in its termination. Quality control provisions normally included in the agreement are: written quality standards, specifications, manuals of practice and provision for proper trademark notices.

In practice, courts have approved a wide range of quality control arrangements, varying from meticulous actual control to that involving little or almost no oversight.[69] The Dawn Donut[70] case, a leading decision on what constitutes quality control, exemplifies the judicial reluctance to find a naked license. Here, the trademark owner sought an injunction of the defendant's use of its registered marks DAWN and DAWN DONUT used on mixes for making baked goods and licensed to third parties. The plaintiff sought to enjoin defendant's use of the mark on donuts. In response, defendant counterclaimed to cancel plaintiff's registrations on the ground that its licensing method violated the Lanham Act,

[66] Crown Fabrics Corp. v. American Viscose Corp., 145 F.2d 246 (CCPA 1944).

[67] Turner v. HMH Publishing Co., 380 F.2d 224 (5th Cir.) cert. denied, 389 U.S. 1006 (1967).

[68] Land O' Lakes Creameries, Inc. v. Oconomowoc Canning Co., 330 F.2d 667 (7th Cir. 1964); Transgo, Inc. v. AJAC Transmission Parts Corp., 768 F.2d 1001 (9th Cir. 1985), cert. denied, 474 U.S. 1059 (1986); Alligator Co. v. Robert Bruce, Inc., 176 F.Supp. 377 (E.D. Pa. 1959).

[69] See Taco Cabana International, Inc. v. Two Pesos Inc., 932 F.2d 1113 (5th Cir 1991); Bureau National Interprofessional Du Cognac v. International Better Drinds Corp., Inc., 6 USPQ2d1610 (TTAB 1988); Nestle Co. Inc. v. Nash-Finch Co., 4 USPQ2d 1085 (TTAB 1987).

[70] Dawn Donut Co. Inc., v. Hart's Food Stores, Inc., 267 F.2d 358 (2d Cir. 1959).

resulting in abandonment of the marks. The injunction was denied for other reasons.[71] The counterclaim, however, was rejected despite the absence of a concerted effort to inspect the operations of the licensees. In addition, there were many instances where the plaintiff had permitted bakers to sell under the DAWN trademark without a written agreement governing the quality of the product.[72] Moreover, bakers were allowed to use the mark after the contracts had expired, and in one instance, the expired franchisee had been allowed to use another's doughnut mix. Despite this evidence, the trial court concluded that by reason of the contracts with its licensees, the plaintiff exercised legitimate control over the nature and quality of the food products on which the plaintiff's licensees used the trademark DAWN. The Second Circuit affirmed, deferring to the trial court's finding of adequate quality control despite all evidence to the contrary. Subsequent decisions have continued this trend of leniency.[73]

The truth is that abandonment has been found only in the most blatant cases of licensing misconduct.[74] Because a finding of insufficient control works as a forfeiture, a person who asserts insufficient control must meet a high burden of proof.[75] Very little is needed to find this quality control. For example, common control of the licensor and licensee by members of the same family can be evidence of adequate quality control. In addition, ownership of the licensee in whole or in part by the licensor is evidence of the control necessary.

Why has this erosion of the naked license doctrine taken place? This flexible, if sometimes lax attitude of the courts is a rational response to a doctrine that lacks clarity, is logically inconsistent and does not mesh with the contemporary marketing environment in which many goods are sold. A fundamental problem with the quality control requirement is that it forces inconsistent treatment of licensing and non-licensing situations. This inconsistency has its parallel in the assignment context. Thus, nothing would prevent the trademark owner from

71 The injunction was based on the geographic separation of the parties' markets.

72 In addition, when written contracts were in effect they did not provide for inspection or control.

73 See e.g. Penta Hotels Ltd. v. Penta Tours Reisen GmbH, 9 USPQ 2d 1081 (D. Conn. 1988).

74 See e.g. First National Bank of Omaha v. Autoteller Systems Service Corp., 9 USPQ2d 1740 (TTAB 1988); Heaton Enterprises of Nevada, Inc. v. Lang, 7 USPQ 1842 (TTAB 1988); First Interstate Bankcorp. v. Stenquist, 16 USPQ2d 1704 (ND Cal. 1990); Embedded Moments, Inc. v. International Silver Co., 648 F. Supp. 187 (EDNY 1986); Universal City Studios, Inc. v. Nintendo Co., 578 F. Supp. 911 (S.D.N.Y. 1983) aff'd on other grounds, 746 F.2d 112 (2d Cir. 1984).

75 Transgo, Inc. v. Ajac Transmission Parts Corp., 768 F.2d 1001, 1017 (9th Cir. 1985).

varying the quality of its product in numerous manufacturing facilities – nothing, that is, except the loss of reputation that the manufacturer would suffer if consumers were disappointed by goods of varying quality. Market discipline, of course, would prevent most manufacturers from causing this result. Whether a mark is licensed or not, there is a certain minimum quality level below which the trademark owner cannot profitably go. For licensors and non-licensors alike, the business decisions are the same.

The quality control requirement is particularly inappropriate in today's marketplace, specifically in merchandizing situations where the trademark owner does not manufacture the licensed goods and endeavors to exploit a mark in new product categories. The quality control requirement makes little sense in such instances where no primary, underlying product exists against which to compare the quality of the trademarked goods. Here, the trademark owner sets its quality standards only through the sale of licensed merchandise.

In these promotional trademark licensing situations, the purchaser is not motivated by the quality level of the product, but rather wishes to identify with the trademark owner.[76] Examples that come readily to mind are universities or other institutions that are constantly finding new products on which to apply their insignia. When a fan buys a coffee mug bearing a football club's insignia, he or she does not expect that that institution itself has manufactured the item.[77] Rather, the consumer who buys the merchandizing item wishes to express affiliation with the institution and is often motivated to buy such items, believing that the institution will reap some benefit from the sale. As one commentator suggested, '[T]o require the owner of the trademark to inaugurate an imaginary quality control program to satisfy legal requirements constructed by courts in dissimilar situations, is to elevate form over substance. The trademark owner is subject to unnecessary expense without any real benefit to consumers.'[78]

Another reason for this liberal tendency to find adequate quality control relates to the way in which the issue arises as an unclean hands defense to allegations of trademark infringement. Often the issue of a naked license originates from a counterclaim for infringement in which a clear infringer of a product is trying to avoid liability and establish free use of the mark. As one might expect,

[76] See University of Pittsburgh v. Champion Products, Inc., 686 F.2d 1040, 1047 (3d Cir.), cert. denied, 459 U.S. 1087 (1982).

[77] National Football League Properties, Inc. v. Wichita Falls Sportswear, Inc., 532 F. Supp. 651, 658–59 (W.D. Wash. 1982).

[78] See W.J. Keating, Promotional Trademark Licensing: A Concept Whose Time Has Come, 89 Dickinson L. Rev. 363, 378 (1985).

the courts have been reluctant to produce an outcome that could foster a greater deception of the public, and at the same time protect a counterclaimant whose hands are perhaps less clean than a lazy trademark licensor's. Peculiarly, application of the naked licensing doctrine may even produce perverse consequences for the consumer. If the trademark owner is denied relief because of its unclean hands, the result is not that the parties will be prohibited from using deceptive marks. Rather, both may use the same mark and the public must now contend with two deceptive marks.

This peculiarity results from the fact that a finding of a naked license will forfeit the licensor's right to enforce the mark against infringers but may not impede its further use. Finding naked licensing in this context transforms a doctrine designed to protect the public into one that results in precisely the same kind of confusion that the Lanham Act was designed to preclude.[79] In this setting, judicial resistance in finding a naked license resulting in an abandonment of the mark comes as no surprise, particularly when courts of equity are notoriously reluctant in declaring a forfeiture of rights, the result of which may cause greater confusion in the marketplace. This judicial resistance is implemented by placing a strict burden of proof on the party asserting abandonment, a hurdle that renders the defense rarely successful.

V. LIKELIHOOD OF CONFUSION: DANCING WITH DILUTION

A. *Introduction*

Once the plaintiff has shown that he owns a valid and protectable mark, the decisive issue in an action for trademark infringement is 'likelihood of confusion'. The Lanham Act defines this key term as an unconsented use of a registered mark that is 'likely to cause confusion, or to cause mistake, or to deceive'.[80] Likelihood of confusion is the universal standard for trademark infringement, cutting across both federal and state trademark and unfair competition law. The federal Lanham Act explicitly recognizes likelihood of confusion as the standard

[79] See Kevin Parks, 'Naked' is Not a Four Letter Word: Debunking the Myth of the 'Quality Control Requirement' in Trademark Licensing, 82 TMR 531 (1992).

[80] Lanham Act section 32, 15 U.S.C. section 1114(1).

in an action for the infringement of registered marks.[81] Courts have adopted likelihood of confusion as the test for infringement in deciding whether a trade symbol is a 'false designation of origin' under section 43(a) of the Lanham Act.[82]

A centerpiece of U.S. trademark law whose roots are anchored in unfair competition, the likelihood of confusion doctrine has gone through a progressive expansion as the commercial environment of branded marketing has evolved over the last sixty years. From an historical standpoint, the doctrine of likelihood of confusion has manifested a remarkable flexibility in its adaptation to these new realities. In retrospect, this enlargement of the doctrine has resulted from a basic realization that trademarks are more than symbols of goodwill. As Schechter would say, they are 'an agency for the perpetuation of good will'.[83]

Advocates of small trademark rights have noted with displeasure that the boundaries of trademark infringement have progressively enlarged through the years, a phenomenon that provides a further indication of how trademark law has deviated from a vehicle for consumer protection to a more absolute property right. This assessment is largely correct and the trend flourished even before Congress passed the federal anti-dilution statute in 1995. As we will see, the likelihood of confusion standard has always been in constant flux, whose contours expand to encompass broader protection for trademark owners. The fact that the likelihood of confusion standard has evolved in this manner is hardly

[81] Lanham Act section 32(1), 15 U.S.C. section 1114(1). Likelihood of confusion also plays a prominent role in ex parte and inter partes proceedings before the Trademark Office. The Trademark Office will reject federal registration of a mark because it is confusingly similar to a previously registered mark. See Lanham Act section 32(1), 15 U.S.C. section 1114(1), requiring the plaintiff to show that the defendant is:

> any person who shall, without the consent of the registrant —
> (1) Use in commerce any reproduction, counterfeit, copy, or colorable imitation of a registered mark in connection with the sale, offering for sale, distribution, or advertising of any goods or services on or in connection with which such use is likely to cause confusion, to cause mistake, or to deceive ...

In addition, likelihood of confusion establishes the basis for which a mark may be opposed or cancelled. Finally, likelihood of confusion is the standard for infringement under both state common and statutory law. State Model Trademark Act section 11.

[82] Lanham Act section 43(a), 15 U.S.C. section 1125(a).

[83] Schecter, note at p.337.

surprising given the changing marketing environment. The phrase 'likelihood of confusion' in itself is a broadly worded standard that provides no more than a starting point in determining trademark infringement and is based on an 'equitable' multifactor test that goes well beyond protecting the consumer against deception in the marketplace. In effect, the case law has filled in the gaps left unanswered by the statutory definition and, in doubtful circumstances, has sided with the trademark owner's interest in protecting the investment in acquiring goodwill in the mark.

In determining likelihood of confusion, three basic questions are at issue: (1) What types of confusion does the Lanham Act prohibit? (2) Who must be confused? and (3) When and where in the purchasing process must the actionable confusion occur? In each of these issues, the courts have progressively enlarged the scope of the doctrine, and have done so in a way consistent with the new economic learning and current marketing realities.

B. Kinds of Confusion

The kinds of actionable confusion generally recognized by the courts are: (1) Confusion of source; (2) Confusion of sponsorship or affiliation; and (3) Reverse confusion. Although some courts and commentators have developed other concepts of confusion,[84] the courts universally recognize these three types of confusion.

The least controversial basis in applying the likelihood of confusion doctrine is source confusion. This occurs when a consumer believes that the junior user's product is the senior user's product or that the junior user's product originates from the same source as the senior user's product. This context has raised little controversy in the world of trademarks. Thus, if the senior user uses the mark GEORGIE on hand lotion and the junior user uses the same mark on the same goods, the public might well believe that the source of the junior user's product is the senior user. Here, the consumer is likely to be confused as to the source of the junior user's goods. When confusion of source occurs, the interests of both the trademark owner and consumer are simultaneously impaired. The junior user's use of the same or similar mark diverts trade from the senior user. At the same time, the consumer, unable to distinguish the goods, is deprived of buying the desired product. A rational purchasing decision on the part of the consumer can only occur absent confusion of source.

[84] William M. Borchard, Reverse Passing Off: Commercial Robbery or Permissible Competition?, 67 Trademark Rep. 1 (1977).

Even as simple and as intuitive a doctrine as source confusion is based on fiction. When a purchaser believes that the junior user's product emanates from the same source as the senior user's product, he may not be able to name the specific source of the goods he is buying. Indeed, more often than not, purchasers do not know the *exact* source of the goods they are buying. They may not know, for example, that SPRITE is manufactured by Coca-Cola, NUTRA-GRAIN by Nabisco or TIDE by Procter & Gamble. In recognizing this basic fact, trademark law has long established as a basic principle that, in actions for infringement, the identity of the source need not be known so long as the article is perceived as emanating from a single, though anonymous, source.[85]

The principle of source confusion must take into account that when a consumer associates a mark with a single anonymous source, this source need not be a manufacturer. In today's marketing world, retailers may have their own private or house brands applied to their goods. Thus, Sears or Radio Shack may place its house mark on television sets or videocassette recorders produced by various manufacturers. Under trademark law, the dealer becomes the 'source' of the goods even though several different manufacturers may fabricate these goods. The dealer who places his mark on these goods that pass through his hands may control their production, or simply verify their quality.[86] This quality control function of our trademark system, as we have seen, means nothing more than that the mark is controlled by a single, though often anonymous, source.

C. *From Source Confusion to Confusion of Sponsorship or Affiliation: The Non-Competing Goods Dilemma*

The likelihood of confusion doctrine is not limited to situations where goods are competing, but is applied as well where the goods are non-competing. In so doing, the courts have recognized that the junior user has not diverted trade from the senior user. Rather, when similar marks are used on goods that do not directly compete – that is, goods that are not substitutes for one another – the courts have justified a finding of infringement based on a theory of confusion of sponsorship or affiliation. In other words, the consumer may be aware that he is

[85] Coty, Inc. v. Le Blume Import Co., 292 F. 264, 267 (S.D.N.Y. 1923), aff'd 293 F. 344 (2d Cir. 1923); Humble Oil & Refining Co. v. American Oil Co., 405 F.2d 803 (8th Cir. 1969); Restatement (First) of Torts section 715 (1938).

[86] See Victor Tool & Machine Corp. v. Sun Control Awnings, Inc., 299 F. Supp. 868 (E.D. Mich. 1968), aff'd, 411 F.2d 792 (6th Cir. 1969).

not buying the senior user's product, but may believe that the senior user has sponsored or authorized the junior user's product, or is otherwise connected with the junior user. Thus, if the senior user uses POLYKUTER on lawnmowers, the public may well be confused as to the sponsorship of the goods if another manufacturer were to use the same mark on tree pruning scissors. The difficulty in cases involving non-competing goods lies in determining whether the goods or services on which the marks are used are sufficiently related so that a consumer could reasonably believe that the senior user has sponsored or is affiliated with the junior user.

In practice, the non-competing goods inquiry has proved to be a difficult, if not impossible task, given the varied marketing contexts in which the issue arises. It is the most litigated issue in trademark law, if not the most troublesome. In practice, it has become increasingly difficult to find convenient boundaries for the doctrine in an era where conglomerate enterprises make an extraordinary number of products, varying from pharmaceuticals to food products and household chemicals, and where an institutional symbol may be found on a diverse range of goods and services.

How far a trademark owner can protect his mark across product lines for distinctly different goods has been a matter of controversy for many years. One conclusion can be drawn when the matter is viewed from a historical dimension: the trademark owner's right to prevent others from using the mark across product lines has progressively enlarged through the years. One only has to look at its progression from its modest origins in the 1905 Trademark Act to today's expansive reinterpretation.

Under the 1905 Trademark Act, the test for trademark infringement required that the marks be confusingly similar and 'be used on goods with the same descriptive properties'.[87] The courts construed 'the same descriptive properties' requirement as providing narrow protection across product lines. For example, in *Borden Ice Cream v. Borden's Condensed Milk Co.*,[88] the court held that the defendant's use of the mark BORDEN on ice cream did not infringe the plaintiff's use of the same mark on milk because the goods were not competing.

Protection of trademarks across products lines was first recognized in *Aunt Jemima Mills Co. v. Rigney & Co*,[89] where the plaintiff's AUNT JEMIMA mark on pancake batter was protected against the defendant's use of the mark on pancake syrup. Although batter and syrup are complementary goods, they have

[87] Act of Feb. 20, 1905, 15 U.S.C. sections 81 et seq.

[88] 201 F.510 (7th Cir. 1912).

[89] 247 F.407 (2d Cir. 1917), cert. denied, 245 U.S. 672 (1918).

distinct properties and are non-competing. Despite the lack of direct injury to the senior user, the court found that the public would assume that the junior user's syrup was made by the senior user. Thus, in benefiting from the senior user's reputation and advertising, the junior user would impede the senior user's potential ability to expand his business into the related product line. As the court stated:

> To use precisely the same mark, as the defendants have done, is, in our opinion, evidence of intention to make something out of it – either to get the benefit of the complainant's reputation or of its advertisement or to forestall the extension of its trade.[90]

The 'Aunt Jemima' doctrine, as it came to be known, recognized the trademark right as a more expansive property right than had been recognized up to that time and regarded the junior user's actions as a trespass on that right.[91] Despite a general acceptance of the 'Aunt Jemima' doctrine, the courts have hardly been unanimous in their approach to protecting trademarks across product lines. The extent to which the courts have protected trademarks across product lines has often depended on each court's general attitude toward trademarks.[92] But once it has become acceptable that trademarks serve other functions than consumer deception, and more importantly operate to reduce search costs for the consumer, the property right rationale for trademarks justifies their expansive scope.

With the passage of the Lanham Act in 1946, Congress reinforced the trend toward more expansive protection of trademarks. The Lanham Act's expanded protection was intended to include any situation in which likelihood of confusion took place among purchasers. The courts, however, were hardly unanimous in their reaction to the new trademark act. Some took an expansionist approach,

[90] Id. at 409.

[91] In the 1920s and 1930s, the Second Circuit broadened its protection to include trademarks on related goods. See e.g. Anheuser-Busch, Inc. v. Budweiser Malt Prod. Corp., 295 F.306 (2d Cir. 1923) (beer trademark on malt syrup); Yale Elec. Corp. v. Robertson, 26 F.2d 972 (2d Cir. 1928) (lock trademark on flashlight batteries); L. E. Waterman Co. v. Gordon, 72 F.2d 272 (2d Cir. 1934) (fountain pen trademark on razor blades).

[92] This history is ably described in David Goldberg and William M. Borchard, Related Goods Trademark Cases in the Second Circuit, 70 Trademark Rep. 287 (1980) and David Goldberg, William M. Borchard and Colby J. Shereff, Mushrooms Revisited: More on Related Goods in the Second Circuit, 74 Trademark Rep. 207 (1984).

focusing on likelihood of confusion as the critical issue.[93] Others took a more constrained approach by balancing the legitimate interests of the senior user with the legitimate interests of the innocent second user. The latter supported the right of third parties to compete and enter markets rather than concentrating on the damage to the senior user's property interest in his trademark.[94] The same tension between the property right of the senior user and the right of the junior user to compete can be found in many non-competing goods cases. This tension is particularly apparent in the Second Circuit,[95] where different panels have vacillated between expansive and constrained protection of trademarks across product lines.[96] The result in close cases will often depend on how the decision maker understands the interests involved when the same or similar trademarks are used on non-competing goods.

D. Confusion of Affiliation or Sponsorship: A Closer Look at the Interests Protected

Determining likelihood of confusion is often a simple process when the goods or services on which the marks are used are competing. Public deception is obvious and damage to the trademark owner is direct. If confusingly similar marks are used on directly competing or closely related goods, the likelihood that they may be attributed to the same or related source is probable and therefore easily proven. The public is likely to be confused about the source or origin of the

[93] See e.g. Triangle Publications, Inc. v. Rohrlich, 167 F.2d 969 (2d Cir. 1948) (publishers of SEVENTEEN magazine were able to enjoin a girdle manufacturer from using the mark MISS SEVENTEEN without having to show damage to their reputation or intention to market girdles).

[94] Avon Shoe Co., Inc. v. David Crystal, Inc., 279 F.2d 607 (2d Cir. 1960), cert. denied, 364 U.S. 909 (1960) (injunction denied for senior user's mark HAYMAKERS for women's shoes against HAYMAKER for women's sportswear).

[95] The Second Circuit Court of Appeals is singled out because it probably has been through the years the most influential court on trademark matters due to the number of cases it has decided and several famous judges.

[96] See McGregor-Donniger, Inc. v. Drizzle, Inc., 599 F.2d 1126 (2d Cir. 1979) (DRIZZLE for women's overcoats and raincoats did not infringe DRIZZLER for men's golf jackets); Vitarroz Corp. v. Borden, Inc., 644 F.2d 200 (2d Cir. 1981) (BRAVOS for tortilla chips did not infringe BRAVOS for crackers); cf., Scarves by Vera, Inc. v. Todo Imports, Ltd., 544 F.2d 1167 (2d Cir. 1976) (VERA for high fashion women's scarves and sportswear protected against VERA for cosmetics and perfumes).

goods. Moreover, damage to the trademark owner is easier to establish. When competing goods are involved, it logically follows that the junior user will divert trade from the senior user. Thus, if both the junior and senior users apply the mark AUDACE on after-shave cologne, consumers will likely be confused about the origin of the goods and trade will likely be diverted from the senior user as a result.

In the non-competing goods setting, determining likelihood of confusion becomes more complicated than when competing goods are at issue. Other interests arise that must be balanced when the marks are used on non-competing goods, that is, goods that are not substitutes. Suppose, for example, the senior user uses the mark GLAMOR on women's shoes while the junior user uses the same mark on a line of women's underwear. Could the defendant be enjoined from its use? Obviously, the two products do not directly compete – they are not substitutes. Because he does not sell shoes, the senior user cannot argue that diversion of trade will occur. Moreover, if the junior user's underwear is of good quality, his presence in the market will not damage the senior user's reputation.

Clearly, protection across product lines confers a more powerful property right on the trademark owners, increasing their market power by allowing them to preserve unanticipated markets for future use. Accordingly, from a consumer deception or unfair competition theory, it is a much more difficult proposition to justify protection of trademarks across product boundaries than in competing goods situations in which both the consumer's and trademark owner's interests clearly coincide.

1. *The Interest Involved In Protecting Goods Across Product Lines*

How is the public interest vindicated when trademark protection is extended across product lines to non-competing goods? Confusion of sponsorship or affiliation is the traditional justification for a broader form of trademark protection. For example, a reasonably prudent purchaser, in seeing the mark GLAMOR on both shoes and underwear, may well believe that the goods either emanate from the same source or that the sellers are related in some way. The consumer's perception that a relationship exists is a reasonable one in today's marketing environment in which firms expand their product lines into associated areas of endeavor. ARM AND HAMMER, for example, now appears not only on baking soda but also on detergents and toothpaste; DOLE appears on both canned and fresh fruit. Thus, a purchaser who sees the same mark on a related good might believe he is buying a product sponsored, affiliated or endorsed by the senior user. Here, the consumer may well make a purchasing decision based on false information. The problem becomes determining whether confusion of sponsorship is likely, as opposed to a vague, speculative possibility.

The interests of the trademark owner often coincide with those of the purchaser when confusion of sponsorship and affiliation occurs. Conferring trademark protection across product lines makes trademark ownership a more valuable property right, encouraging the trademark owner to invest in promoting her product or service under the mark. Commercially successful products known for their high quality are rewarded by such protection. If the junior user's goods are of poor quality, and confusion of sponsorship takes place, the senior user's reputation may be damaged. In this way, the incentive to invest in a trademark is undermined when consumers identify the senior user's mark with poorer quality products, resulting in the tarnishment of the senior user's reputation. When tarnishment occurs, loss of patronage will follow and the senior user's investment in promoting the trademark and acquiring goodwill is undermined. Thus, the courts in a non-competing goods case will scrutinize the quality of the junior user's product. If the goods are of poor quality (as compared with the senior user's), a finding of infringement is enhanced.[97]

Even if the junior user's products are not inferior in quality, protecting marks across product lines increases the value of trademark rights in another way. It allows the senior user breathing room to extend his trademark into a related endeavor. Thus, if the owner of GLAMOR on shoes has a product that consumers desire, he may well want to expand the mark into a related goods line (women's underwear) and build on the goodwill already established under the mark. Courts in non-competing goods cases recognize this concept by examining whether the senior user would bridge the gap by extending use of the mark to the related product line.[98]

[97] Learned Hand was one of the first judges to articulate the tarnishment and quality control rationale of trademark protection. See Yale Elec. Corp. v. Robertson, 26 F.2d 972 (2d Cir. 1928). Many other cases have referred to the trademark owner's right to control the reputation of the product. See e.g. James Burroughs, Ltd. v. Sign of the Beefeater, Inc., 540 F.2d 266 (7th Cir. 1976); Scarves by Vera, Inc. v. Todo Imports, Ltd., 544 F.2d 1167 (2d Cir. 1976).

[98] See e.g. Scarves by Vera, Inc. v. Todo Imports, Ltd., 544 F.2d 1167 (2d Cir. 1976) (women's scarves and perfume); E. I. Dupont de Nemours & Co. v. Yoshida, Inc., 393 F. Supp. 502 (E.D.N.Y. 1975) (non-stick resin and zippers).

2. The Expansion of the Likelihood of Confusion Standard and the Dilution Doctrine

The legal standard for both competing and non-competing goods cases is likelihood of confusion. For confusion to occur, the purchaser must believe that the junior user's goods or services emanate from the senior user or are sponsored by, affiliated with or connected to the senior user. To make this determination, the courts use a multifactor test that takes into account the similarity of the marks as well as other aspects of the marketing environment. These factors include the similarities in the goods or services, the intent of the defendant to cause confusion, the extent of actual confusion, the sophistication of the purchasers, the strength of the plaintiff's mark, the quality of the junior user's product, and the likelihood that the senior user will expand into the junior user's product line.[99]

According to theory, the 'likelihood of confusion', as implemented by the multifactor test, imposes a limit on the rights of a trademark owner. It simultaneously confers a boundary around this intangible property right and harmonizes it with the public interest in making rational purchasing decisions. In reality, however, the multifactor test has inevitably led to an expansion of the likelihood of confusion standard, which has had the practical effect, in large part, of incorporating into trademark law a de facto dilution standard.

Until 1996, Congress had declined to amend the Lanham Act to incorporate the anti-dilution concept[100] and the courts uniformly have rejected dilution as a basis for trademark protection. Despite this explicit renunciation, the anti-dilution principle has insinuated itself into U.S. law. The outcomes in certain cases are difficult to explain on any other but an anti-dilution basis. There appear to be two patterns of cases that tend to incorporate de facto the anti-dilution concept. In the first pattern, the anti-dilution principle is embodied implicitly in cases involving merchandising rights. In these cases, some courts have given expansive protection to names of sports teams, colleges, motion pictures, television programs and magazines against their use on goods sold by third parties under the name or title.[101] In each of these cases, the court will use

[99] See discussion infra at note 143.

[100] The original version of the Trademark Revision Act of 1988 Pub. L. 100–667, 102 Stat 3935 (Nov. 16, 1989) contained an anti-dilution provision. See 77 Trademark Rep. 454–62 (1987).

[101] See e.g. National Football League v. Governor of Delaware, 435 F. Supp. 1372 (D. Del 1977) (use of team logos in conjunction with state lottery enjoined); Boston Professional Hockey Assoc. v. Dallas Cap & Emblem Mfg., Inc., 510 F.2d 1004 (5th

a likelihood of confusion rationale even though there may be only a remote possibility of confusion. For example, a court has enjoined the sale of t-shirts with BOSTON MARATHON on the front, finding likelihood of confusion of sponsorship because consumers would believe that the goods were sponsored by the official organizers of the event.[102]

A second pattern of cases departing from the confusion rationale are those in which the defendant has 'tarnished' the reputation of a trademark. When a court enjoined use of the slogan WHERE THERE'S LIFE THERE'S BUGS on insecticides, a take-off on the famous Budweiser Beer slogan WHERE THERE'S LIFE THERE'S BUD, it emphasized that the consumer might believe that Budweiser was in the insecticide business, and as a result of this association, the brewer's reputation would be injured.[103] In other cases, courts have enjoined use of trademark parodies, particularly those that involve sexual allusions or are in 'bad taste'.[104] Although courts invariably give likelihood of confusion of sponsorship as their rationale when the possibility of confusion is so strained, the decision can only be explained on an anti-dilution rationale. Here, the implication is that the defendant's use constitutes a whittling away of a trademark's distinctiveness by placing it in an unwholesome context – a context that tarnishes the mark's reputation, uniqueness or prestigious connotations.[105]

Of course, not all courts have been amenable to extending the boundaries of likelihood of confusion in their reconfirmation that trademark protection is

Cir) cert. denied, 423 U.S. 868 (1975) (use of sports emblem on a variety of products, e.g. pennants, t-shirts, etc., enjoined); Warner Bros. v. Gay Toys, Inc., 658 F.2d 76 (2d Cir. 1982) (toy based on television show creates likelihood of confusion); Boston Athletic Assoc. v. Sullivan, 867 F.2d 22 (1st Cir. 1989) (t-shirts with mark BOSTON MARATHON enjoined). Robert Denicola, Institutional Publicity Rights: An Analysis of the Merchandising of Famous Trade Symbols, 62 N. Car. L. Rev. 603 (1984).

102 Boston Athletic Assoc. v. Sullivan, 867 F.2d 22 (1st Cir. 1990).

103 Chemical Corp. of America v. Anheuser-Busch, Inc., 306 F.2d 433 (5th Cir. 1962).

104 See Georgia Athletic Assoc. v. Laite, 756 F.2d 1535 (11th Cir. 1985) (BULLDOG beer infringes University of Georgia's BULLDOGS football team); Coca-Cola Co. v. Gemini Rising, Inc., 346 F. Supp. 1183 (E.D.N.Y. 1972) (poster ENJOY COCAINE imitating Coca-Cola's ENJOY COCA-COLA enjoined on a questionable likelihood of confusion rationale).

105 See e.g. General Electric Co. v. Alumpa Coal Co., 205 USPQ 1063 (D. Mass. 1979) (GENITAL ELECTRIC on underwear infringes GE – confusion of sponsorship). A possible First Amendment defense to cases of trademark parody and other referential uses of trademarks is discussed elsewhere. See section infra.

essentially based on a concept of preventing public deception and that a trademark, unlike a patent or copyright, is not a 'right in gross'.[106] Despite this mainstream position, the clear trend has seen the boundaries of trademark rights continuously expanded, particularly in cases dealing with merchandising rights and situations involving the tarnishment of a trademark's reputation.

E. Reverse Confusion

Under the Lanham Act, likelihood of confusion ordinarily occurs when the junior user of a mark creates the false impression that the senior user is the source or sponsorship of the junior user's goods. Recently the courts have begun to recognize a new kind of confusion called 'reverse confusion', a variety of confusion that departs from the common law 'passing off' model of trademark infringement. Reverse confusion occurs when the junior user creates the false impression that he is the source of the senior user's goods.[107] Both types of confusion, 'passing off' and 'reverse passing off', may exist at the same time; they are not mutually exclusive, but reverse confusion has come to be recognized as an independent basis for trademark infringement. To establish reverse confusion, the senior user must prove that the junior user's selection of a mark is likely to lead consumers to believe that the goods marketed by the senior user originated with the junior user. In short, reverse confusion occurs when the junior user leads consumers to the false impression that it is the source of the senior user's goods.

The interest protected in 'reverse confusion' cases differs from that protected in source or sponsorship confusion cases. In the traditional trademark infringement case, the court prevents the junior user from appropriating the senior user's reputation, limiting his expansion or causing loss of patronage. By contrast, in a reverse confusion case, consumers who are initially aware of the junior user's goods may believe that the senior user's mark they later see originates with the junior user. Accordingly, consumers may believe that the senior user is an infringer. In this way, the junior user's use of the mark may injure the senior

[106] See Bi-Rite v. Button Master, 555 F. Supp. 118 (S.D.N.Y. 1982) (trademark rights should be limited to likelihood of confusion rationale); American Footwear Corp. v. General Footwear Co., 609 F.2d 655, cert. denied 445, U.S. 951 (2d Cir. 1979) (trademark rights unlike copyrights and patents, are not rights in gross).

[107] Restatement of Unfair Competition, section 20(1) (c) and comment f, at 174 (1988); Banff, Ltd. v. Federated Dep't. Stores, Inc., 841 F.2d 486, 490 (2d Cir. 1988) (reverse confusion is the misimpression that the junior user is the source of the senior user's goods).

user's reputation and damage his goodwill. In addition, if the junior user's goods are of inferior quality, the damage is enhanced. One court defined reverse confusion as follows:

> A reverse confusion claim differs from the stereotypical confusion of source or sponsorship claim. Rather than seeking to profit from the goodwill captured in the senior user's trademark, the junior user saturates the market with a similar trademark and overwhelms the senior user. The public comes to assume the senior user's mark or that the former has become somehow connected to the latter. The result is that the senior user loses the value of the trademark – its product identity, corporate identity, control over its goodwill and reputation, and ability to move into a new market.[108]

In proving reverse confusion, there must be evidence establishing that the confusion could inflict commercial injury by diverting sales, damaging goodwill or causing loss of control over reputation.[109]

The leading case finding infringement through reverse confusion is *Big O Tire Dealers, Inc. v. Goodyear Tire & Rubber Co.*[110] In *Big O*, a small tire manufacturer sold BIGFOOT tires in a local market. Goodyear, a large national tire company and seller, began selling BIGFOOT tires with an extensive national publicity campaign. Goodyear's advertising inundated the regional user's brand recognition, inducing purchasers to believe that Goodyear, the junior user, produced Big O's tires. In these circumstances, the court found that Goodyear had infringed Big O's trademark by causing reverse confusion.

Courts have decided other reverse confusion cases in similar fashion. Most of these cases follow the familiar pattern in which a well-known junior user causes reverse confusion, injuring the lesser-known senior user.[111] For example, in *Banff Ltd. v. Federated Department Stores*,[112] Banff had marketed women's clothing under the mark B AND B WEAR to retail consumers since 1971. In 1986, Bloomingdale's began to sell BEE\WEAR on women's clothing in its retail

[108] See Ameritech, Inc. v. American Info. Tech. Corp., 811 F.2d 960 (6th Cir. 1987).

[109] Doe Lang v. Retirement Living Publishing Co., No. 96, Docket 91-7336, 1991 WL 243595 (2d Cir. 1991) (Westlaw, Federal Library, 2nd Circuit File).

[110] 408 F. Supp. 1219 (D. Colo. 1976), 561 F.2d 1365 (10th Cir. 1977).

[111] Ameritech Inc. v. American Info. Tech. Corp., 811 F.2d 960 (6th Cir. 1987) (Ohio law); Fuji Photo Film Co., Inc. v. Shinohara Shoji Kabushiki Kaisha, 754 F.2d 591 (5th Cir. 1985) (Texas law); but see Westward Coach Mfg. Co. v. Ford Motor Co., Inc., 388 F.2d 627 (7th Cir.), cert. denied, 392 U.S. (1968).

[112] 841 F.2d 486 (2d Cir. 1988); Sands, Taylor & Wood Co. v. Quaker Oats Co., 998 F.2d 947 (7th Cir. 1992); IHSA v. GTE, 99 F.3d 244 (7th Cir. 1996), cert. denied, 117 S. Ct. 1083 (1997).

stores. Banff filed suit for infringement to enjoin Bloomingdale's use of the mark. The District Court granted the preliminary injunction allowing Bloomingdale's to use the mark in the lower case (bee\wear). The Court of Appeals not only upheld the injunction but also granted a broader one based on reverse confusion. It reasoned that the junior user, Bloomingdale's, was bigger and better known in the marketplace, and, as such, consumers would view it as the source of the senior user's goods.

Although a relatively new development in the law, the principle of reverse confusion now effectively covers the entire domain of trademark and unfair competition law.[113] It has been adopted not only in trademark infringement cases but also under section 43(a) of the Lanham Act (false designation of origin),[114] and is grounds for an opposition before the Trademark Office.[115] In addition, reverse confusion is not limited to cases involving competing goods, but has also been extended to cases involving non-competing goods.[116] In embracing the doctrine of reverse confusion, the courts have once again opted for the primacy of protecting the trademark owner's ability to capitalize on the goodwill associated with its mark. Here goodwill is protected even though the consumer confusion is negligible and diversion of trade nonexistent.

F. Proving Likelihood of Confusion: The Illusory 'Probability' of Confusion Standard

The term 'likelihood' has been interpreted to mean a 'probability' of confusion. The courts are unanimous in declaring that probability of confusion means

[113] See Harlem Wizards Ent. Basketball v. NBA Properties, Inc., 952 F. Supp. 1084 (D.N.J. 1997).

[114] Banff, Ltd. v. Federated Dep't. Stores, Inc., 841 F.2d 486, 490 (2d Cir. 1988).

[115] See e.g., American Hygenic Laboratories, Inc. v. Tiffany & Co., 12 U.S.P.Q.2d 1979 (TTAB 1989).

[116] See Plus Prod. v. Plus Discount Foods, Inc., 772 F.2d 999 (2d Cir. 1983) (senior user of PLUS mark on various expensive health products, such as vitamins, beauty aids and food fortifiers, infringed on reverse confusion grounds by junior user of PLUS mark in discount supermarket for its inexpensive house brand); MasterCard Int'l., Inc. v. Arbel Corp., 13 U.S.P.Q.2d 1958 (S.D.N.Y. 1989) (possibility of reverse confusion found for use of slogan 'Master the Travel Possibilities' where senior user was a local, religion-oriented travel agency and junior user was MasterCard financial services).

more than a mere possibility of confusion.[117] Although the trademark owner need not prove that actual confusion has occurred to prevail in an action for trademark infringement, proof of actual confusion constitutes strong (in some instances the strongest) evidence of likelihood of confusion. In addition, the senior user need not prove the junior user's intent to deceive, even though proof of the junior user's bad faith in adopting a mark can constitute strong evidence of likelihood of confusion. The test for likelihood of confusion focuses on the results of the defendant's conduct in the marketplace, rather than on his motivation in adopting a mark. That being said, a strong showing of actual confusion and intent to deceive on the part of the defendant can play a critical role in infringement litigation. Such evidence can be the basis for which a court will extend the scope of relief accorded the trademark owner.[118]

The courts have explicitly relaxed the 'probability' of confusion requirement in certain instances. For example, when pharmaceutical products are involved, some courts have held that a mere 'possibility' of confusion is sufficient to prove likelihood of confusion.[119] The reason for this reduced standard is one of public health: to protect the consumer from injury resulting from ingesting the wrong drug. Beyond this narrow exception, however, the courts uniformly insist that the plaintiff show more than a 'possibility' of confusion. Strict adherence to probability standard is less than uniform. When one examines the actual percentages of confused purchasers required in case law, the likelihood of confusion determination falls far short of the probability standard. In practice, the threshold falls very short of a majority of the purchasing public. One court has held that confusion among eight-and-a-half percent of those surveyed was

[117] Carter-Wallace, Inc. v. Procter & Gamble Co., 434 F.2d 794 (9th Cir. 1970).

[118] In addition, intent to deceive may create an inference that the prior user's mark is distinctive and that the defendant's use creates a likelihood of confusion. Moreover, certain equitable defenses may be denied the defendant for intentional deception.

[119] See e.g. Morgenstern Chem. Co. v. G.D. Searle & Co., 253 F.2d 390 (3d Cir.), cert. denied, 358 U.S. 816 (1958); Syntex Laboratories, Inc. v. Norwich Pharmaceutical Co., 437 F.2d 566 (2d Cir. 1971); American Cyanamid Corp. v. Connaught Laboratories, Inc., 800 F.2d 306 (2d Cir. 1986) (although no infringement found, court rearticulated the 'possibility of confusion' doctrine for drug products); but see Smithkline Beckman Corp. v. Procter & Gamble Co., 591 F. Supp. 1229 (N.D.N.Y. 1984) (no infringement found for mark on an over-the-counter drug product because reasonably prudent purchaser is more careful in buying this category of product).

strong evidence of likelihood of confusion.[120] Other courts have accepted similar percentages.[121]

G. *Expanding the Confusion Standard Beyond Actual Purchasers: The 1962 Amendments*

Under the Lanham Act of 1946 as originally passed, a trademark was infringed if the defendant's use of a mark was 'likely to cause confusion or mistake or to deceive purchasers as to the source of origin of such goods or services'.[122] This original language defining likelihood of confusion was construed to mean likelihood of confusion at the point of sale among *actual purchasers* as to the producer of the defendant's product. Because of the overly constrained interpretation, Congress in 1962 amended this basic provision, deleting the phrase 'purchasers as to the source of origin of such goods or services'. The pertinent language of the Act now reads 'likely to cause confusion or mistake or to deceive'.[123]

It has never been entirely clear exactly what Congress had in mind when it deleted the pre-1962 phrase 'purchasers as to the source and origin of such goods or services' and simplified the statutory language. Consequently, this lack of clarity has not led to judicial uniformity in interpreting this key standard. One thing is certain, however. At a minimum, Congress wished to broaden likelihood of confusion to encompass not only actual purchasers but potential purchasers as well. It is generally accepted that liability for initial confusion among potential purchasers is fully justified by the 1962 amendment of sections 32(a) and 2(d) of the Lanham Act. Consistent with this view, the Senate report states that by omitting the word 'purchasers', the intent of Congress was to extend the confusion concept to potential purchasers as well as to actual purchasers.[124]

Despite the apparent intent of the 1962 amendments to the Lanham Act to include potential as well as actual purchasers, some courts have insisted that likelihood of confusion be focused on the actual purchaser at the point of

[120] Grotrian, Helfferich, Schulz, Th. Steinweg Nachf. v. Steinway & Sons, 365 F. Supp. 707 (S.D.N.Y. 1973), modified, 523 F.2d 1331 (2d Cir. 1975).

[121] James Burroughs, Ltd. v. Sign of the Beefeater, Inc., 540 F.2d 266 (7th Cir. 1976) (15% confusion sufficient); Exxon Corp. v. Texas Motor Exchange of Houston, Inc., 628 F.2d 500 (5th Cir. 1980) (15% confusion sufficient).

[122] 15 U.S.C. section 1114(1) (1946).

[123] 15 U.S.C. section 1114(1), Lanham Act section 32.

[124] S. Rep. No. 2107, 87th Cong., 2d Sess. 2847, 2850–51 (1962).

sale.[125] The trend, however, has enlarged the confusion doctrine to encompass other values than that of purchaser deception. In fact, courts have extended protection well beyond what takes place at the point of sale; that is, beyond the behavior of the actual and potential purchaser. In adopting this view, they have enlarged the likelihood of confusion to encompass any confusion concerning any commercial relationship between an allegedly infringing mark and an established mark.[126]

H. Post-sale and Pre-sale Confusion

A significant body of case law has extended likelihood of confusion analysis beyond immediate purchasers. Courts have held that likelihood of confusion can occur among users of the product,[127] among actual or potential investors,[128] among suppliers,[129] or among the general public who are not necessarily potential purchasers.[130] For these courts, likelihood of confusion at the point of sale is not a prerequisite for infringement.[131] Once the confusion concept is

125 See e.g. Keebler Co. v. Rovira Biscuit Corp., 624 F.2d 366, 378 (1st Cir. 1980); McKee Baking Co. v. Interstate Brands Corp., 738 F. Supp. 1272, 1275 (E.D. Mo. 1990); American Greetings Corp. v. Easter Unlimited, Inc., 579 F.Supp. 607, 616 (S.D.N.Y. 1983); Black & Decker, Inc. v. North Am. Phillips Corp., 632 F. Supp. 185, 194 (D. Conn. 1986); Beneficial Corp. v. Beneficial Capital Corp., 529 F. Supp. 445, 450 (S.D.N.Y. 1982).

126 See e.g. Dallas Cowboys Cheerleaders, Inc. v. Pussycat Cinema, Ltd., 604 F.2d 200 (2d Cir. 1979) (maker of pornographic film was found liable for trademark infringement in movie that featured actresses in cheerleader costumes similar to those used by the Dallas Cowboys Cheerleaders, suggesting commercial cooperation or at least tacit approval).

127 In re Arctic Elec. Co., 220 USPQ 836 (TTAB 1983) (users of video games in arcades may be confused, even though purchasers of the machines may not be confused).

128 Communications Satellite Corp. v. Comcet, Inc., 429 F.2d 1245 (4th Cir. 1970), cert. denied, 400 U.S. 942 (1970).

129 Bishop v. Hanenburg, 39 Wash. App. 734, 695 P.2d 607 (Wash. Ct. App. 1985).

130 AMP, Inc. v. Foy, 540 F.2d 1181 (4th Cir. 1976); Lois Sportswear, U.S.A., Inc. v. Levi Strauss & Co., 799 F.2d 867 (2d Cir. 1986).

131 For an excellent overview of post- and pre-sale confusion, see Michael J. Allen, The Scope of Confusion Actionable Under Federal Trademark Law: Who Must Be Confused and When?, 26 Wake Forest L. Rev. 321, 339–48 (1991).

expended to post- and pre-sale events, the contours of the confusion are extended well beyond a consumer deception model.[132]

Post-sale confusion is one form of non-point-of-sale confusion that may constitute trademark infringement. The doctrine of post-sale confusion refers to confusion by persons who have not yet bought the goods at issue. Such confusion arises on the part of observers of the goods that are already purchased and in use. This concept was recognized in *Mastercrafters Clock & Radio Co. v. Vacheron & Consenting-Le Coultre Watches, Inc.*[133] In *Mastercrafters*, the plaintiff was an importer and distributor of expensive Swiss timepieces, one of which was the Atmos clock. The defendant sold a similar looking imitation for less than a quarter of the price. The purchasers of defendant's cheap imitation of plaintiff's famous and distinctive clock knew exactly what they were buying. Nevertheless, the court found likelihood of confusion and trademark injury. Thus, as this case indicates, actionable confusion can take place in a post-sale context when, for example, a guest in the home of a purchaser might believe that the imitation clock on display is in fact the Atmos timepiece.[134] In sum, although the initial purchaser of a product may not be confused, observers of the item bearing the junior user's mark may well be.

Post-sale confusion may arise when initial purchasers buy a product that is distinguishable at the point of sale by labels and explanatory literature, but when put in use, the goods become indistinguishable because confusion-avoiding devices are no longer apparent to the observer. In *Lois Sportswear, USA, Inc. v. Levi Strauss & Co.*,[135] Levi Strauss brought suit against Lois Sportswear's use of a rear pocket design on its blue jeans, alleging that this use was confusingly similar to its own pocket design. Even though the defendant's blue jeans were properly labeled at the point of sale, the court found a likelihood of confusion because non-purchasers would be confused when seeing the jeans once the labels had been discarded.[136]

[132] For a recent overview see Anne M. McCarthy: The Post-Sale Confusion Doctrine: Why the General Public Should be Included in the Likelihood of Confusion Inquiry, 67 Ford. L. Rev. 333 (1999).

[133] 221 F.2d 464 (2d Cir. 1955).

[134] See also, Rolex Watch U.S.A., Inc. v. Canner, 645 F. Supp. 484 (S.D. Fla. 1986) (the immediate purchaser of a $25 ROLEX watch at a flea market may know he is not getting the real thing, but confusion could take place among others who may see the watch later on).

[135] 799 F.2d 867 (2d Cir. 1986).

[136] 799 F.2d 867(2d Cir. 1986); other courts have allowed the post-sale confusion argument as well. See Keds Corp. v. Renee Int'l Trading Corp., 888 F.2d 215, 222 (1st

The post-sale confusion doctrine is difficult to reconcile with the traditional deception model of trademark rights. So long as the actual purchaser is not confused regarding the source of the goods, why should it make a difference if a purchaser's friends, acquaintances or unknown third parties are misled? Of course, confusion is really not the issue in post-sale confusion cases. The doctrine rewards the investment in acquiring goodwill in the mark, particularly where the junior user is ostensibly free riding on the prestige image of a well-known mark. In other words, the post-sale doctrine implicitly recognizes the property value that may develop in a trademark due to the efforts of the trademark owner. The same rationale appears in cases adopting the related, but less widely applied, 'pre-sale' confusion doctrine.

Adopted by a small number of courts, pre-sale confusion is another developing concept that has extended the boundaries of trademark law.[137] Pre-sale confusion[138] may occur at the early stages of negotiation in which a plaintiff's trademark is used as a door opener to initiate contact with a prospective purchaser. Courts have found trademark injury in the pre-sale context even though purchaser confusion is soon resolved. In *Mobil Oil v. Pegasus Petroleum Corp.*,[139] the court found a likelihood of confusion between 'Pegasus Petroleum' used by an oil trading company and Mobil Oil's well-known flying horse symbol (Pegasus), even though an oil trader would quickly realize that Pegasus Petroleum was not connected with Mobil. Despite a lack of ultimate confusion, the initial interest engendered through the brief period of confusion constituted sufficient injury for the court to grant injunctive relief.[140]

Cir. 1989) (mark on sneakers); Polo Fashions, Inc. v. Craftex, Inc., 816 F.2d 145 (4th Cir. 1989) (polo figure on shirts). Courts have recognized the post-sale confusion doctrine under the Trademark Counterfeiting Act, 18 U.S.C. section 2320; see United States v. Torkington, 812 F.2d 1347 (11th Cir. 1986); United States v. Hon, 904 F.2d 803 (2d Cir. 1990) (defendants in trademark counterfeiting actions have attempted without success to argue that the initial purchaser knows he is not getting the authentic item).

137 See Charles E. Bruzga, Sophisticated Purchaser Defense Avoided Where Pre-Sale Confusion is Harmful – A Brief Note, 78 Trademark Rep. 659, 665 (1988).

138 Pre-sale confusion often involves confusion of sponsorship. See Grotrian, Helfferich, Schultz Th. Steinweg Nachf. v. Steinway & Sons, 523 F.2d 1331 (2d Cir. 1975) ('Steinway' infringed by 'Grotrian-Steinweg' on expensive pianos. 'The Grotrian-Steinweg name ... would attract potential customers based on the reputation built up by Steinway in this country for many years'. Id. at 1342).

139 818 F.2d 254 (2d Cir. 1987).

140 Id. See also, Arrow United Indus., Inc. v. Hugh Richards Assoc., Inc., 678 F.2d 410, 414–15 (2d Cir. 1982); Dreyfus Fund, Inc. v. Royal Bank of Canada, 525 F. Supp.

To explain the trademark injury in pre-sale confusion cases, some courts engaged in dubious conceptual gymnastics to protect the goodwill of the trademark owner beyond the strict confines of the consumer deception model. The theory of 'subliminal confusion' is one such doctrine of doubtful worth that protects the accrued value of the mark. Subliminal confusion is defined as confusion that affects the buyer's perception of a product through an unconscious or subliminal association of marks even though there may be no immediate confusion of source or sponsorship.[141] For example, in *Koppers Co. v. Krupp-Koppers GMBH*,[142] the plaintiff, who used KOPPERS on coal gasification plants, brought an action against the use of KRUPP-KOPPERS on a similar commercial endeavor. The court rejected the defendant's argument that purchasers of expensive coal gasification plants are discriminating and that few, if any, of these purchasers would be confused by the defendant's use of the mark. The court used the 1962 amendments to the Lanham Act[143] to support its view that where confusion takes place on a *subliminal* level, a finding of likelihood of confusion should not be restricted to purchasers but should be extended to non-purchasers as well.[144]

Subliminal confusion is a murky concept from both a theoretical and practical standpoint. To critics of expansive trademark rights, it is an aberrant notion in U.S. trademark law because it has little to do with likelihood of confusion. The courts appear to use the concept when they believe that value of the senior

1108 (S.D.N.Y. 1981) ('the law requires that some form of confusion be proved likely, not that it be shown to persist and to cause lost sales'. Id. at 1122); Grotrian, Helfferich, Schultz Th. Steinweg Nachf. v. Steinway & Sons, 523 F.2d 1331 (2d Cir. 1975); Communications Satellite Corp. v. Comcet, Inc., 429 F.2d 1245, 1251 (4th Cir 1970); Television Enter. Network, Inc. v. Entertainment Network, Inc., 630 F. Supp. 244, 247 (D.N.J. 1986).

141 For an overview of the concept of subliminal confusion, see Steven H. Hartman, Subliminal Confusion: The Misappropriation of Advertising Value, 78 Trademark Rep. 506 (1988).

142 517 F. Supp. 836 (W.D. Pa. 1981).

143 The infringement sections of the Lanham Act formerly required that there be a likelihood of confusion among purchasers as to the source and origin of such goods and services. (Formerly codified at 15 U.S.C. section 1114(1). The 1962 amendment deleting this language shows a clear congressional intent to outlaw the use of trademarks which are likely to cause confusion, mistake or deception of any kind. Likelihood of confusion is not limited to purchasers.) Syntex Laboratories, Inc. v. Norwich Pharmacal Co., 437 F.2d 566, 568 (2d Cir. 1971).

144 Koppers Co. Inc. v. Krupp-Koppers GMBH, 517 F. Supp. 836 (W.D. Pa. 1981).

user's advertising is misappropriated, even though no source confusion has occurred. Thus, rather than protecting the source-identifying function of a mark, the courts have used the doctrine to protect the advertising value of the mark and to impede a new entrant from free riding on the favorable associations produced by a well-known mark. In this sense, subliminal confusion is an anti-dilution notion smuggled into federal trademark law. Consistent with the dilution concept, it would protect a trademark as an absolute property interest without requiring the senior user to show public deception. In many of these cases, the harm to the trademark owner brought about by consumer confusion is sometimes difficult to see, particularly when the product is expensive, sold to sophisticated purchasers, or bought directly from the manufacturer after protracted negotiations. Post- and pre-sale confusion concepts are another instance where courts smuggled into trademark law de facto anti-dilution law rather than a body of law based on consumer deception.

Of course, from a practical standpoint, the concept of subliminal confusion defies application. Simply stated, how does one prove subliminal confusion? For example, what kind of survey could one use to prove subliminal confusion? Because of these problems, subliminal confusion has had little place in a practical litigation context. The interests protected under this dubious concept are better supported directly under anti-dilution law. The subliminal confusion doctrine illustrates once more how ripe U.S. law had become for the adoption of the federal anti-dilution law in 1996.

VI. CONCLUSION

If one were to a pick an official date for the demise of trademark monopoly phobia, it would clearly be the year 1996 when the Federal Dilution Act went into effect. But as I have attempted to show, this pivotal date reflects only the inevitable culmination of a long process whose rationale became ever more persuasive during the sixty years of the Lanham Act's existence. These forces resulted from current realities of the global marketplace: the necessities of the new marketing environment, the influence of the new economic learning, and the push toward the harmonization of trademark law worldwide. By focusing on the assignment of trademark rights and the likelihood of confusion doctrine, trademark doctrine could no longer sustain the inconsistencies and shortcomings of a purely consumer deception model of trademark law. These inconsistencies are particularly apparent in the rules regarding the assignment and licensing of trademarks, where insistence on an anachronistic version of quality control could no longer be reconciled with the case law and actual practice. Similarly, the likelihood of confusion has manifested the same inescapable progression from confines of a rigid consumer deception model to reflect the marketing needs and realities of contemporary industrial organization.

POSTSCRIPT

Since this article was written, developments under the Lanham Act reflect a marked disposition toward a property centered rationale of trademark law. With the passage of time, one can safely say that the heyday of monopoly phobia is becoming ever more a distant memory. In sum, the developments in trademark law during this period have accelerated the trends referred to in the article. These trends are manifest in the case law and particularly in Congressional activity.

Two such efforts to retool trademark law to the realities of marketing in the digital age reflect the strong property rights view of trademark law. In November 1999, Congress passed the Anticybersquatting Consumer Protection Act and added a new section 43(d) in the Lanham Act (15 U.S.C. section 1125(d)). It has created a cause of action against anyone who, with bad faith intent to profit from a mark, registers, trafficks in or uses a domain name that is identical or confusingly similar to a distinctive mark, or is identical or confusingly similar to or dilutive of a famous mark. Among its battery of remedies (including treble damages and attorneys' fees), the Anticybersquatting Consumer Protection Act authorizes *in rem* actions against the domain name itself, in instances where the trademark owner is unable to establish personal jurisdiction.

Also in 1999, the Internet Corporations for Assigned Names and Numbers (ICANN) established a dispute resolution process, which now exists as another means to combat cybersquatting. The ICANN adopted a Uniform Name Dispute Resolution Policy (UDRP). The Policy requires domain registrants to submit to mandatory administrative proceedings when a third party asserts that the registrant's domain name is identical or confusingly similar to a mark in which the complainant has rights, and either that the registrant has no rights or legitimate interests in the domain name, or that the registrant's domain name has been registered and is being used in bad faith. Both the Anticybersquatting Act and ICANN's Dispute Resolution Policy are significant steps in bolstering the acquisition and maintenance of robust and stable property rights in trademarks.

In addition to domain name practice, developments in the international arena illustrate the basic themes discussed in the article. As indicated, an expansive, property rights basis of trademark law has come about through the inexorable pressures for harmonization of trademark law in a global marketing environment. For some years, most observers anticipated that the United States would soon become a member of the Madrid Protocol, a multinational agreement that facilitates the registration of trademarks in member countries. On 2 November 2002, after a century of resisting the Protocol and its predecessor, the Madrid Agreement, the United States joined other Madrid Protocol member countries. Now, U.S. trademark owners by 2 November 2003 will have access to an international procedure, one that will facilitate the simultaneous registration of their trademarks in some 56 member countries. In the years ahead, trademark practice will change irrevocably as the Trademark Office tries to retool its procedures to the increased influx of trademark registrations originating from member countries.

On 5 July 2006 the Lanham Act turned sixty years old. Through the years it has revealed a remarkable ability for adaptability. Nonetheless, it has come to exhibit the wear and tear of middle age. One sees this in the complexity of its basic terms, particularly in the multiplicity of court-made provisions concerning likelihood of confusion, and the on-going anachronistic provisions relating to the assignment and licensing of trademarks. Perhaps it is time to consider an overhaul of the Lanham Act, to express more explicitly a contemporary basis for protection of trademark law. Thus, if likelihood of confusion includes concepts of reverse confusion, initial interest confusion or post-sale confusion, it would be better to state so clearly in the statute. Similarly, concepts such as 'assignment in gross' and 'naked license' have outlived their original rationale and should be retooled to reflect contemporary commercial practice. Whatever form this updated version of the Lanham Act may take, it will reflect a more sophisticated understanding of how trademarks function in our contemporary marketing environment.

Chapter 5

Discharging the Canons of Claim Construction: Exercises in Interpretation at the United States Court of Appeals for the Federal Circuit

*John R. Thomas**

Two great crises plague the United States patent system. The familiar issues of patent eligibility and claim interpretation continue to frustrate both the United States Patent and Trademark Office (PTO) and the United States Court of Appeals for the Federal Circuit (Federal Circuit), diminishing the value of judicial precedent, defeating the expectations of industry, and denying the elusive goal of certainty. A review of Federal Circuit precedent demonstrates two contrasting approaches to these fundamental tenets of the patent law.

In recent years we have seen a devolution of patent eligibility principles, to the extent that our rudderless regime appears ready to appropriate any tangible manifestation of human intelligence. The Federal Circuit has steadily dismantled doctrines denying patents to such inventions as mathematical algorithms, mental steps, printed matter and methods of doing business. Stripped of limiting principles, the subject matter for patenting in the United States now appears as broad as the range of human experience.[1]

The Federal Circuit's reaction to claim interpretation stands in high relief to its approach to statutory subject matter. The construction of the patent instrument, whether in the context of literal infringement and the doctrine of equivalents, has become increasingly doctrinal. The court has launched an aggressive campaign to control the reader's encounter with the text of patent claims, erecting ever more detailed interpretational protocols to augment

* Professor of Law, George Washington University, Washington, D.C.

[1] See John R. Thomas, *The Patenting of the Liberal Professions*, 40 Boston College L. Rev. 1139 (1999).

longstanding canons of claim construction. Yet this strategy has been marked by numerous failures: many of the canons have been extremely short-lived, while the surviving canons remain surrounded by ambiguities of application.

This article offers an account of the Federal Circuit's increasing tendency towards interpretative rulemaking. Along with the judges of the Federal Circuit, it takes as a given that a goal of any patent system is the consistent interpretation of claims. Contrary to certain deconstructionist and reader-response schools associated with postmodernism, this article also urges that accuracy in interpretation is a goal at least partially realizable in the context of the patent system. But this article also offers a critical perspective on the increasing canonization of claim interpretation protocols in the United States. It seeks new techniques for enhancing textual understanding within the patent community.

This article begins by reviewing the essential U.S. law governing patent claim construction. In Part I, it briefly discusses the seminal *Markman* and *Warner-Jenkinson* opinions and considers their impact on claim interpretation methodologies. Part I next introduces the concept of canons of claim construction: the basic rules of interpretation intended to dictate the reader's encounter with the text of patent claims. It offers a brief catalogue of the principal canons and considers the possibility of conflicting canons in particular cases.

Part II of this article recounts a handful of episodes in Federal Circuit jurisprudence where the court has sought to augment the traditional canons. Part II examines the birth and, in many cases, rapid decline of new canons: the All Elements Rule, Public Dedication Principle, Foreseeable Alteration Rule, *Dolly* Doctrine and All Advantages Rule. Part III then offers a critical assessment of the U.S. experience with proscriptivism in claim interpretation. This article instead reasons that the best hope for clarity in claim construction lies in the continued acculturization of patent attorneys towards the reading and writing of texts. As a discrete corps of professionals writing within a restricted genre, the patent bar provides an ideal community in which administrative rule-making, training and dialogue could develop shared norms of interpretation. This article also calls upon the U.S. courts to unpack the traditional equivalency formula that balances protection to the patentee with notice to competitors. By inquiring into whether an accused infringer had actual notice of the asserted claims, the courts can better assess the scope of protection they should be accorded.

I. FUNDAMENTALS OF CLAIM INTERPRETATION

A. *Patent Claim Interpretation After* Markman *and* Warner-Jenkinson

Markman v. Westview Instruments[2] and *Warner-Jenkinson v. Hilton Davis*[3] have already come to hold a central place in modern patent law. In combination these decisions expound the basic scheme of claim interpretation in the United States. Although *Markman* and *Warner-Jenkinson* are already well known, a brief review sets the stage for the Federal Circuit's current efforts to refine the construction of patent claims.

As issued by the *in banc* Federal Circuit and sanctioned by the Supreme Court, the *Markman* opinion developed an interpretational protocol intended for use in all future claim interpretations. The patented technology that so engaged the twenty jurists of these two courts was a rather humble one, an inventory tracking system for a dry cleaning shop. The invention deployed a computer and bar code technology to minimize lost garments and employee theft during the dry cleaning process. As such, the claimed 'inventory and control and reporting system' required the detection of 'spurious additions to inventory as well as spurious deletions therefrom'.[4]

Markman's assertion of the patent against a competitor led to a jury trial. Although the jury had found for the patentee, the trial judge instead directed a verdict of noninfringement. Asserting that claim interpretation was a matter of law for the court, the trial judge determined that the term 'inventory' referred exclusively to articles of clothing. Because the accused device merely maintained a listing of invoices, it could not track the location of individual garments as they were moved about the shop and therefore could not infringe.[5]

On appeal, the *in banc* Federal Circuit affirmed. The court agreed that claim interpretation presented solely legal issues appropriate for judicial resolution. As to Markman's argument that the Seventh Amendment had been violated, the court held that patents resembled statutes in that 'these public instruments may create liability in third persons who were not participants in the legislative process or the [PTO] proceedings'.[6] Because statutory interpretation was a matter of law, so too was patent claim construction. The Federal Circuit also upheld

[2] 52 F.3d 967 (Fed. Cir. 1995), *aff'd*, 517 U.S. 370 (1996).

[3] 520 U.S. 17, 41 USPQ2d 1865 (1997).

[4] 52 F.3d at 972.

[5] 52 F.3d at 972–73.

[6] 52 F.3d at 987.

the trial court's reading of the claims, citing numerous statements in the specification and prosecution indicating that both Markman and the examiner understood the term 'inventory' to consist of articles of clothing.[7] The Supreme Court affirmed in a short opinion principally devoted towards Seventh Amendment concerns.[8]

The Federal Circuit had gone further, however, seeking to influence future claim interpretations by developing a bipolar regime of favored and disfavored texts. Dominant in this hierarchy were so-called 'intrinsic evidence' – the claims, specification, drawings and prosecution history – that comprised the principal revealers of meaning. All evidence external to the patent and prosecution history was deemed 'extrinsic evidence', which courts had discretion to admit but were not mandated to receive.[9] While extrinsic evidence could inform the court of the technical subject matter at hand, it could not vary or contradict the terms of the claims.[10]

The Federal Circuit's subsequent decision in *Vitronics Corp. v. Conceptronic, Inc.*[11] further articulated patent claim interpretation protocols. Although the Federal Circuit has had numerous occasions to apply and refine *Markman*, the magisterial *Vitronics* opinion remains among the court's most valued restatements of the *Markman* cosmology.[12] The *Vitronics* decision continued to discount the use of extrinsic evidence in claim interpretation, reasoning that 'competitors are entitled to review the public record, apply the established rules of claims construction, ascertain the scope of the patentee's claimed invention and, thus, design around the claimed invention'.[13] The court further opined that, in most cases, intrinsic evidence alone would yield the proper interpretation; therefore the use of extrinsic evidence was most often improper. In a footnote, the *Vitronics* court suggested a more favorable posture towards learned treatises and dictionaries. According to the court, '[j]udges are free to consult

[7] 52 F.3d at 982–83.

[8] 517 U.S. 370 (1996).

[9] 52 F.3d at 980.

[10] 52 F.3d at 981.

[11] 90 F.3d 1576, 39 USPQ2d 1573 (Fed. Cir. 1996).

[12] E.g. Robert D. Flam, *Patently A Civil War*, Legal Times Special Report on Intellectual Property 13, 13 (3 August 1998) (noting that *Vitronics* is 'widely cited'); John M. Romary & Arie M. Michelson, *Patent Claim Interpretation After Markman: How the Federal Circuit Interprets Claims*, 46 Am. U. L. Rev. 1887, 1901 (1997) ('The post-*Markman* case[] of *Vitronics* ... provide[s] considerable guidance as to how the Federal Circuit interprets technical terms of art').

[13] 90 F.3d at 1583.

such resources at any time in order to better understand the underlying technology and may also rely on dictionary definitions when construing claim terms', so long as they were not in conflict with the intrinsic evidence of record.[14]

Markman was a literal infringement case. In *Warner-Jenkinson*, the Supreme Court considered claim construction in connection with the doctrine of equivalents. That litigation involved the enforcement of a patented purification process useful in the manufacture of food dyes. The claimed 'ultrafiltration' process employed a membrane 'at a pH from approximately 6.0 to 9.0'.[15] The accused process operated at a pH of 5. Following lengthy opinions from a deeply divided *in banc* Federal Circuit,[16] the Supreme Court granted *certiorari* and ultimately issued a magisterial opinion with far-reaching commentary of the doctrine of equivalents.

According to the Court, the doctrine of equivalents was to be applied to individual elements of a claim, not to the invention as a whole.[17] The Court thus maintained the so-called All Elements Rule, about which more will be said shortly.[18] The Court also upheld the doctrine of prosecution history estoppel, concluding that where a patentee cannot establish a reason for a claim amendment unrelated to patentability, prosecution history would bar the application of the doctrine of equivalents with regard to that element.[19] The Court next rejected the argument that a finding of equivalency required that the accused infringer have copied the patentee's invention or otherwise engaged in bad faith conduct.[20]

The Court then made short work of the defendant's argument that the doctrine of equivalents should be limited to either equivalents known at the time the invention issued, or equivalents disclosed within the patent instrument itself. The Court rejected both propositions, concluding that assessing equivalency from the perspective of a skilled artisan placed sufficient limits on the concept of equivalency.[21] The Court concluded by establishing that the test for equivalency was one of insubstantial differences.[22] The *Warner-Jenkinson* opinion suggested that such factors as known interchangeability, independent experi-

[14] 90 F.3d at 1584 n.6.

[15] 517 U.S. at 22–23.

[16] 62 F.3d 1512, 35 USPQ2d 1641 (Fed. Cir. 1995).

[17] 517 U.S. at 28–30.

[18] See infra notes 37–47 and accompanying text.

[19] 517 U.S. at 30–34.

[20] 517 U.S. at 34–36.

[21] 517 U.S. at 37.

[22] 517 U.S. at 39–41.

mentation and the traditional function-way-result test would inform the equivalency inquiry.

B. The Canons of Claim Construction

Beyond the basic principles of claim interpretation delineated in *Markman* and *Warner-Jenkinson*, numerous Federal Circuit cases have intoned that 'a number of canons ... guide our construction of all patent claims'.[23] A review of the Federal Circuit's jurisprudence reveals a modest set of these interpretational protocols. Perhaps the most fundamental of these is that a term should be accorded a consistent meaning throughout the patent instrument. Courts have maintained this doctrine even though the term appears in different claims within the same patent, or even in distinct but related patents.[24]

Another frequently invoked canon is the doctrine of claim differentiation. Under this canon, the reader should presume that each claim of a patent conveys a different meaning. In an exemplary decision applying the claim differentiation doctrine, *Transmatic, Inc. v. Gutton Industries, Inc.*,[25] the Federal Circuit considered a patented light fixture for buses and other public transit vehicles. Claim 1 of the asserted patent called for a 'light housing' but recited no other structural limitations on that claim element.[26] In contrast, claim 3 of the patent-in-suit, which depended from claim 1, required that the light housing have 'a horizontal wall with an inward securement formation' for securing the light fixture to a vehicle. The Federal Circuit applied the doctrine of claim differentiation to hold that claim 1 did not require the specific structure recited in claim 3.[27]

That these competing canons of identity and difference might occasionally work at cross purposes should not be unsurprising. If a patent contains two claims with the same wording then the reader plainly could not apply both canons during the act of interpretation. Beyond this trite example, these fundamental canons may lead to divergent results because they are not the only ones available. Other sources of meaning, such as the evidentiary inputs specified in *Vitronics*, place strain upon these interpretative canons.

[23] *Athletic Alternatives, Inc. v. Prince Mfg., Inc.*, 73 F.3d 1573, 1578, 37 USPQ2d 1365, 1370 (Fed. Cir. 1996).

[24] *Fonar Corp. v. Johnson & Johnson*, 821 F.2d 627, 632, 3 USPQ2d 1109, 1113 (Fed. Cir. 1987).

[25] 53 F.3d 1270, 35 USPQ2d 1035 (Fed. Cir. 1995).

[26] 53 F.3d at 1272.

[27] 53 F.3d at 1277.

The Federal Circuit's recent opinion in *O.I. Corp. v. Tekmar Co.*[28] is representative of this conundrum. The patented invention involved in that appeal concerned the removal of water vapor from a sample to be analyzed in a gas chromatograph. One of the asserted claims, claim 17, recited a 'first means for passing the analyte slug through a passage' without further limitations as to the configuration of the passage.[29] Claims dependent upon claim 17 did provide further limitations, requiring that the passage produce swirling or spiraling of the analyte slug.

The written description of the patent seemed to offer a different view of the invention. It persistently referred to a ridged or abraded passage. Exemplary was one passage from the specification that explained that the patented invention concerned passages 'having an irregular shaped surface or noncylindrical shape. In contrast, the prior art has generally specified that the [passages] are smooth-walled'. Under these circumstances, if the Federal Circuit applied the canon of claim differentiation, then claim 17 would necessarily embrace smooth passages. But if the court instead opted for the canon of consistency, then the term 'passage' would connote a coarse and uneven geometry even as used in claim 17.[30]

In *O.I. Corp.*, the Federal Circuit did what most courts seem to do in this situation: it abandoned the canon of claim differentiation. The canon of consistency prevailed because the patentee had committed to meaning of the term 'passage'. That some of the claims dependent upon claim 17 were redundant was of secondary concern. In the words of the court: 'We believe that the description provides a clear meaning for the language of the claim in this case and that it trumps the doctrine of claim differentiation.'[31]

The decision in *O.I. Corp.* also exposes the canon of claim interpretation that claims are to be read in light of the specification. But reciting this canon immediately brings to mind another familiar tenet of the patent law, that limitations from the written description should not be imported into the claims. The Federal Circuit opinion in *Unique Concepts, Inc. v. Brown* illustrates the tension between these two competing canons.[32]

Unique Concepts held an exclusive license on a patented assembly of border pieces used to fasten fabric wall coverings to walls. The patent's claims included

[28] 115 F.3d 1576, 42 USPQ2d 1777 (Fed. Cir. 1997).

[29] 115 F.3d at 1579.

[30] 115 F.3d at 1581–82.

[31] 115 F.3d at 1582.

[32] 939 F.2d 1558, 19 USPQ2d 1500 (Fed. Cir. 1991).

a limitation calling for 'linear border pieces and right angle corner border pieces'.[33] Unique Concepts brought a patent infringement suit against Brown, but lost the trial after the district court held that Brown's assembly did meet this limitation. The trial court noted that Brown's assembly provided only mitered linear pieces. Brown apparently formed border pieces simply by joining the linear pieces together on the fly during the installation of the wall coverings. Unique appealed to the Federal Circuit, which affirmed over a dissent by Judge Rich.

The majority opinion of the Federal Circuit agreed with the trial court that Brown did not infringe. According to Judges Lourie and Mayer, the claim limitation referred to two distinct parts of the assembly: 'linear border pieces' and 'right angle corner border pieces'. The majority viewed the specification as demonstrating that the claim language 'right angle corner border pieces' referred to a single preformed piece. The fact that linear border pieces could be arranged to form a right angle corner did not convert them into 'right angle corner border pieces'.[34]

The dissenting opinion of Judge Rich viewed the patent's written description differently. Judge Rich pointed to language in the patent's written description that provided: 'Instead of using preformed right-angle corner pieces of the type previously disclosed, one may improvise corner pieces by miter-cutting the ends of a pair of short linear border pieces placed at right angles to each other ...' According to Judge Rich, the specification demonstrated that mitered, linear pieces could be placed at right angles and joined to form borders.[35]

In sum, the majority contended that it interpreted the claim term 'right angle corner border pieces' in light of the specification. The dissent instead charged the majority with importing limitations from the specification into the claims. At the end of the day, *Unique Concepts* demonstrates that the difference between using the specification to alter the scope of a claim term and importing claim scope from the specification is a subtle one. Because no neutral principles govern this distinction, interpreting or importing becomes largely a subjective exercise – exactly the sort of practice the canons of claim construction would have us avoid.

There are other canons of claim construction,[36] but this brief review should suffice to show that the canons often do not live up to their billing as objective

[33] 939 F.2d at 1560.

[34] 939 F.2d at 1562.

[35] 939 F.2d at 1564.

[36] For a concise discussion see Kimberly Pace Moore et al., *Patent Litigation and Strategy*, 206–19 (1999).

indicators of meaning. The ideal of self-validating principles that invariably lead the reader to the correct construction should strike most observers as naive. Even in the insular patent community, the school of legal realism is too well entrenched for such positivist principles to gain much currency. We have also learned far too much about literary criticism to believe in transcendent interpretational principles. Yet despite these apparent flaws, the Federal Circuit seems intent upon enlarging the canon, a venture this article takes up next.

II. AUGMENTING THE CANON

Federal Circuit jurisprudence pertaining to claim interpretation has displayed an increasingly doctrinal tendency. The court seems no longer content to resolve the interpretative dispute before it, but seeks to influence future readers and drafters by pronouncing canons of claim construction. Especially noteworthy are five of these canons, known as the All Elements Rule, Public Dedication Principle, Foreseeable Alteration Rule, *Dolly* Doctrine and All Advantages Rule. The origin and, in some cases, speedy demise of these canons teaches us valuable lessons about prescriptivism in the interpretative task.

A. *The All Elements Rule*

The All Elements Rule is the best known and most robust of the Federal Circuit's canons of claim construction. A sort of structuralism, the All Elements Rule causes readers to stress aspects of claim drafting earlier assumed to be latent.[37] As such this canon has also proven to be the most controversial. Although the rule arguably has ancient origins in U.S. law, the Federal Circuit's *in banc* decision in *Pennwalt Corp. v. Durand-Wayland, Inc.*[38] achieved the canonization of the All Elements Rule.

Pennwalt's '628 patent bore the title 'Sorter for Fruit and the Like'. The '628 patent disclosed a mechanism that rapidly sorted fruit or other items based upon color, weight or a combination of these traits. A hard-wired network, including hardware registers, followed each piece of fruit as it moved down a track. Among the claimed elements were first and second 'position indicating means' that

[37] See John R. Thomas, *On Preparatory Texts and Proprietary Technologies: The Place of Prosecution Histories in Patent Claim Interpretation*, 47 UCLA L. Rev. 183, 185 n.7 (1999).

[38] 833 F.2d 931, 4 USPQ2d 1737 (Fed. Cir. 1987).

shifted the data corresponding to the fruit as it was conveyed along the sorting mechanism.

Pennwalt brought an infringement suit against Durand-Wayland, asserting that its '628 patent claims read on the accused Microsizer product. The district court held for the defendants. According to the trial judge, the Microsizer lacked the claimed 'position indicating means' because it never shifted data. The Microsizer instead employed random access memory that stored the color and weight data in a discrete location. Thus, rather than shuffling data down a queue to match the progression of a piece of fruit, the Microsizer managed queue pointers. According to the trial court, because the accused device wholly lacked a claimed element of the '628 patent, it could not infringe either literally or under the doctrine of equivalents.

The Federal Circuit agreed to hear Pennwalt's appeal *in banc*. The majority of the court agreed with the trial court that the Microsizer's lack of a 'position indicating means' was fatal to Pennwalt's contention of infringement. According to the majority, an accused technology must embody every element of a claimed invention, either literally or equivalently, to be judged an infringement. To hold otherwise would divest the infringement inquiry from the language of the claims themselves. A lengthy opinion offering the 'additional views' of Judge Nies dubbed this canon the All Elements Rule.

A dissenting opinion from Judge Bennett and supplementary 'commentary' from Judge Newman stridently disagreed with the All Elements Rule. According to the dissenters, the majority had devised an analytical framework for the doctrine of equivalents that was little more than a redundant literal infringement inquiry. The dissenters viewed the doctrine of equivalents as an equitable creation designed to work justice in individual cases, a goal that would be undone by such a restrictive and inflexible canon of construction.

Much has been written for and against the All Elements Rule.[39] The British Patents Court went so far as to characterize the *Pennwalt* opinion as an 'emotional' matter,[40] but the consequences of *Pennwalt* are of great practical significance. Consider the example of the following, simplified claims:

[39] E.g. William E. Eshelman, Comment, *The Doctrine of Equivalents in Patent Law: Post-*Pennwalt *Developments*, 65 Tul. L. Rev. 883 (1991); Paul N. Katz, Note, *The Federal Circuit, in Determining Whether Patent Infringement Exists, Is Divided Over Whether to Utilize 'As-A-Whole' or 'Element-By-Element' Analysis When Applying The Doctrine of Equivalents*, 30 S. Tex. L. Rev. 441 (1989); Frank S. Molinaro, Note, *Pennwalt Corp. v. Durand-Wayland, Inc. – The Federal Circuit Redefines the Doctrine of Equivalents*, 38 DePaul L. Rev. 787 (1989).

[40] *Beloit Technologies, Inc. v. Valmet Paper Machinery, Inc.*, [1995] RPC 705.

1. A fork comprising:
   a cylindrical handle; and
   four tines attached to said handle.
2. A fork comprising:
   a cylindrical handle;
   a first tine attached to said handle;
   a second tine attached to said handle;
   a third tine attached to said handle; and
   a fourth tine attached to said handle.

These claims appear to provide the same scope of protection in terms of literal infringement. But suppose a competitor markets a fork with three tines. The holding of *Pennwalt* would not bar a finding of equivalent infringement with regard to claim 1. But with respect to claim 2, the absence of the final recited element – 'a fourth tine attached to said handle' – would violate the All Elements Rule and prove fatal to the case of equivalency.

Although this example is straightforward enough, application of the All Elements Rule has proven rather more difficult in the litigated cases. The most notorious episode concerning this canon arose in the Federal Circuit's later opinion in *Corning Glass Works v. Sumitomo Electric USA, Inc.*[41] That appeal concerned a patented fiber optic cable with a low signal attenuation rate. The claim at issue recited a fiber with a cladding and a core, the former comprising a glass coating to help prevent scratching. The core was 'positively' doped to create the appropriate refraction index differential. The claim read in part as follows:

> An optical waveguide comprising
> (a) a cladding layer ..., and
> (b) a core formed of fused silica to which a dopant material on at least an elemental basis has been added to a degree in excess of that of the cladding layer so that the index of refraction thereof is of a value greater than the index of refraction of said cladding layer ...[42]

In what proved to be a fascinating set of circumstances, the defendants obtained the appropriate index of refraction differential by negatively doping the cladding. The district court found the defendants liable for infringement. The defendants appealed, citing the *Pennwalt* rule, and with a rather surprising opinion the Federal Circuit affirmed. According to the opinion authored by Judge

[41] 868 F.2d 1251, 9 USPQ2d 1962 (Fed. Cir. 1989).
[42] 868 F.2d at 1256.

Nies, the defendants misunderstood the sense of the term 'element' in the All Elements Rule:

> 'Element' may be used to mean a single limitation, but it has also been used to mean a series of limitations which, taken together, make up a component of the claimed invention. In the All Elements Rule, 'element' is used in the sense of a limitation of a claim ... [T]he determination of equivalency is not subject to a rigid formula. An equivalent must be found for every limitation of the claim somewhere in the accused device, but not necessarily in a corresponding component, although that is generally the case.[43]

Many commentators have doubted whether *Pennwalt* and *Corning Glass* can be reconciled.[44] *Pennwalt* pronounces an elemental equivalency standard, while *Corning Glass* seemingly reverts to a holistic view of the doctrine of equivalents. Some observers have attempted to distinguish *Corning Glass* as involving unusual facts. For example, Judge Lourie's subsequent opinion in *Ethicon Endo-Surgery, Inc. v. United States Surgical Corp.*[45] speaks of *Corning Glass* as involving a special case: the 'simultaneous substitution of two reciprocal limitations (cladding for core and negative dopant for positive)'.[46]

Another way to consider these cases is to consider the options of the claims drafter in these two opinions. *Pennwalt* strikes many observers as a case of including too many claim limitations. A watchful drafter likely would have been able to define a patentable advance by incorporating fewer limitations into the claim. In contrast, the claims drafter in *Corning Glass* possessed a number of options in terms of claim drafting. Consider the following three possibilities:

(1) 'adding dopant to the core'
(2) 'adding dopant to change the refraction index'
(3) 'altering the refraction index differential'

Of course, the patentee chose option (1). This claim language appears to give the defendants the better of the argument in light of *Pennwalt*. Yet had Corning Glass obtained claims reciting the modified refraction index limitation in terms of options (2) or (3), the defendants would properly be judged infringers.

This hypothetical illustrates that the identification of a missing limitation may depend upon the generality or specificity applied to claim interpretation.

[43] 868 F.2d at 1259.

[44] E.g. Toshiko Takenaka, *Interpreting Patent Claims: The United States, Germany and Japan*, 124–25 (VCH Publishers, NY, 1995).

[45] 149 F.3d 1309, 47 USPQ2d 1272 (Fed. Cir. 1998).

[46] 149 F.3d at 1319.

Obviously the Federal Circuit deleted from the claim the words 'to the core'. The basis on which it could remove this limitation is less certain. But the court's opinion plainly was impressed with Corning's landmark invention, and likely considered the patentee to have limited unduly the scope of its claims. Perhaps *Corning Glass* suggests that the doctrine of equivalents can be used to correct claim scope in the case of landmark inventions.

Whatever the merits of the All Elements Rule, the Supreme Court opinion in *Warner-Jenkinson* broadly upheld it. There the Court pronounced:

> Each element contained in a patent claim is deemed material to defining the scope of the patented invention, and thus the doctrine of equivalents must be applied to individual elements of the claim, not to the invention as a whole. It is important to ensure that the application of the doctrine, even as to an individual element, is not allowed such broad play as to effectively eliminate that element in its entirety.[47]

The facts of *Warner-Jenkinson* did not provide an apt vehicle for this approving statement. The crucial claim limitation identified the pH at which a dye purification process should be performed. No one doubted that the accused process occurred at some acidity – it could hardly be otherwise. *Warner-Jenkinson* simply wasn't a case of a missing claim limitation. Nor did the Court see fit to discuss or even cite the crucial *Pennwalt* and *Corning Glass* opinions. The lower courts have always found the dicta of the Supreme Court extremely persuasive, however, and the All Elements Rule remains with us for the time being. But as we shall see, not all of the canons of patent claim construction introduced by the Federal Circuit have proven so robust.

B. The Public Dedication Principle

The Federal Circuit again endeavored to lend some consistency to the interpretation of patent claims in its 1996 opinion in *Maxwell v. J. Baker, Inc.*[48] The claim at issue in that appeal recited 'a system for attaching together mated pairs of shoes'. Manufacturers often attach pairs of shoes by using plastic filaments threaded through each shoe's eyelets. This technique is unavailable where the shoes lack eyelets, however. Maxwell solved this problem by securing tabs inside of each shoe. This additional feature allowed shoes to be connected by threading a filament through a loop or hold in each tab.

Maxwell obtained United States Patent No. 4,624,060. Its lengthy claims included the limitation that a 'fastening tab' extend 'horizontally between the

[47] 520 U.S. at 29.

[48] 86 F.3d 1098, 39 USPQ2d 1001 (Fed. Cir. 1996).

inside surfaces of the outer sole and the inner sole of the shoe'.[49] During trial before the United States District Court for the District of Minnesota, the district court interpreted this claim language to require that the fastening tab form a discrete component of the shoe, distinct from other parts such as the interior lining structure. The trial court was unwilling to find infringement either literally or under the doctrine of equivalents. This ruling had the effect of exempting from infringement a number of accused fastening systems that did not involve a separate fastening tab.

On appeal, Maxwell urged the Federal Circuit to consider language found in the specification of the '060 patent. There, Maxwell had noted various fastening schemes in which fastening tabs could be 'stitched into the lining seam of the shoes'. According to Maxwell, the inclusion of an alternative description in the specification supported a finding of equivalency.

The Federal Circuit disagreed. In sweeping language, the court promulgated a new canon of claim construction: that 'subject matter disclosed in the specification, but not claimed, is dedicated to the public'.[50] Judge Lourie reasoned that patentees should not be allowed to obtain claims of narrow scope from the PTO, yet then obtain a broader scope of protection from the courts through the doctrine of equivalents. He also quoted from the 1881 Supreme Court opinion in *Miller v. Bridgeport Brass*, which called for the 'dedication to the public of that which is not claimed'.[51]

The canon of claim construction, that what is not claimed is disclaimed, has some resonance in the patent law. Similar language appears in opinions of the British courts.[52] The U.S. patent law draws a similar distinction between what an earlier filed application claims, as compared to what it merely discloses, for purposes of prior art. Under section 102(e), subject matter that is disclosed, but not merely claimed, is a source of novelty-defeating prior art. But if the subject matter is claimed in both patents or applications, then the PTO will conduct an interference under section 102(g).

But despite this pedigree, the Public Disclosure Principle has never been applied with great rigor in the infringement inquiry. As well, the venerable *Miller* opinion did not address infringement issues at all, but actually considered whether an earlier application supported later-filed claims. The Supreme Court's

[49] 86 F.3d at 1102.

[50] 86 F.3d at 1107.

[51] 104 U.S. 350, 352 (1881).

[52] See *Electrical & Musical Industries Ltd v. Lissen Ltd*, 56 RPC 23, 39 (1939); see also *Glaverbel SA v. British Coal Corp.*, [1995] FSR 254, [1995] RPC 255.

opinion in *Warner-Jenkinson*, issued about nine months after *Maxwell*, cast further doubt upon the Public Disclosure Principle. There, the Court 'reject[ed] the ... proposition that equivalents must not only be known, but must be actually disclosed in the patent in order for such equivalents to infringe upon the patent'.[53] The Court's recognition that equivalents are not limited to those disclosed in the written description appeared to foreclose the possibility that equivalents could not be contained in the written description at all. As a result, despite the Federal Circuit's subsequent confirmation of the *Maxwell* rule in its *en banc* decision in *Johnson & Johnson Associates Inc. v. R.E. Service Co.*,[54] Supreme Court rejection of the Public Dedication Doctrine remains a very real possibility.

C. *The Foreseeable Alteration Rule*

A third novel canon of construction appears to have originated in the Federal Circuit's 1997 opinion in *Sage Products, Inc. v. Devon Industries, Inc.*[55] The patent at issue concerned a container for disposing of hazardous medical waste. Although the disclosure of the patent was robust, the patentee had opted to draft narrow claims closely linked to the structure of its commercial embodiment. In particular, the claims called for 'an elongated slot at the top' that allowed access to the inside of the container, as well as complementary constricting barriers that extended 'over said slot' and 'beneath said slot'. These barriers limited access to waste that had already been deposited within the container.

The patentee brought suit against a competitor that marketed a device configured differently from the claimed disposal container. One distinction was that the container slot was not at the top of the container, but rather within the container body. Another was that the accused device featured a hinge mechanism over the slot rather than complementary constricting barriers. The trial court issued a summary judgment of noninfringement, and on appeal the Federal Circuit affirmed. Judge Rader reasoned that:

> The claim at issue defines a relatively simple structural device. A skilled patent drafter would foresee the limiting potential of the [claim limitations]. No subtlety of language or complexity of the technology obfuscated the significance of this limitation at the time of its incorporation into the claim. If Sage desired broad

[53] 520 U.S. at 37.

[54] 285 F.3d 1046, 62 USPQ2d 1225 (Fed. Cir. 2002).

[55] 126 F.3d 1420, 44 USPQ2d 1103 (Fed. Cir. 1997).

> patent protection for any container that performed a function similar to its claimed container, it could have sought claims with few structural encumbrances.[56]

Sage Products suggests that if the applicant could have readily envisioned a competing technology within the scope of his disclosure, then he should have drafted claims to read literally upon them. Under this view, the doctrine of equivalents is not available to correct mere errors in claim drafting. The doctrine should instead be seen as applying to technologies developed after the patent issued or in other circumstances that a skilled patent solicitor could not have foreseen.[57]

At least for the time being, the precedential status of *Sage Products* is secure. No domestic opinion has yet to cast significant doubt upon the Foreseeable Alteration Rule it pronounced. But a comparison of the Foreseeable Alteration Rule with approaches to equivalency abroad reveals an extremely sharp divide. In particular, the purposive construction rule favored by the British courts seems completely at odds with the approach of *Sage Products*.

Recall that in *Catnic Components Ltd. v. Hill and Smith Ltd.*,[58] Lord Diplock announced that:

> The question in each case is: whether persons with practical knowledge and experience of the kind of work in which the invention was intended to be used, would understand that strict compliance with a particular descriptive word or phrase appearing in a claim was intended by the patentee to be an essential requirement of the invention so that any variant would fall outside the monopoly claimed, even though it would have no material effect upon the way the invention worked.

This quotation reveals that the focus of purposive construction is what the patentee intended to claim at the time the patent application was filed. Under *Sage Products* and the Foreseeable Alteration Rule, the question is not so much what the patentee intended, but what he could not have foreseen.

The distinction between the approaches is admittedly a subtle one, but can be of great practical consequence. Cases where technology arises after the inventor files a patent application provide the best illustration of how the approaches of *Catnic* and *Sage Products* differ. Suppose that an inventor obtains patent protection in the United States and the United Kingdom upon a tool made out of a strong, smooth metal such as iron, nickel or cobalt. Several years after the patents issue, a competitor markets that tool, but fabricated out of a new titanium-tungsten alloy. Suppose further that the particular alloy employed was not developed until well after the patents were filed.

[56] 126 F.3d at 1425.

[57] See Thomas, supra note 37, at 227–28.

[58] [1981] FSR 60, [1982] RPC 183.

In the United States, a court applying the Foreseeable Alteration Rule would ask whether the inventor should have claimed a titanium-tungsten tool. Plainly the inventor could not have claimed a futuristic metal alloy, for under § 112 each claim must be supported by an enabling disclosure in the patent's specification. So a U.S. court would consider this hypothetical as an ideal case for the application of the doctrine of equivalents. But in the United Kingdom, the purposive construction focuses upon the intent of the drafter. Inevitably, the patentee could not have intended its claims to cover technology that was unknown at the time an application was filed. In sum, the *Catnic* standard does not provide much room for future technologies. Given that the new canons of claim construction have not displayed a particular endurance, and that the British courts have questioned the continued vitality of *Catnic* following UK participation in the European Patent Convention, it remains to be seen whether there will be much need to debate the propriety of either rule in coming years.

D. The Dolly *Doctrine*

The *Dolly* Doctrine is another canon of construction with recent origins and a dubious future. The Federal Circuit announced this rule in its 1994 opinion in *Dolly Inc. v. Spalding & Evenflo Co. Inc.*[59] This appeal arose following an infringement trial between competitors in the children's furniture market. The claims at issue recited a portable, adjustable child's play-chair. The claims called for a stable, rigid frame to which an assembler added a seat panel and a back panel. In the accused chair, the seat and back fit together to form a fixed frame.

The United States District Court for the Southern District of Ohio found infringement under the doctrine of equivalents. On appeal, the Federal Circuit reversed. Judge Rader reasoned that the absence of a rigid frame in the accused device was so fundamental as to preclude a finding of equivalent infringement. In language that caught the attention of many in the patent bar, the court noted that the doctrine of equivalents 'cannot embrace a structure that is specifically excluded from the scope of the claims'.[60] Under the facts, a fixed frame assembled from the seat and back panels was not equivalent to the claimed stable, rigid frame.

Thus was born the *Dolly* Doctrine. Under this canon, there can be no non-textual infringement when the claim language itself specifically excludes the patentee's equivalency theory. An apparent problem with the *Dolly* Doctrine is

[59] 16 F.3d 394, 29 USPQ2d 1767 (Fed. Cir. 1994).

[60] 16 F.3d at 400.

that the inclusion of any element within a claim necessarily works to exclude others. No objective principle informs the reader when a particular claim limitation rises to the level of negating the doctrine of equivalents. If the *Dolly* Doctrine were given an expansive reading, the court would lend preclusive effect to each recited claim limitation and utterly negate the doctrine of equivalents. Once the court held that the accused technology did not literally infringe a claim, under this reading of the *Dolly* Doctrine a finding of equivalent infringement would also be precluded.

The 1996 Federal Circuit opinion in *Athletic Alternatives, Inc. v. Prince Manufacturing, Inc.*[61] exemplifies these concerns. The claim at issue called for a sports racket with numerous string segments spanning a frame. The string segments were offset from another by variable lengths. Specifically, the claim called for the distances to vary 'continuously between minimums as small as about zero for the ends of lateral strings near the tip and heel portions of said frame, and a maximum of up to about ½-inch for the ends of the lateral string segments near the center of said side portions of said frame'.

The trial court held, and the Federal Circuit agreed, that this claim's requirement of continuous variation required a gradual change in the offset between strings. This limitation mandated that the offset distance between strings differed from that of both adjacent strings. According to both courts, then, the claim literally called for at least three offset distances between strings: a minimum, maximum and intermediate interval. Because the accused racket had only two discrete string spacings, it could not literally infringe.

The Federal Circuit also agreed with the trial court's conclusion of non-infringement under the doctrine of equivalents. Quoting from the *Dolly* decision, Judge Michel reasoned that 'the intermediate offset distance required by the properly construed claims cannot have an equivalent in a racket with only two offset distances. In other words, the two-distance splayed string system was '"specifically excluded from the scope of the claims"'.[62] The difficulty with this application of the *Dolly* Doctrine is that anything not expressly covered by the claims is excluded from the claims. Absent some unarticulated limiting principle, the *Dolly* Doctrine appears to swallow the doctrine of equivalents whole.

The 1998 Federal Circuit opinion in *Ethicon Endo-Surgery, Inc. v. United States Surgical Corp.* recognized as much.[63] Responding to the accused

[61] 73 F.3d 1573, 37 USPQ2d 1365 (Fed. Cir. 1996).

[62] 73 F.3d at 1582.

[63] 149 F.3d 1309, 47 USPQ2d 1272 (Fed. Cir. 1998).

infringer's vigorous reliance upon the *Dolly* Doctrine, Judge Lourie dealt with the *Dolly* Doctrine with the following language:

> [A]ny analysis of infringement under the doctrine of equivalents necessarily deals with subject matter that is 'beyond,' 'ignored' by, and not included in the literal scope of the claim. Such subject matter is not necessarily 'specifically excluded' from coverage under the doctrine unless its inclusion is somehow inconsistent with the language of the claim. Literal failure to meet a claim limitation does not necessarily amount to a 'specific exclusion.'[64]

Ethicon Endo-Surgery appears to announce the end of the *Dolly* Doctrine, at least to the extent that it enjoyed the status as a cognizable canon of claim construction. The *Dolly* Doctrine now appears to do no more than alert patentees not to espouse equivalency theories with regard to one claim limitation that would slight another limitation. For example, suppose that a claimed chemical process calls for an increase in pressure of an isolated gas. The accused process does not involve this step, but instead involves an increase in temperature. In both processes the volume and mass of the gas are held constant.

Recalling Boyle's Law,[65] the patentee might assert that an increase in temperature bears a known relationship to an increase in pressure, at least for an ideal gas, and thus the accused process should be judged an equivalent of the claimed process. What little is left of the *Dolly* Doctrine would seem to bar the patentee's equivalency theory only if the claims expressly recited a *decrease* in temperature. Whether this vitiated rule of textual consistency deserves recognition as a distinct canon seems doubtful. But the Federal Circuit was quick to make up for any perceived absence, for in 1998 it presented a fifth novel canon to the patent bar: the All Advantages Rule.

E. *The All Advantages Rule*

A final innovative canon arose in the Federal Circuit's opinion in *Vehicular Technologies Corp. v. Titan Wheel Int'l, Inc.*[66] That case concerned a locking differential for use in the axle of an automobile. The claims at issue called for a 'spring assembly consisting of two concentric springs bearing against one end of said pin'. The accused device employed only a single spring placed in parallel

[64] 149 F.3d at 1317.

[65] Boyle's Law provides that for an ideal gas at constant temperature, the volume is inversely proportional to the pressure. See Francis W. Sears et al., *University Physics*, 6th edition, 329–30 (Addison Wesley, 1984).

[66] 141 F.3d 1084, 46 USPQ2d 1257 (Fed. Cir. 1998).

with a plug. The District Court for the Central District of California found infringement likely under the doctrine of equivalents and awarded a preliminary injunction.

Following an appeal, the Federal Circuit reversed the trial court determination. Judge Clevenger wrote the majority opinion, which Judge Plager joined. The majority observed that the patent's written description repeatedly noted that the inner spring served as a backup to the outer spring in the event the latter device failed. As such, Judge Clevenger reasoned that spring back-up was a key function sought by the patentee. Because the accused differential mechanism consisted of a spring-plug structure, it was entirely incapable of performing this function. Finding it likely that the accused device substantially differed from the claimed invention, the Federal Circuit vacated the grant of a preliminary injunction.[67]

Judge Newman authored a blistering dissent. According to Judge Newman, the majority created a new canon of claim interpretation: that the advantages mentioned in the specification, although not included in the claims, must be possessed by the accused device before there can be a finding of infringement by equivalency. Terming this canon the All Advantages Rule, the dissent reasoned that advantages discussed in the specification should not become per se claim limitations.[68] At best, whether spring backup was a key function of the patented invention was a question of fact, not a legal imperative that should restrain the doctrine of equivalents.

The difficult birth of the All Advantages Rule suggests that it too might experience the controversial and brief existence of some of the other fledgling canons of claim construction, such as the Public Dedication Principle and the *Dolly* Doctrine. At bottom, *Vehicular Technologies* calls for limitations to be imported from either the specification or the prosecution history into the claims, a practice heretofore declared impermissible. With the All Advantages Rule in mind, accused infringers possess strong incentives to comb through an asserted patent's specification and prosecution history, searching for a function performed by the patented invention that the accused infringement does not achieve. Given the broad applicability of this maxim and its opposition to one of the traditional canons of claim construction, we will likely hear more about the All Advantages Rule in the near future.

[67] 141 F.3d at 1090–92.
[68] 141 F.3d at 1093.

III. EXPLORING ALTERNATIVES TO THE CANONS

These episodes from U.S. patent jurisprudence suggest that the Federal Circuit is struggling to generate consistent protocols of textual interpretation. But experience has taught us that earnestly pronounced canons that seem sensible under one set of facts do not always transplant well. The particularized disputes that are the subject of appellate court opinions do not provide an optimal vehicle for the articulation of a comprehensive method of interpretation. Canons suffer from another infirmity: courts apply them against claims that were written long before the drafter could have known about them.

Instead of a comprehensive set of canons, the U.S. patent community instead is left with a patchwork of practices, heuristics and tactics for determining the meaning of claims. Readers must reason by analogy from the existing case law, yet the words and grammars at play in the precedents invariably differ from those before subsequent readers. With no final meeting fully present in the text, and no established technique for approaching it, the interpretative freedom granted to readers in the patent community undermines the patent system's ability to bring stability to its regime of appropriation.

There is no reason to believe that even the most precisely detailed set of canons will ever change a fundamental reality in the U.S. patent system: that the withering gaze of high stakes litigation will forever expose gaps and ambiguities in the text of patent claims. But we likely could do a better job of ensuring that the text of claims conveys a meaning shared by members of the patent community. Rather than relying wholly on Federal Circuit proscriptivism, we should make more fundamental efforts towards improving the way we write and read claims.

This article suggests two ways of going about this task. The first, best taken up by the PTO, is to increase emphasis upon drafting and interpretational norms within the patent community. The second calls for two reforms within the patent enforcement system: attentiveness to whether an accused infringer possessed actual notice of the claims, and judicial ability to amend claims during litigation.

A. *Promotion of Interpretative Norms at the PTO*

The promotion of interpretative norms within the patent community seems a worthwhile endeavor for at least two reasons. First, patent claims are not a robust medium. Although claims are notorious for their stilted language, they remain but single sentences. The ends of patent claims are also quite modest.

These technological aphorisms do no more than paint verbal portraits of physical artifacts or behavioral engagements. It stands to reason that within this formalized, limited genre, improvements could be obtained in the mapping of the tangible to the text of patent claims.

Second, the U.S. patent community already possesses both a long tradition and an internal cohesiveness. The group of patent agents and attorneys comprises a relatively small set of formally licensed professionals. Its members frequently interact with one another and with PTO examiners. As textually oriented communities go, the patent bar is a discrete, accessible group that seems susceptible to improving its drafting and interpretative skills.

The PTO should take the lead in providing readers and writers of patent claims with additional interpretative norms. Thanks to an aggressive campaign by PTO management throughout the 1990s, culminating with a Supreme Court victory in the *Dickinson v. Zurko* litigation, PTO practice has been placed squarely into the mainstream of U.S. administrative law.[69] The Federal Circuit now appears obliged to accord PTO rule-making substantial weight. As never before, the PTO is in a position to normalize the reading and writing of patent claims.

An initial step towards augmenting interpretational norms is to standardize the vocabulary of patent claims. Although cases like *Vitronics* encourage jurists to consult technical dictionaries, these references suffer from their comprehensiveness. Traditional technical dictionaries, encyclopedias and manuals typically associate each entry with a number of alternative definitions. A PTO-sponsored dictionary, structured to provide a single, default definition alongside a number of electives, would surely enhance communication within the patent community.

The PTO should also ensure that members of the patent bar receive training in technical drafting skills. Currently, patent solicitors must pass an examination in order to receive a license to represent others before the PTO. Traditionally, the patent agent's examination required would-be patent attorneys to draft a passable set of claims. Citing burdens in administering this test, the PTO recently opted to administer the examination wholly in multiple-choice format.[70]

[69] See *Dickinson v. Zurko*, 527 U.S. 150 (1999).

[70] See *Registration Examination for Patent Practitioners and the Establishment of a Continuing Education Requirement and an Annual Fee for Registered Patent Practitioners*, 61 Fed. Reg. 51,072 (1996).

With respect, this shift in examination tactics moves the patent bar in the wrong direction. The current crisis in interpretation calls for claims drafting skills to be emphasized, not ignored. The PTO should also mandate, and perhaps sponsor directly, preparatory training in claims drafting for would-be patent attorneys and agents. The PTO should also require continuing education for practicing members of the patent bar subsequent to the agent's examination. By opening a dialogue with patent practitioners concerning their drafting skills, the PTO could help to achieve consistent claims drafting and interpretation.

More particularly, the PTO should also bear a special solicitude towards claims that recite ranges of some physical trait. The *Warner-Jenkinson* and *YBM Magnex* opinions suggest that courts continue to be confronted with infringements that include physical characteristics, such as temperature, weight or acidity, narrowly outside a claimed range.[71] Both of these litigations resulted in findings of infringement under the doctrine of equivalents, demonstrating that courts will not necessarily adhere to the recited end points. Surely the patent community could develop an improved protocol for managing this common sort of claim limitation? Perhaps each patent instrument should incorporate an explanation of how the end points of a recited range were chosen. The PTO might also notify applicants of the presence of ranges within a particular set of patent claims and advise them to consider whether the noted range merely delineates ranges preferred by the applicant, or instead defines a patentable advance over the prior art.

As well, the PTO should consider altering the mechanisms it employs when issuing patent claims. The U.S. patent regime has always relied heavily on the efforts of applicants to draft coherent claims. Typically a lone examiner provides the entirety of the review that these claims will receive. The case can be made that the PTO should place the same stress on the issuance of individual patent claims as it does its own body of regulations. For the regime of patents amounts to a regime of private regulation, with each patent instrument governing the behavior of other market participants. Given that patents issue without the usual cycle of notice and public commentary associated with administrative law, we should consider whether more resources should be devoted towards the production of well-drafted claims.

One possible solution would call for the review of claims on the verge of allowance by a panel of experienced examiners, technical writers and possibly even industry representatives. Obviously, limitations on PTO resources and the entirely appropriate demands of industry for timely issuance of patents will

[71] See supra notes 15–22 and 54–58.

constrain the ability of the PTO to enhance its examination procedures in this manner. But if a substantive legal benefit in keeping, say, with the uncontestability provisions of the Lanham Act accompanied any enhanced examination, then the benefits of such a proceeding might be considerable.[72] The most important inventions in terms of potential licensing and litigation would receive in essence a pre-grant reissue, lending additional certainties to the interpretational task.

Finally, the PTO should consider alterations to the U.S. patent instrument itself. A recent writing by this author advocated several changes in this regard, including changes that would better represent inventorship and the written description requirement.[73] Perhaps the patent instrument should make itself more amenable to claim interpretation efforts as well. A first claim drafted as broadly as the abstract would avoid disconnects between the written description and claims, as occurred in cases like *Johnson & Johnson*.[74] As well, such reforms as obligatory definitions of key terms in the claims or identification of embodiments of the claimed invention available on the market may lead to greater uniformity of results when others interpret the patent instrument.

B. Patent Enforcement Reform in the Courts

Judicial reforms could also be implemented with an eye to improving our current regime of claim interpretation. An initial reform would require the unpacking of the competing values traditionally viewed as at stake during equivalency determinations. These values are succinctly stated in the Protocol to Article 69 of the European Patent Convention, which calls for nonliteral claim interpretations in a way 'which combines a fair protection for the patentee with a reasonable degree of certainty for third parties'. United States Supreme Court opinions also encourage the balancing of these norms during equivalency interpretations. In *Graver Tank & Mfg. Co. v. Linde Air Products Co.*, the Court concluded that 'to permit imitation of a patented invention which does not copy every literal detail would be to convert the protection of the patent grant into a hollow and useless thing'.[75] Fifty years later, in *Warner-Jenkinson,* the Court also sensed that 'the doctrine of equivalents, when applied broadly, conflicts

[72] See 15 U.S.C. § 1065 (1994).

[73] See Thomas, supra note 37, at 230–32.

[74] See supra notes 48–53 and accompanying text.

[75] 339 U.S. 605, 607 (1950).

with the definitional and public-notice functions of the statutory claiming requirement'.[76]

The difficulty with this usual paean is that although it is often recited, it is most often quickly discarded in judicial opinions. The level of protection that balances notice and fair protection is precisely the question to be resolved, not some sort of analytical pathway. Academic analysis has not been of much assistance either. Most often appealing to an economic rationale, scholarly discussion of the scope of equivalency has found little practical application in the courts.

It is time that the U.S. patent system rethinks the notice component of this formulation. Indeed, the U.S. patent system should simply abandon the wearying mantra that patent claims provide notice to competitors of artifacts or behaviors they must avoid. Notice has never been guaranteed by the U.S. patent regime because the PTO has traditionally been obliged to maintain applications in secrecy.[77] Even after the Domestic Publication of Foreign Filed Patent Applications Act of 1999, applications that have not been published abroad will not be published in the United States. Inventors maintain the ability to hold their applications in secrecy and file suit on the day the patent issues.[78] Further, even if some delay accompanies enforcement of a patent, neither the patentee nor the PTO need inform potential infringers prior to the filing of suit.

The suggestion that notice comprises a core purpose of patent claims strains credulity.[79] As applied during patent litigation, any notice to the defendant is typically of a presumptive or constructive variety. This recognition does not suggest that the patent law should not be concerned for competitors that made marketplace decisions based upon an analysis of a competitor's patent position. In that case the patent system should protect the defendant's reliance interest by employing an estoppel theory or similar mechanism to deny the patentee protection under the doctrine of equivalents. But there is little cause for such heavy reliance upon a constructive notice rationale when the very structure of

[76] 520 U.S. at 29.

[77] See 35 U.S.C. § 122 (1994).

[78] Examples of patent infringement suits filed on the same day the patent issued include *Robotic Vision Sys., Inc. v. View Eng'g, Inc.*, 112 F.3d 1163, 1164 (Fed. Cir. 1997); *GAF Building Materials Co. v. Elk Corp.*, 90 F.3d 479, 480 (Fed. Cir. 1996); *National Presto Indus., Inc. v. West Bend Co.*, 76 F.3d 1185, 1193 (Fed. Cir. 1996); *Exxon Chem. Patents, Inc. v. Lubrizol Corp.*, 935 F.2d 1263, 1264 (Fed. Cir. 1991); and *Amgen, Inc. v. Chugai Pharm. Co.*, 927 F.2d 1200, 1204 (Fed. Cir.), *cert. denied*, 502 U.S. 856 (1991).

[79] See Thomas, supra note 37, at 200–04.

the patent system does not guarantee industry participants warning of any of the patents they might infringe.

Instead of proceeding along a dubious inference of constructive notice, the U.S. courts should inquire into whether an accused infringer actually knew of the asserted patent. In many, and possibly most cases, the defendant did not know of the patent until the day the suit was filed. In some circumstances the accused infringer could not have known about the patent, as many patentees file infringement suits on the day the patent issued. In others, the defendant simply was neither perceptive nor legally sophisticated enough to learn of the patent.

If the accused infringer had no actual notice of the patent's claims prior to the filing of suit, then there seems little reason to accord the value of notice any weight at all during infringement analyses. In such cases, concerns over notice within the equivalency inquiry act to penalize inventors without corresponding benefit obtained by other industry actors. Therefore, in cases where the accused infringer had no actual notice of the patent, the prior art should form the principal restraint upon the scope of equivalency. Following the principles of such cases as *Wilson Sporting Goods Co. v. David Geoffrey & Associates*[80] or *Formstein*,[81] patent claims should be accorded a range of equivalents as broad as the prior art allows.

Alternatively, the court may determine that the accused infringer knew about the patent prior to suit. Perhaps a parallel application had been published abroad, an event that following the Domestic Publication of Patent Applications Published Abroad of 1999 will cause the PTO to republish the identical information domestically. Or time may have passed between the date the U.S. patent issued and the date an infringement suit was filed. In such cases, if the accused infringer concluded that its products or processes were noninfringing based upon a considered judgment, then the courts should assess the accused infringer's reliance interest. If the court judges that an accused infringer responsibly exercised its duty to avoid the patented technology, then the range of equivalents accorded to such a patent should be less generously awarded. Not only should the constraining effect of the prior art upon the scope of equivalency be accounted for, the court should also assess why the patentee did not obtain a claim that literally embraces the accused infringement. In cases where claims of the proper scope could have been readily obtained, the court may wish to award intervening rights[82] or otherwise alleviate the harshness of a judgment of infringement by equivalency.

[80] 904 F.2d 677, 14 USPQ2d 1942 (Fed. Cir.), *cert. denied*, 498 U.S. 992 (1990).

[81] [1991] RPC 597 (German Federal Supreme Court 1986).

[82] See 35 U.S.C. § 252 (1994).

A claim interpretation regime based upon actual notice might also cause the PTO to get into the business of supporting potential patent infringers as well as inventors. For example, the PTO might generate a database in which innovative commercial actors would be permitted to register their areas of interest. Upon the publication of relevant applications or issuance of pertinent patents by the PTO, copies could be forwarded to registrants. Taking this possibility even further, the PTO could maintain a confidential database of products and processes available on the market. The content of the database would consist of industry submissions, with each entry comprising a textual description of a trade secret or otherwise unpatented technology. Again, when the PTO issues an apposite patent or publication, a copy could be sent to the database entrant.

A second judicial reform would call for reconsideration of the sanctity of claims during patent litigation. U.S. courts have historically been unable to reform patent instruments during enforcement proceedings. They must either uphold the asserted claims or declare them invalid. Only the PTO possesses the authority to modify patents during post-grant proceedings.[83] This regime can be a rigorous one, particularly for deserving patentees who find themselves with a set of overbroad claims.

This enforcement structure runs headlong into the complexity of the current claims drafting environment. In a passage worthy of extensive quotation, Magistrate Judge Brazil has noted that:

> inventor and counsel must consider how broad to make the claims (a decision influenced by legal, business, and technical considerations). They are trying to carve out a protectable niche in an already crowded environment. In deciding where to carve, they are simultaneously attempting to be broad enough to maximize their position in the market but not so broad as to create an unacceptable risk of invalidity. They must make judgments about what to claim, which words to use in articulating the claims, which matters to emphasize, which arguable prior art to cite, etc ... [W]hen lawyer and inventor make these judgments they choose between different alternatives. They select some items for inclusion and decide to exclude others. They choose certain words (instead of others) to articulate their claims and describe their product or process. These judgments are not simple, linear, technical undertakings. They are intellectually dense, and the density is both technical and legal. To appreciate that density, one only needs to consider the huge number of patents already on file, the increasing technical complexity of the subjects of patents, the subtlety of the distinctions and refinements that can exist among abstractly comparable products and processes, and the inherently arbitrary and elusive character of the process of selecting which words to attach to physical

[83] See *Wolens v. F. W. Woolworth Co.*, 703 F.2d 983, 991, 218 USPQ 100 (7th Cir. 1983).

things (an arbitrariness and an elusiveness that seem to increase in direct proportion to the complexity and subtlety of the physical things that are offered as potential subjects of patents).[84]

The arbitrariness noted by Judge Brazil looms especially large in the case of the more narrow claims within a typical U.S. patent. As those schooled in the patent law will recognize, U.S. claims drafters typically craft a series of claims in each application, forming a reverse pyramid of successively narrower claims. The first claim of the patent is very broad and abstract. The most narrow claim usually describes a product the inventor would actually consider putting into commercial practice. Intermediate claims are set to varying levels of abstraction, each taking a place on the spectrum of technologies surrounding the narrowly focused commercial embodiment of the invention.

By drafting claims in this manner, the patentee wishes to enforce the narrowest possible claim against an accused infringer: the narrower the claim, the greater the likelihood that such a claim will withstand a defense of invalidity. The greater the number of limitations in a claim, the more unlikely it is that prior art will render that claim anticipated or obvious. Importantly, experienced claims drafters recognize that not all the pertinent prior art may be before them, and that they must speculate as to the sorts of references they may bear upon the claimed invention. Also, the narrower the claim, the greater the difficulty an accused infringer will have in making an attack based upon enablement.

On the other hand, the patentee also wants the broadest claim possible in order to have the possibility of reaching as many competitors as possible. Competitors find efforts to design competing technologies that do not fall within the scope of the claims more difficult, and thus avoid literal infringement less easily. So a claims drafter will attempt to write the broadest claim the PTO will allow, allowing a range of potential technological protection in each patent instrument.[85]

Although the claim drafting consequences of a multiple claiming regime are apparent, a determination of which basis to define the more narrow claims typically is not. Patentable subject matter ordinarily may be expounded through an enormous number of defining traits. Picking among possible characteristics often amounts to an arbitrary exercise.

84 *Advanced Cardiovascular Systems, Inc. v. C.R. Bard, Inc.*, 25 USPQ2d 1354, 1357 (N.D. Cal. 1992).

85 See Martin J. Adelman et al., *Patent Law: Cases and Materials* 641–42 (LexisNexis, 1998).

Suppose, for example, a broad claim is drafted towards a simple electrical circuit known as a peak detector.[86] The claim recites a voltage source, diode and a parallel RC circuit. Even for this elementary circuit, the number of combinations susceptible to distinct claiming is enormous. The drafter might specify a particular capacitance; range of resistance; characteristics on the input signal; threshold voltage of the diode; the precise electrical connections between individual circuit components; and so on. Further, when the possibility of sub-combinations of these more particular characteristics is considered, the number of claiming options grows enormous even for this most simple of circuits. Whether these more narrowly circumscribed claims are of any value is often not apparent to either inventor or claims drafter. The PTO's fee schedule and concerns for overclaiming mean that only so many combinations may be selected in advance. Yet these necessarily uninformed choices are often of great moment in infringement litigation.

The U.S. patent system should at long last recognize the arbitrariness that occurs in claim drafting. The post-grant proceedings of reissue and reexamination to some extent alleviate this harm: as the passage of time reveals weaknesses in the particular claim language chosen, the patentee may seek modifications. But serious consideration should be given to allowing courts to reform patent claims during litigation, as they occasionally do to the text of individual contracts.[87] Again, in cases where the accused infringer has had no actual notice of the patent instrument, then the defendant could hardly be in a position to assert that he could be harmed by any redrafting that occurs in the courts. Concerns should instead focus upon preserving the benefit of the invention to the patentee, as well as providing better notice to subsequent competitors accused of infringing the patent.

IV. CONCLUSION

A review of recent episodes involving the canons of claim constructions suggests that this sort of proscriptivism may be counterproductive. The lives of most of the fledgling canons have been cut short, and the remainder seem to cast long shadows over claims that were drafted well before the newborn canons were ever

[86] See Stephen D. Senturia & Bruce D. Wedlock, *Electronic Circuits and Applications* 489–92 (John Wiley, 1975).

[87] E.g. *Donohue v. Picinich*, 852 F. Supp. 144 (D. Conn. 1994) (reforming real estate sales contract due to mutual mistake of the parties).

pronounced. Instead, we should consider working improvements upon the current regime of claiming. This article has advanced specific mechanisms through which the U.S. administrative and judicial regimes can improve upon our current regime of claim interpretation.

In forming these proposals this article has recognized that the set of patent professionals are in a sense a community of translators. The public relies upon the patent bar to transmit its specialized knowledge of this sophisticated legal regime, as well as to explain the mandates that individual patent instruments contain. Like traditional translators, the patent bar should be encouraged to serve the text.[88] For only through the careful drafting of particular patent instruments, and honesty in their interpretation, may we maintain the integrity of the totality of the regime of patents.

[88] Cf. Hans-Georg Gadamer, *Text and Interpretation*, in Michelfeld & Palmer (Eds.), *Dialogue and Deconstruction: The Gadamer-Derrida Encounter*, 31 (1989).

Chapter 6

Economic and Constitutional Influences on Copyright Law in the United States

*Pamela Samuelson**

1. INTRODUCTION

In the aftermath of the accession of the United States to the Berne Convention for Artistic and Literary Works,[1] European copyright professionals have had the pleasure of watching the law of this once renegade nation move toward greater conformity with the longstanding norms of authors' rights jurisdictions.[2] One example is the ruling of the United States Supreme Court in *Feist Publications,*

* Chancellor's Professor of Law and Information Management, University of California at Berkeley. The author wishes to thank Jason Schultz and Leah Theriault for their research work on this article. Research support for this article was provided by NSF Grant No. SES 9979852. This essay (sans postscript) was first published 23 Eur. Intell. Prop. Rev. 409 (Sept. 2001).

1 See Berne Convention for the Protection of Literary and Artistic Works, 9 September 1886, as last revised at Paris, 24 July 1971, and amended in 1979, 828 U.N.T.S. 221 [hereinafter Berne Convention]; the U.S. acceded to the Paris revision of the Berne Convention on March 1, 1989.

2 See Berne Implementation Act, Pub.L. No. 100-568, 102 Stat. 2853 (1988); Visual Artists Rights Act of 1990, Pub.L. No. 101-650, tit. VI, 104 Stat. 5128 (codified as 17 U.S.C. § 106A (Supp. II 1990)) [hereinafter VARA]; Architectural Works Copyright Protection Act, Pub.L. No. 101-650, tit. VII, 104 Stat. 5133. Foreign copyrights that had fallen into the public domain in the U.S. because of a failure to comply with formalities were restored by two acts: the North American Free Trade Agreement Implementation Act, Pub. L. No. 103-182, Sec. 334(a), 107 Stat. 2115 (gave protection to public domain motion pictures of NAFTA signatories); and the Uruguay Round Agreements Act, Pub. L. No. 103-465, Sec. 514, 108 Stat. 4976 (restored the copyright in all works which had entered the public domain due to a failure to comply with formalities, treating them as if they had never entered the public domain for the purposes of calculating their term of protection).

Inc. v. Rural Telephone Service Co.[3] By holding that the white pages listings of telephone directories lacked sufficient originality to warrant copyright protection, U.S. courts reached the same legal conclusion as authors' rights jurisdictions.[4] With officials of the European Union and the United States working together in international forums to establish ever higher minimum standards for intellectual property rights[5] and with the increasingly global trade in intellectual property products and services,[6] European copyright professionals may think that U.S. and European copyright laws will become ever more harmonious.[7] Who knows? Perhaps the United States will finally embrace the moral rights of authors, as it is obliged to do under Article 6bis of the Berne Convention.[8]

Despite the many signs of convergence of European and U.S. copyright laws, this article contends that copyright law in the United States will continue to differ in two significant respects from authors' rights laws of member states of the European Union. One difference is that economic reasoning sometimes

[3] 499 U.S. 340 (1991).

[4] See, e.g. George Metaxas, *Protection of Databases: Quietly Steering in the Wrong Direction?*, 7 Eur. Intell. Prop. Rev. 227, 228, 233 (1990) (electronic databases not sufficiently protected by the copyright law of most European Union members because they do not meet the originality requirement); *accord*, Jean Hughes & Elizabeth Weightman, *EC Database Protection: Fine Tuning the Commission's Proposal*, 5 Eur. Intell. Prop. Rev. 147 (1992).

[5] See Agreement on Trade-Related Aspects of Intellectual Property Rights, 15 April 1994, Marrakesh Agreement Establishing the World Trade Organization, Annex 1C, Legal Instruments – Results of the Uruguay Round vol. 31, 33 I.L.M. 81 (1994); WIPO Copyright Treaty, adopted Dec. 20, 1996, WIPO Doc. CRNR/DC/94; WIPO Performances and Phonograms Treaty, adopted Dec. 20, 1996, WIPO Doc. CRNR/DC/95; Agreed Statements Concerning the WIPO Copyright Treaty, adopted Dec. 20, 1996, WIPO Doc. CRNR/DC/96.

[6] See, e.g. International Intellectual Property Alliance, Copyright Industries in the U.S. Economy: *The 1998 Report* (exports of copyright-related products and services are increasing at an impressive rate – in 1996 their value surpassed that of every other export sector in the United States).

[7] Alain Strowel, *Droit d'auteur and Copyright: Between History and Nature*, in Brad Sherman & Alain Strowel (Eds.) *Of Authors And Origins: Essays On Copyright Law* 235 (OUP, 1994) (discussing the historical development of commonalities between *droit d'auteur* and utilitarian copyright regimes); Jane C. Ginsburg, *A Tale of Two Copyrights: Literary Property in Revolutionary France and America*, in Sherman & Strowel, ibid, 137–38 (noting that historical origin of American copyright law contains both natural rights and utilitarian impulses).

[8] Berne Convention, *supra* note 1, Art. 6bis. Don't hold your breath.

exerts a powerful influence on the contours of U.S. copyright law.[9] A second is that the U.S. Constitution exerts a strong, if somewhat erratic, influence on the understanding of the bounds of U.S. copyright law.[10] Economic and constitutional influences sometimes intermix,[11] in part because of certain historical experiences underpinning the Constitution.[12] This essay will consider these differences between the traditions of U.S. copyright law and those of authors' rights jurisdictions.

2. ECONOMIC INFLUENCES IN AMERICAN COPYRIGHT LAW

An extensive literature in the United States discusses the economic underpinnings of copyright law.[13] This literature justifies not only the grant of exclusive rights to authors,[14] but also certain limitations on authors' rights that differentiate American copyright law from European authors' rights law.[15] Utilitarian considerations underlie, for example, the U.S. 'work made for hire' rule that confers authorship status on employers for works prepared by employees in the scope of their employment.[16] This rule starkly contrasts with rules in Continental Europe where, in deference to the cultural importance of authorship, employees are treated as 'authors' and therefore as the initial owners of exclusive rights in works they produce.[17]

[9] See *infra* notes 13–110 and accompanying text.

[10] See *infra* notes 111–57 and accompanying text.

[11] See *infra* notes 165–67 and accompanying text.

[12] See, e.g. L. Ray Patterson, *Free Speech, Copyright, and Fair Use*, 40 Vand. L. Rev. 1 (1987); Mark Rose, *Authors And Owners – The Invention Of Copyright* (Harvard University Press, 1993).

[13] See, e.g. Wendy J. Gordon, *Asymmetric Market Failure and Prisoner's Dilemma in Intellectual Property*, 17 U. Dayton L. Rev. 853 (1992); Peter S. Menell, *Intellectual Property: General Theories, in* Encyclopedia Of Law & Economics (Edward Elgar, forthcoming); Robert P. Merges, *The End of Friction? Property Rights and Contract in the 'Newtonian' World of On-Line Commerce*, 12 Berkeley Tech. L.J. 115 (1997); J.H. Reichman, *Legal Hybrids Between The Patent and Copyright Paradigms*, 94 Colum. L. Rev. 2432 (1994).

[14] See, e.g. Gordon, *supra* note 13 at 854–55.

[15] See, e.g. Menell, *supra* note 13.

[16] 17 U.S.C. sec. 201. See, e.g. Rochelle C. Dreyfuss, *The Creative Employee and the Copyright Act of 1976*, 54 U. Chi. L. Rev. 590, 594–97 (1987).

[17] In France, for example, the only exception to this rule arises in the case of collective works. See Paul Geller & Melville Nimmer, *International Copyright Law &*

A far starker contrast between U.S. and European laws lies in their stances on the moral rights of authors. U.S. law is concerned with providing economic incentives to authors to induce them to invest in creative work; a grant of moral rights seems unnecessary to induce such investment.[18] Major copyright industries in the U.S. strongly object to moral rights because they may interfere with certain economic arrangements that these industries wish to make.[19] Utilitarian reasons also explain why American firms and policymakers have sought to persuade moral rights jurisdictions to make these rights waivable by contract.[20]

Concerns about economic consequences of protection also underlie the 'useful article' rule of U.S. copyright law that denies copyright protection to pictorial, sculptural and graphic works if they have a utility beyond merely conveying information or displaying an appearance.[21] This too contrasts with some European jurisdictions that provide copyright protection to artistic designs for toasters, teapots and the like.[22]

Practice § 4[1] (Matthew Bender, 1988) [hereinafter Geller & Nimmer]. However, the widespread practice in Europe of employees assigning rights to employers may, as a practical matter, lessen the practical differences.

18 See, e.g. Roberta R. Kwall, *Copyright And The Moral Right: Is An American Marriage Possible?*, 38 Vand. L. Rev. 1, 27–28 (1985) (discussing why U.S. law has resisted moral rights). VARA, *supra* note 2, which provides moral rights to creators of certain types of visual art, is an exception to the general absence of explicit moral rights in U.S. copyright law.

19 American movie executives, for example, would certainly regard the fate of colorized movies in French courts as an impediment to their legitimate business arrangements. See *Huston v. Societe de l'Exploitation de la Cinquieme Chaine*, 1991 Cass. le civ., 149 Revue Internationale Du Droit D'auteur 197 (1991) (granting injunction barring the broadcast of colorized John Huston movie because it impaired author's right of integrity – even though the author no longer owned the copyright in the film).

20 See, e.g. Information Infrastructure Task Force Working Group On Intellectual Property Rights, Intellectual Property Rights And The National Information Infrastructure, 133–34, 145–47 (Sept. 1995) available at http://www.uspto.gov/web/offices/com/doc/ipnii/ [hereinafter White Paper] (discussing the difficulty of reconciling moral rights with the business practices of American entertainment and publishing industries).

21 17 U.S.C. sec. 101, 113. For an explanation, see, e.g. Jerome H. Reichman, *Design Protection in Domestic and Foreign Copyright Law: From the Berne Revision of 1948 to the Copyright Act of 1976*, 1983 Duke L.J. 1143 (1983).

22 In France, for example, this aspect of copyright law arises from the 'unity of art' principle, which eschews dividing works of art into categories based on use. See Geller & Nimmer, *supra* note 17 at § 2[1][b][i][D].

Still another U.S. rule commonly justified on economic grounds that starkly contrasts with European law is the fair use defense of American copyright law.[23] European intellectual property specialists surely know that the U.S. Supreme Court held that home taping of television programs was fair use in its decision *Sony of America v. Universal City Studios*.[24] What Europeans may not know is how deeply economic is a prevalent rationale for this decision. The Supreme Court in *Sony* did not express its views on fair use in market failure terms, but in the aftermath of this decision, commentators have pointed out that the Court's ruling was justified, in economic terms, because the costs of having each individual with a VCR negotiate with all pertinent copyright owners for rights to make home copies from television broadcasts of their copyrighted programs far outweighed the returns likely to be obtained.[25] Because a market for home taping rights could not operate in an efficient way, fair use was, in the view of these commentators, a reasonable resolution to this dispute.

Economically minded American commentators also regard parody cases such as *Campbell v. Acuff-Rose Music, Inc.*[26] (in which fair use was raised in defense to a copyright claim based on Campbell's rap music parody of Roy Orbison's popular song 'Pretty Woman') as instances of market failure. Few copyright owners, the theory goes, will set a reasonable market price to license parody or critical commentary. This will thwart the operation of an efficient market in parodies.[27] Fair use can cure this market failure. Although parody exceptions exist in some national European authors' rights laws,[28] the existence of such exceptions in Europe is unlikely to be based on an economic rationale. Thus, even when U.S. and European law would reach the same result, they may do so for different reasons.

Nowhere has economic reasoning played a more substantial role in shaping the contours of the law than in cases attempting to define the proper scope of copyright protection for computer programs. In four major U.S. software copy-

[23] 17 U.S.C. sec. 107. See, e.g. Wendy J. Gordon, *Fair Use as Market Failure: A Structural and Economic Analysis of the Betamax Case and Its Predecessors,* 82 Colum. L. Rev. 1600 (1982); Merges, Friction, *supra* note 13 at 133.

[24] 464 U.S. 417 (1984).

[25] See, e.g. Gordon, *supra* note 23, at 1618.

[26] 510 U.S. 569 (1994).

[27] See, e.g. Robert P. Merges, *Are You Making Fun of Me? Notes on Market Failure and the Parody Defense in Copyright*, 21 AIPLA Q.J. 305 (1993).

[28] France, for example, has a codified parody exception, but it is often difficult to invoke because it requires a comic intent. See Geller & Nimmer, *supra* note 17 at § 8[2][a][iii].

right decisions discussed below, economic analysis played a particularly key role in the interpretation of copyright law. U.S. commentators have, for the most part, expressed approval for the use of economic analysis as an aid to interpretation of copyright rules, especially when, as in these cases, courts have been confronted with questions for which the copyright case law provided essentially no meaningful precedent.[29]

The trend of relying on economic reasoning in software copyright cases has not been without its critics, some of whom suggest that such an approach is inappropriate.[30] It is certainly true that reliance on economic reasoning can sometimes lead courts astray, as proved true in the *Whelan* case. Most commentators believe the errors in *Whelan* have been corrected by subsequent cases, such as *Altai*, *Sega* and *Borland*.[31] While European courts might reach the same conclusions as American courts in some of these cases, they might reach different conclusions in others. Even when reaching the same conclusion, European courts might well use different reasoning than the American courts. In particular, judges in European software copyright cases are far less likely than American judges to employ economic reasoning to justify their rulings in a particular case.

Whelan Associates v. Jaslow Dental Labs., Inc. was the first American appellate decision to consider whether the 'structure, sequence and organization' ('SSO') of computer programs could be protected by copyright law.[32] Because this decision was much discussed at the time the European Commission was working on the Directive on the Legal Protection of Computer Programs,[33] it

[29] See, e.g. Mark A. Lemley, *Convergence in the Law of Software Copyright?*, 10 High Tech. L.J. 1 (1995) [hereinafter Convergence]; Peter S. Menell, *An Analysis of the Scope of Copyright Protection for Application Programs*, 41 Stan. L. Rev. 1045 (1989); Glynn S. Lunney, Jr., *Essay Lotus v. Borland: Copyright and Computer Programs*, 70 Tul. L. Rev. 2397 (1996).

[30] See, e.g. Jane C. Ginsburg, *Comment: Four Reasons and a Paradox: The Manifest Superiority of Copyright Over Sui Generis Protection of Computer Software*, 94 Colum. L. Rev. 2559 (1994); Arthur R. Miller, *Copyright Protection for Computer Programs, Databases, and Computer-Generated Works: Is Anything New Since CONTU?*, 106 Harv. L. Rev. 977 (1993).

[31] See, e.g. Dennis S. Karjala, *A Coherent Theory for the Copyright Protection of Computer Software and Recent Judicial Interpretations*, 66 U. Cin. L. Rev. 53 (1997); Lemley, Convergence, *supra* note 29; Pamela Samuelson, *Fair Use for Computer Programs and Other Copyrightable Works in Digital Form: The Implications of Sony, Galoob and Sega*, 1 J. Intell. Prop. L. 49, 91–95 (1993).

[32] 797 F.2d 1222 (3rd Cir. 1986).

[33] See Council Directive 91/250 on the Legal Protection of Computer Programs, 1991 O.J. (L 122) 42 [hereinafter European Software Directive].

became a model U.S. software copyright decision that American officials hoped European law would emulate.[34] European policymakers were quite receptive to the idea of protecting structural design elements of programs, and the European Directive embodies this principle.[35]

The Third Circuit Court of Appeals in *Whelan* decided that 'SSO' was protectable under U.S. copyright law on both doctrinal and economic grounds. The doctrinal analysis relied on this syllogism: computer programs are literary works under U.S. copyright law, and since the structure, sequence and organization of literary works are generally protectable by copyright law, so the structure, sequence and organization of programs should be protected by copyright law as well.[36] This aspect of the *Whelan* analysis would likely resonate with European intellectual property specialists.[37]

Complementing this doctrinal analysis, however, was an economic argument that focused on the need for software developers to have sufficient protection to recoup development costs. A second economic concern was the locus of value in computer programs. Consider, for example, this excerpt from the *Whelan* decision:

> By far the larger portion of the expense and difficulty in creating computer programs is attributable to the development of the structure and logic of the program, and to debugging, documentation and maintenance, rather than to the coding. See Frank, Critical Issues in Software 22 (1983) (only 20% of the cost of program development goes into coding); Zelkowitz, Perspective on Software Engineering, 10 Computing Surveys 197–216 (June, 1978). See also InfoWorld, Nov. 11, 1985 at 13 ('the "look and feel" of a computer software product often involves much more creativity and often is of greater commercial value than the program code which

[34] See, e.g. Pamela Samuelson, *Comparing U.S. and EC Copyright Protection for Computer Programs: Are They More Different Than They Seem?*, 13 J.L. & Com. 279, 290–91 (1994).

[35] See, e.g. Bridget Czarnota & Robert J. Hart, *Legal Protection Of Computer Programs In Europe – A Guide To The EC Directive* 35–36 (Butterworths, 1991) (explaining that the protection of computer programs goes beyond the literal code and encompasses the 'structure, sequence and organization of the work as a whole').

[36] 797 F.2d at 1239–40.

[37] See, e.g. Czarnota and Hart, *supra* note 35 at 36: 'This is entirely in keeping with the jurisprudence, not only in the field of computer programs, but also of literary works more generally, where courts have found that protection of originality lies not only in the words used to express an idea, but in other elements which demonstrate the personal choice of the author, such as the detailed story line or plot.'

> implements the product ...'). The evidence in this case is that Ms. Whelan spent a tremendous amount of time studying Jaslow Labs, organizing the modules and subroutines for the Dentalab program, and working out the data arrangements, and a comparatively small amount of time actually coding the Dentalab program.[38]

The Third Circuit seems to have been persuaded to this position by a friend-of-the-court brief submitted by a software industry organization which argued that if copyright protection did not extend to the structure, sequence and organization of a program, the software industry would be jeopardized because the law would provide too little protection to induce an optimal level of investment in the development of computer programs.[39] The Third Circuit directly responded to this plea: 'The rule proposed here, which allows copyright protection beyond the literal computer code, would provide the proper incentive for programmers by protecting their most valuable efforts, while not giving them a stranglehold over the development of new computer devices that accomplish the same end.'[40]

Between 1986 and 1992, the *Whelan* decision was influential in subsequent U.S. cases, both in its doctrinal and economic reasoning.[41] The first decision to seriously challenge *Whelan*'s hegemony was *Computer Associates v. Altai, Inc.* in 1992.[42] On at least one important point, the Second Circuit Court of Appeals agreed with *Whelan*: the structure, sequence and organization of a program could, in an appropriate case, be protected by copyright law.[43] Unlike *Whelan*, which regarded program structure as exempt from infringement only when there was essentially no other way to structure the program,[44] the court in *Altai* reasoned that similarities in the structure of two programs might be due, for example, to functional constraints such as the need to develop a program that would interoperate with another program, efficiency considerations or use of the same standard programming techniques, none of which was protected by

[38] 797 F.2d at 1231.

[39] See Brief Amicus Curiae of ADAPSO, The Computer Software and Services Industry Association, Inc., *Whelan Associates, Inc. v. Jaslow Dental Laboratory, Inc.* (Civ. A. No. 85-1358) (1986).

[40] 797 F.2d at 1237.

[41] See, e.g. *Johnson Controls, Inc. v. Phoenix Control Systems, Inc.*, 886 F.2d 1173 (9th Cir. 1989); *Lotus Development Corp. v. Paperback Software Int'l*, 740 F. Supp. 37 (D. Mass 1990).

[42] 982 F.2d 693 (2nd Cir. 1992).

[43] See *id.* at 702–03.

[44] 797 F.2d at 1240.

copyright law.[45] The court in *Altai* directed that these and other unprotectable elements of programs be 'filtered out' before infringement analysis began[46] to ensure compliance with the directive of section 102(b) of the U.S. copyright statute, which states that '[i]n no case shall copyright protection for an original work of authorship extend to any idea, procedure, process, system, method of operation, concept, principle, or discovery, regardless of the form in which it is described, explained, illustrated, or embodied in such work'.[47] The court ultimately ruled that some structural similarities in *Altai* were attributable to the fact that both Computer Associates (CA) and Altai were developing programs to interoperate with the same three IBM operating system programs, and other structural similarities were to be expected in programs of that kind.[48] Hence, it affirmed the lower court's finding of noninfringement.

As in *Whelan*, the plaintiff and its amici predicted dire economic consequences for the software industry if courts did not provide strong protection to program structure. However, the Second Circuit took a different view than had the court in *Whelan*:

> [The Supreme Court's decision in] *Feist* teaches that substantial effort alone cannot confer copyright status on an otherwise uncopyrightable work. *** [D]espite the fact that significant labor and expense often goes into computer program flowcharting and debugging, that process does not always result in inherently protectable expression. Thus, *Feist* implicitly undercuts the *Whelan* rationale, 'which allow[ed] copyright protection beyond the literal computer code ... [in order to] provide the proper incentive for programmers by protecting their most valuable efforts ...'. [citation omitted]. We note that *Whelan* was decided prior to *Feist* when the 'sweat of the brow' doctrine still had vitality. In view of the Supreme Court's recent holding, however, we must reject the legal basis of CA's disincentive argument.[49]

The Second Circuit went on to offer some economic counterarguments to those made by CA and its amici:

> [W]e are unpersuaded that the test we approve today will lead to the dire consequences for the computer program industry that plaintiff and some amici predict. To the contrary, serious students of the industry have been highly critical of the sweeping scope of copyright protection engendered by the *Whelan* rule, in that it

45 982 F.2d at 708–11.
46 *Id*. at 707.
47 17 U.S.C. sec. 102(b).
48 982 F.2d at 710.
49 *Id*. at 711–12.

'enables first comers to "lock up" basic programming techniques as implemented in programs to perform particular tasks'.[50]

The Second Circuit warned that if courts heeded purely economic arguments for broadening the scope of copyright protection for computer programs, this would impair the integrity of copyright law:

> While incentive based arguments in favor of broad copyright protection are perhaps attractive from a pure policy perspective, *** ultimately, they have a corrosive effect on certain fundamental tenets of copyright doctrine. If the test we have outlined results in narrowing the scope of protection, as we expect it will, that result flows from applying, in accordance with Congressional intent, long-standing principles of copyright law to computer programs.[51]

The Second Circuit pointed out that patent protection might be a more suitable way to protect some program innovations than copyright.[52] If copyright proved to be too 'thin' to provide proper incentives to program developers, this was a matter for Congress, not the courts, to consider.[53]

A few months after the *Altai* decision, the Ninth Circuit Court of Appeals in the well-known decision, *Sega Enterprises, Ltd. v. Accolade, Inc.*, endorsed the *Altai* ruling and its approach to analyzing infringement in software copyright cases, thereby implicitly repudiating its earlier endorsement of *Whelan*.[54] Both *Altai* and *Sega* are significant developments, in part because they were the products of a judicial decisionmaking process that reached essentially the same legal conclusions on compatibility and decompilation issues as the European Commission and Council had reached in promulgating the software directive.

Altai and the European software directive both adopt the view that copyright protection is unavailable to elements of programs necessary for interoperation with other programs (that is, program interfaces).[55] Judged purely in terms of

[50] *Id.* at 712 (citation omitted).

[51] *Id.*

[52] *Id.*

[53] *See id.*

[54] 977 F.2d 1510 (9th Cir. 1992). The Ninth Circuit had endorsed *Whelan* in *Johnson Controls*. It repudiated its analysis in *Sega*, *id.* at 1524–25.

[55] 977 F.2d at 1527–28; European Software Directive, *supra* note 33 at 1.2. Note, however, that the exact status of interfaces under the Directive is not without uncertainty: see, e.g. Alan K. Palmer & Thomas C. Vinje, *The EC Directive On The Legal Protection Of Computer Software: New Law Governing Software Development*, 2 Duke J. Comp. & Int'l L. 65, 85 (1992): 'In general, as long as only the rules and methods of interoperability established by the interface are used and implemented

the creativity and judgment required to design them, program interfaces might initially seem to be 'original' enough to be protectable expression as a matter of copyright law.[56] However, once developed, program interfaces unquestionably constrain the design choices of subsequent programmers seeking to develop software capable of successfully interacting with an existing program.[57] The competition policy significance of protecting interfaces was recognized in Europe in part because the Competition Policy Directorate of the European Commission had taken action against IBM arising from its practice of changing interfaces in a manner that had exclusionary impacts on European developers of computer peripherals.[58] If European software developers were going to have a fair chance to compete with U.S. software in the European as well as the world market, these developers would need to be able to use interface information from American programs. The intervention of the Competition Policy Directorate in negotiations surrounding the drafting of the software directive resulted in these economic considerations being brought to bear on the contours of copyright protection for software in Europe.[59]

It is, of course, one thing for a legislative body to decide that competition policy considerations should narrow the scope of copyright protection for an original work of authorship. It may seem quite another thing for courts to use economic considerations in interpreting copyright law so as to narrow the scope of protection. However, this is not as aberrational in U.S. law as it would be in European law because of the judicially created 'merger' doctrine of U.S. copyright law.[60] If an idea is capable of being expressed in only one or a very limited number of ways, American judges will tend to regard the 'idea' and

independently in the program code, the program should be held to be noninfringing under the Software Directive. There is, however, one further twist: to make an interface work, meaning to make a product interoperable, it is sometimes necessary to use small portions of a program code that are very similar or identical to expressions found in the program code of existing copyrighted products. The Software Directive does not explicitly address this issue, and there is room for divergence among the member states' laws on this point. However, while the precise legal theory employed may vary from country to country, it seems likely that such similarities in expression will be deemed noninfringing.'

[56] See, e.g. Miller, *supra* note 30.

[57] *Altai*, F.2d at 710.

[58] See Palmer & Vinje, *supra* note 55, n. 34.

[59] *Id.* at 71–78.

[60] See, e.g. *Baker v. Selden*, 101 U.S. 99, 25 L. Ed. 841 (1879); *Morrissey v. Proctor & Gamble Co.*, 379 F.2d 675, 678–79 (1st Cir. 1967) (discussing 'merger doctrine').

'expression' in a work as having 'merged', and in order not to give an author a monopoly on that idea, judges will tend to give no or only the thinnest scope of protection to what would otherwise be protectable expression.[61] Other American cases have recognized that the existence of significant constraints on the design choices faced by subsequent authors may narrow the scope of copyright protection because authors in a constrained design space will tend to produce similar expression.[62] The merger and significant constraints doctrines are consistent with the utilitarian rationale for copyright protection in the U.S. that seeks to promote, as Professor Goldstein has put it, 'abundant' rather than 'efficient' expression: that is, a wide variety of new literary and artistic works.[63]

The unprotectability of program interfaces was not the only difficult interoperability-related issue that legal decision makers have had to confront. An equally, if not more difficult, question was whether to allow programmers to decompile or disassemble other firms' programs if necessary to get access to information needed to develop an interoperable program. This was a dicey issue for copyright law because the decompilation and disassembly process inevitably requires the making of a number of intermediate copies of the target program.[64] Such copies would seem to run afoul of the exclusive right that copyright law confers on authors to control the reproduction of their works in copies. Yet unless copyright law recognized at least a limited right to decompile or disassemble programs, the decision not to protect interface information would be significantly undermined. The plain fact is that although some software developers openly publish APIs (application programming interfaces) for their programs, many do not.[65] The willingness of program developers to license APIs to other firms varies considerably, and some firms only license APIs on terms that

[61] See, e.g. *Herbert Rosenthal Jewelry Corp. v. Kalpakian*, 446 F.2d 738, 742 (9th Cir. 1971).

[62] See, e.g. *Apple Computer, Inc. v. Microsoft Corp.*, 35 F.3d 1435 (9th Cir. 1994).

[63] Paul Goldstein, *Infringement of Copyright in Computer Programs*, 47 U. Pitt. L. Rev. 1119, 1123 (1986).

[64] See, e.g. Andrew Johnson-Laird, *Software Reverse Engineering In The Real World*, 19 U. Dayton L. Rev. 843 (1994).

[65] See, e.g. *Court's Findings of Fact, U.S. v. Microsoft*, 65 F.Supp.2d 1 (D.D.C. 1999) (No. Civ. 98-1232 (TPJ), Civ. 98-1233 (TPJ)) *available at* http://www.microsoft.com/presspass/trial/c-fof/ (detailing various instances in which Microsoft did not make its APIs publicly available).

some developers regard as unacceptable (e.g. giving up the right to make a version of the same program for other platforms).[66]

As with the interface issue, U.S. and European legal decision makers reached very similar results by very different means. Once again, the European decision was legislative, and the U.S. decision was the product of judicial interpretation of copyright law in the kind of case-by-case decisionmaking process that typifies the American common law tradition. As European readers will surely know, the European software directive mandates that member states provide a limited exception to the reproduction right to enable decompilation of computer programs when necessary for interoperability purposes.[67] *Sega v. Accolade* and companion U.S. decisions rely upon the U.S. fair use doctrine to reach the conclusion that no infringement occurs when a firm makes intermediate copies of programs for a legitimate reason such as to get access to information necessary to create an interoperable program.[68] Economic considerations undergird both decisions.

Because American fair use law is so foreign to the European intellectual property tradition, it may be instructive for European readers to see how economic reasoning can influence scope-of-copyright analysis in American case law, as it did in *Sega v. Accolade*.[69] To set the stage for this discussion, a brief overview of fair use law may be helpful.

The U.S. copyright statute now codifies the judicially created fair use doctrine. The fair use provision directs courts to consider four factors when determining whether a use is fair and therefore noninfringing: (1) the purpose and character of the defendant's use; (2) the nature of the copyrighted work; (3) the amount and substantiality of the defendant's appropriation; and (4) the harm, if any, to the actual or potential market for the copyrighted work if the use is determined to be fair.[70] All factors must be weighed together, and in a typical fair use case, some factors will weigh in favor of fair use and some against. European

[66] See, e.g. *Sony Computer Entertainment, Inc. v. Connectix Corp*, 53 U.S.P.Q.2d 1705 (9th Cir. 2000).

[67] European Software Directive, *supra* note 33, art. 6.

[68] See, e.g. *Sega*, 977 F.2d 1510, 1527–28; *Atari Games Corp. v. Nintendo of America Inc.*, 975 F.2d 832, 843 (Fed. Cir. 1992); *Connectix*, 53 U.S.P.Q.2d 1705.

[69] See also Julie E. Cohen, *Reverse Engineering and The Rise Of Electronic Vigilantism: Intellectual Property Implications of 'Lock-Out' Programs*, 68 S. Cal. L. Rev. 1091 (1995).

[70] 17 U.S.C. sec. 107. See generally, William F. Patry, *The Fair Use Privilege In Copyright Law* 2nd ed, 413–569 (Bureau of National Affairs, Washington D.C., 1995).

commentators sometimes criticize American fair use law because this balancing of factors can make fair use determinations somewhat unpredictable.[71] However, fair use decisions often fall into predictable patterns of analysis so that a well-informed person can judge whether a fair use defense has a reasonable chance of success in any particular case. Fair use also has the advantage of providing American copyright law with a flexible mechanism with which to adapt to unforeseen circumstances in an era of rapid technological change, as the *Sega v. Accolade* case itself demonstrates.[72]

With this background, let us consider the fair use defense in *Sega v. Accolade*. Sega persuaded the trial court that Accolade's disassembly of Sega's programs was not fair use because Accolade had a commercial purpose in performing it, namely to develop videogames that would compete in the market with Sega games.[73] Sega pointed out that the U.S. Supreme Court decision in *Sony Corp. of America v. Universal City Studios, Inc.* had said that courts should presume uses to be unfair if done for commercial purposes.[74] Although the U.S. Supreme Court later repudiated the presumption of unfairness when uses were commercial,[75] the Ninth Circuit decided that Accolade's commercial intent was not the only purpose-of-use consideration. On balance, the court decided that the purpose-of-use factor weighed in Accolade's favor, as this excerpt from the decision makes clear:

> The declarations of Accolade's employees indicate, and the district court found, that Accolade copied Sega's software solely in order to discover the functional requirements for compatibility with the Genesis console – aspects of Sega's programs that are not protected by copyright. 17 U.S.C. § 102(b). With respect to the video game programs contained in Accolade's game cartridges, there is no evidence in the record that Accolade sought to avoid performing its own creative work. Indeed, most of the games that Accolade released for use with the Genesis console were originally developed for other hardware systems. Moreover, with respect to the interface procedures for the Genesis console, Accolade did not seek to avoid paying a customarily charged fee for use of those procedures, nor did it simply copy Sega's code; rather, it wrote its own procedures based on what it had learned through disassembly. Taken together, these facts indicate that although Accolade's ultimate purpose was the release of Genesis-compatible games for sale,

[71] See, e.g. Herman Cohen Jehoram, Remarks at the ALAI Study Days (Sep. 14–17 1998).

[72] See, e.g. Samuelson, Fair Use, *supra* note 31 at 55.

[73] See 785 F. Supp. 1392, 1398, rev'd on appeal, 977 F.2d 1510 (9th Cir. 1992).

[74] 464 U.S. 417, 451, 104 S.Ct. 774, 793, 78 L.Ed.2d 574 (1984).

[75] *Campbell v. Acuff-Rose Music, Inc.*, 510 U.S. 569, 584 (1994).

> its direct purpose in copying Sega's code, and thus its direct use of the copyrighted material, was simply to study the functional requirements for Genesis compatibility so that it could modify existing games and make them usable with the Genesis console. Moreover, as we discuss below, no other method of studying those requirements was available to Accolade. On these facts, we conclude that Accolade copied Sega's code for a legitimate, essentially non-exploitative purpose, and that the commercial aspect of its use can best be described as of minimal significance.[76]

Thus did economic considerations, particularly the absence of evidence of unfair free-riding, come into play in the purpose-of-use analysis in *Sega v. Accolade*.

Sega's main argument concerning the nature-of-the-copyrighted-work factor was that Accolade had unfairly sought access to Sega's unpublished work, that is, to the source code form of Sega's program where interface information was to be found.[77] Here too, Sega relied upon an earlier U.S. Supreme Court decision for a presumption of unfairness. In *Harper & Row Pub. v. The Nation Enterprises, Inc.*, the Court had rejected *The Nation*'s fair use defense mainly because the magazine had published excerpts from Gerald Ford's as yet unpub-

[76] 977 F.2d at 1522–23. The court went on to say:

> We further note that we are free to consider the public benefit resulting from a particular use notwithstanding the fact that the alleged infringer may gain commercially. See *Hustler*, 796 F.2d at 1153 (quoting *MCA, Inc. v. Wilson*, 677 F.2d 180, 182 (2d Cir. 1981)). Public benefit need not be direct or tangible, but may arise because the challenged use serves a public interest. Id. In the case before us, Accolade's identification of the functional requirements for Genesis compatibility has led to an increase in the number of independently designed video game programs offered for use with the Genesis console. It is precisely this growth in creative expression, based on the dissemination of other creative works and the unprotected ideas contained in those works, that the Copyright Act was intended to promote. See *Feist Publications, Inc. v. Rural Tel. Serv. Co.*, 499 U.S. 340, 111 S. Ct. 1282, 1290, 113 L. Ed. 2d 358 (1991) (citing *Harper & Row*, 471 U.S. at 556–57). The fact that Genesis-compatible video games are not scholarly works, but works offered for sale on the market, does not alter our judgment in this regard. We conclude that given the purpose and character of Accolade's use of Sega's video game programs, the presumption of unfairness has been overcome and the first statutory factor weighs in favor of Accolade.

Id. at 1523.

[77] *Id.* at 1526 n. 9.

lished memoirs, thereby unfairly 'scooping' the right of first publication.[78] The Ninth Circuit contrasted the widespread availability of Sega programs with the unavailability of the Ford memoirs, no copy of which had been distributed to the general public at the time of *The Nation*'s publication of the excerpts.[79] The Ninth Circuit's analysis of the nature-of-the-work factor focused on the fact that decompilation or disassembly of a program was sometimes the only way to get access to information contained in the text of this kind of copyrighted work:

> If disassembly of copyrighted object code is per se an unfair use, the owner of the copyright gains a *de facto* monopoly over the functional aspects of his work – aspects that were expressly denied copyright protection by Congress. 17 U.S.C. § 102(b). In order to enjoy a lawful monopoly over the idea or functional principle underlying a work, the creator of the work must satisfy the more stringent standards imposed by the patent laws. [citation omitted] Sega does not hold a patent on the Genesis console. Because Sega's video game programs contain unprotected aspects that cannot be examined without copying, we afford them a lower degree of protection than more traditional literary works.[80]

Here too is evidence that the court considered the economic impact of a ruling in Sega's favor when analyzing the nature-of-the-copyrighted-work factor of fair use.

Sega met with more success in its argument on the third fair use factor. Making a copy of the whole of a copyrighted work, as typically occurs in the process of decompiling or disassembling a program, unquestionably weighs against fair use. Moreover, decompilation and disassembly typically involve making numerous copies of the program being studied. However, as the Ninth Circuit pointed out, the amount and substantiality of the taking is only one factor in the fair use determination and does not by itself dictate a finding that a use is unfair.[81] Moreover, the substantiality of the copying was undercut to some degree by the intermediate nature of the copies. That is, the copies were made in order to study the text of the program, not in order to extract expression from the Sega program for reuse in a competing work. The economic significance of these intermediate copies was minimal.[82]

The harm-to-the-market factor is often said to be the most important of the fair use factors.[83] Unsurprisingly, analysis of this factor is where economic reasoning tends to be most visible in fair use analysis. While harm to the market

[78] 471 U.S. at 553–55, 105 S.Ct. at 2226–28.

[79] 977 F.2d at 1526 n. 9.

[80] *Id.* at 1526.

[81] *Id.* at 1526–27.

[82] *Id.* at 1527.

[83] See *Harper & Row*, 471 U.S. at 566.

has sometimes been presumed in cases involving commercial uses of copyrighted works,[84] Sega did not rely on presumptions alone to argue that the fourth factor weighed against a finding of fair use. Rather, it insisted that the directly competitive nature of Accolade's programs would harm the actual or potential market for Sega's own games.[85] However, the Ninth Circuit took a different view of the harm factor.

> By facilitating the entry of a new competitor, the first lawful one that is not a Sega licensee, Accolade's disassembly of Sega's software undoubtedly 'affected' the market for Genesis-compatible games in an indirect fashion. *** [But] there is no basis for assuming that Accolade's 'Ishido' has significantly affected the market for Sega's 'Altered Beast', since a consumer might easily purchase both; nor does it seem unlikely that a consumer particularly interested in sports might purchase both Accolade's 'Mike Ditka Power Football' and Sega's 'Joe Montana Football', particularly if the games are, as Accolade contends, not substantially similar. In any event, an attempt to monopolize the market by making it impossible for others to compete runs counter to the statutory purpose of promoting creative expression and cannot constitute a strong equitable basis for resisting the invocation of the fair use doctrine.[86]

If Accolade's programs did harm the market for some Sega games because the consuming public found them to be more enjoyable than the Sega games, the court regarded this as the very kind of economic competition among noninfringing works that copyright law sought to promote.[87]

In *Sega* the Ninth Circuit considered more than the four statutory fair use factors in determining that decompilation or disassembly was fair use. The fair use provision makes clear that other factors can be considered in an appropriate case.[88] This excerpt reveals other factors on the court's mind:

> In determining whether a challenged use of copyrighted material is fair, a court must keep in mind the public policy underlying the Copyright Act. 'The immediate effect of our copyright law is to secure a fair return for an "author's" creative labor. But the ultimate aim is, by this incentive, to stimulate artistic creativity for the general public good.' Sony Corp., 464 U.S. at 432 (quoting *Twentieth Century Music Corp. v. Aiken*, 422 U.S. 151, 156 (1975)). When technological change has rendered an aspect or application of the Copyright Act ambiguous, 'the Copyright Act must be construed in light of this basic purpose.' Id. As discussed above, the

[84] See *supra* notes 73–78 and accompanying text.

[85] See *Sega*, 977 F.2d at 1523–24.

[86] *Id.*

[87] *Id.* at 1524.

[88] 17 U.S.C. sec. 107.

> fact that computer programs are distributed for public use in object code form often precludes public access to the ideas and functional concepts contained in those programs, and thus confers on the copyright owner a de facto monopoly over those ideas and functional concepts. That result defeats the fundamental purpose of the Copyright Act – to encourage the production of original works by protecting the expressive elements of those works while leaving the ideas, facts, and functional concepts in the public domain for others to build on.[89]

Neither Congress nor the National Commission on New Technological Uses of Copyrighted Works (CONTU) that recommended the use of copyright law to protect computer programs[90] had considered whether decompilation should be lawful for interoperability or other purposes, but the fair use doctrine provided a framework within which this question could be dealt with in a manner consistent with the underlying purposes of copyright law.[91] *Sega v. Accolade* is, in fact, one of several new technology cases to employ fair use as an adaptive mechanism for copyright law.[92]

[89] *Sega*, 977 F.2d at 1527.

[90] See National Commission on New Technological Uses of Copyrighted Works, Final Report (1978).

[91] The Ninth Circuit also rejected Sega's 'sweat of the brow' argument as inconsistent with *Feist*:

> Sega argues that the considerable time, effort, and money that went into development of the Genesis and Genesis-compatible video games militate against a finding of fair use. Borrowing from antitrust principles, Sega attempts to label Accolade a 'free rider' on its product development efforts. In *Feist Publications*, however, the Court unequivocally rejected the 'sweat of the brow' rationale for copyright protection. 111 S. Ct. at 1290–95. Under the Copyright Act, if a work is largely functional, it receives only weak protection. 'This result is neither unfair nor unfortunate. It is the means by which copyright advances the progress of science and art.' *Id.* at 1290; see also *id.* at 1292 ('In truth, "it is just such wasted effort that the proscription against the copyright of ideas and facts ... [is] designed to prevent."') (quoting *Rosemont Enterprises, Inc. v. Random House, Inc.*, 366 F.2d 303, 310 (2d Cir. 1966), cert. denied 385 U.S. 1009, 87 S. Ct. 714, 17 L. Ed. 2d 546 (1967)); *CAI*, 23 U.S.P.Q. 2d at 1257. Here, while the work may not be largely functional, it incorporates functional elements which do not merit protection. The equitable considerations involved weigh on the side of public access. Accordingly, we reject Sega's argument.

Sega, 977 F.2d at 1527.

[92] See also *Religious Technology Center v. Netcom On-Line Communication Services, Inc.*, 907 F.Supp 1361 (N.D. Cal. 1995); *Kelly v. Arriba Soft Corp.*, 77 F. Supp.2d 1116 (C.D. Cal. 1999); and cases cited in Samuelson, Fair Use, *supra* note 31.

Concerns about the monopolistic effects of an overbroad scope of copyright protection for computer programs also influenced the First Circuit Court of Appeals decision in *Lotus Dev. Corp. v. Borland Int'l, Inc.*[93] Lotus sued Borland because the latter's Quattro Pro (QP) program provided users with an 'emulation' interface allowing those accustomed to Lotus 1-2-3 to invoke the same commands to perform the same functions. Borland asserted that its incorporation of the Lotus command hierarchy into the QP emulation interface was necessary to enable users who had invested in constructing macros in the 1-2-3 macro command language to be able to continue to make use of these macros to perform previously specified sequences of spreadsheet functions. Reproducing the same commands in the same order was, as the trial judge had indicated in a previous ruling, 'a fundamental part of the functionality of the Lotus macro system'.[94] Borland argued that the Lotus macro system was the kind of 'system' that Congress had meant to make unprotectable when enacting section 102(b). Although the First Circuit agreed that users should be able to make use of macros constructed through use of Lotus 1-2-3, the First Circuit rejected Borland's 'system' argument, deciding instead that the Lotus command hierarchy was an unprotectable 'method of operation' under section 102(b).[95] Judge Stahl's majority opinion pointed out that users operate spreadsheet programs by invoking commands presented by the programs' user interface in much the same way as users operate VCRs by pushing buttons presented by that machine's user interface.[96]

Judge Boudin's concurring opinion in *Lotus v. Borland* made explicit some economic considerations that were implicit in Judge Stahl's opinion. Particularly of concern to him were the societal costs of 'mistakes' as to the scope of copyright protection in different kinds of cases.

[93] 49 F.3d 807 (1st Cir. 1995), aff'd by an equally divided court, 516 U.S. 233, 116 S.Ct. 804 (1996).

[94] *Lotus v. Borland*, 799 F.Supp. 203, 213 (D. Mass 1992) (quoting *Lotus v. Paperback*, 740 F.Supp. 37, 65 (D. Mass. 1990)). Once the court recognized the functionality of this command hierarchy, it became unprotected as a matter of American copyright law: see, e.g. Pamela Samuelson, *Computer Programs, User Interfaces, and Section 102(B) of The Copyright Act of 1976: A Critique of Lotus v. Paperback*, 55, Law & Contemp. Probs. 311, 333–34 (Spring 1992) ('This statement demonstrates that the court recognized that the structure of the commands was part of the Lotus macro system, which, if one was taking section 102(b) seriously, would need to be regarded as outside the bounds of copyright protection').

[95] 49 F.3d at 816.

[96] *Id.* at 817.

> Most of the law of copyright and the 'tools' of analysis have developed in the context of literary works such as novels, plays and films. In this milieu, the principal problem – simply stated, if difficult to resolve – is to stimulate creative expression without unduly limiting access by others to the broader themes and concepts deployed by the author. The middle of the spectrum presents close cases; but a 'mistake' in providing too much protection involves a small cost: subsequent authors treating the same themes must take a few more steps away from the original expression.
>
> The problem presented by computer programs is fundamentally different in one respect. The computer program is a means for causing something to happen; it has a mechanical utility, an instrumental role, in accomplishing the world's work. Granting protection, in other words, can have some of the consequences of patent protection in limiting other people's ability to perform a task in the most efficient manner. Utility does not bar copyright (dictionaries may be copyrighted), but it alters the calculus.[97]

Judge Boudin thought that 'the "cost" side of the equation may be different where one places a very high value on public access to a useful innovation that may be the most efficient means of performing a given task.'[98]

This thought led Judge Boudin to consider whether legal protection for the Lotus command hierarchy might better be provided by the patent system.

> Requests for the protection of computer menus present the concern with fencing off access to the commons in an acute form. A new menu may be a creative work, but over time its importance may come to reside more in the investment that has been made by users in learning the menu and in building their own mini-programs – macros – in reliance upon the menu. Better typewriter keyboard layouts may exist, but the familiar QWERTY keyboard dominates the market because that is what everyone has learned to use. [citation omitted] The QWERTY keyboard is nothing other than a menu of letters.
>
> Thus, to assume that computer programs are just one more new means of expression, like a filmed play, may be quite wrong. The 'form' – the written source code or the menu structure depicted on the screen – look hauntingly like the familiar stuff of copyright; but the 'substance' probably has more to do with problems presented in patent law or, as already noted, in those rare cases where copyright law has confronted industrially useful expressions. Applying copyright law to computer programs is like assembling a jigsaw puzzle whose pieces do not quite fit.
>
> * * *

[97] *Id.* at 819.
[98] *Id.*

> If Lotus is granted a monopoly on this pattern, users who have learned the command structure of Lotus 1-2-3 or devised their own macros are locked into Lotus, just as a typist who has learned the QWERTY keyboard would be the captive of anyone who had a monopoly on the production of such a keyboard. Apparently, for a period Lotus 1-2-3 has had such sway in the market that it has represented the de facto standard for electronic spreadsheet commands.[99]

Although Judge Boudin does not use the term 'network effects' to describe the 'lock-in' to a single product that can occur when users have invested a great deal in learning and using a particular command hierarchy, commentators on the *Borland* decision have used this term to explain the economic effects that broad copyright protection for program innovations such as command hierarchies may have.[100]

As long as the Lotus product was superior in design and functionality, Judge Boudin did not find it objectionable that Lotus should enjoy the benefits of these network effects. However, the Borland program had won numerous awards for its innovations. This caused the judge to think that 'if a better spreadsheet comes along, it is hard to see why customers who have learned the Lotus menu and devised macros for it should remain captives of Lotus because of an investment in learning made by the users and not by Lotus. Lotus has already reaped a substantial reward for being first; assuming that the Borland program is now better, good reasons exist for freeing it to attract old Lotus customers: to enable the old customers to take advantage of a new advance, and to reward Borland in turn for making a better product'.[101] For Judge Boudin, the question was not whether Borland should win the lawsuit, but on what basis. He considered whether the court should create a new privilege to allow significant improvements on existing software products, the nearest analog to which was the fair use doctrine.[102] However, Judge Boudin realized that creating a new privilege would produce problems of its own,[103] and ultimately concluded that the majority opinion had found a plausible way to achieve the desired result.[104]

It is difficult to know how a European court would rule on claims such as those presented by Lotus against Borland. The European software directive does

[99] *Id.* at 821.
[100] See, e.g. Mark Lemley and David McGowan, *Legal Implications of Network Economic Effects*, 86 Calif. L. Rev. 479 (1998).
[101] *Borland*, 49 F.3d at 821.
[102] *Id.*
[103] *Id.*
[104] *Id.* at 822.

not really address user interface issues.[105] Because Continental European nations tend to have a relatively high originality standard,[106] courts in these countries might conclude that a command hierarchy, particularly one that used many terms common to spreadsheet programs, would not qualify for protection. However, some creativity and judgment went into the design of the command hierarchy, perhaps enough to qualify for protection. Whether a macro compatibility defense based on the unprotectability of program elements necessary for interoperability would succeed is also difficult to predict.

Even if European courts reached the same result in *Lotus v. Borland*, they would be unlikely to do so for reasons given in either the Stahl or Boudin opinions. Some subsequent cases have followed the *Borland* ruling,[107] while others have questioned it.[108] What is noteworthy is that *Borland*, along with *Altai* and *Sega*, has validated drawing upon economic reasoning to consider how broad or narrow the scope of copyright should be for computer programs. Some American commentators suggest that economic analysis should more frequently be used in resolving a wide range of copyright matters.[109] Although economic analysis is unlikely to displace traditional doctrinal analysis in American copyright cases, increasing reliance on economic reasoning is likely to supplement traditional doctrinal analysis. Most American commentators would regard this as a healthy and positive development.[110]

105 See, e.g. Czarnota and Hart, *supra* note 35 at 39–43 (explaining that the explicit reference to interfaces that was included in article 1.3 of the Commission's Proposed Software Directive was removed from the final text of the European Software Directive, *supra* note 33, art. 1.3). Although user interfaces are mentioned in art. 1.2 of the Directive, they are referred to only as regards the general idea/expression distinction, which governs the eligibility for protection of all aspects of computer programs. See European Software Directive, *supra* note 33, art. 1.2.

106 See, e.g. Metaxas *supra* note 4; Hughes & Weightman, *supra* note 4.

107 See, e.g. *MiTek Holdings, Inc. v. Acre Engineering Co., Inc.*, 89 F.3d 1548, 1554 (11th Cir. 1996).

108 See, e.g. *Mitel, Inc. v. Iqtel, Inc.*, 124 F.3d 1366 (10th Cir. 1997).

109 See, e.g. Glynn S. Lunney, Jr., *Reexamining Copyright's Incentives-Access Paradigm*, 49 Vand. L. Rev. 483 (1996).

110 See, e.g. Stephen Breyer, *The Uneasy Case for Copyright: A Study of Copyright in Books, Photocopies, and Computer Programs,* 84 Harv. L. Rev. 281 (1970) (economic arguments should be employed to circumscribe the scope of and role for copyright in many industries); William W. Fisher, *Reconstructing The Fair Use Doctrine,* 101 Harv. L. Rev. 1659 (1988) (advocating the use of economics to determine the contours of the fair use defense).

3. CONSTITUTIONAL INFLUENCES IN AMERICAN COPYRIGHT LAW

Another respect in which American copyright law is distinguishable from European authors' rights laws is in the grounding of American copyright law in that nation's Constitution. The influence of the U.S. Constitution on American copyright law mainly comes from Article I, section 8, clause 8, which grants power to the Congress to enact legislation 'to promote the progress of science and useful arts by securing for limited times to authors and inventors the exclusive right in their respective writings and discoveries'. However, the First Amendment's free speech and free expression guarantees also have implications for the contours of copyright law in the United States.[111] At least two other constitutional provisions occasionally manifest themselves in copyright and other intellectual property disputes, namely the Supremacy Clause of the U.S. Constitution, which U.S. courts sometimes invoke to strike down state laws that conflict with federal law or policy,[112] and the Eleventh Amendment, which the Supreme Court recently decided limited the power of federal courts to order state governments to pay damages for infringement of federal intellectual property rights, such as copyright.[113]

The Constitution not only grants power to Congress enabling it to enact intellectual property legislation, but it also limits that power.[114] Rights, for example, can only be granted 'for limited times'.[115] Another check on constitutional power arguably lies in the purpose for which Congress can pass such legislation: to promote the progress of science and useful arts.[116] Courts have also perceived

[111] U.S. Const., 1st A. See, e.g. *Harper and Row Publishers, Inc. v. Nation Enterprises*, 471 U.S. 539 (1985) (considering 1st Amendment defense to claim of copyright infringement).

[112] See, e.g. *Vault Corp. v. Quaid Software Ltd*, 847 F.2d 255 (5th Cir. 1988) (refusing to enforce shrinkwrap license statute because it conflicted with federal copyright policy).

[113] *Florida Prepaid Postsecondary Educ. Expense Bd. v. College Sav. Bank*, 527 U.S. 627, 119 S.Ct. 2199 (1999).

[114] See, e.g. *Graham v. John Deere Co. of Kansas City*, 383 U.S. 1, 5 (1966) ('The clause is both a grant of power and a limitation.')

[115] U.S. Const. Art I, § 8, cl. 8. Eldred Press is relying on this provision as a basis for its challenge to the constitutionality of the Sonny Bono Copyright Term Extension Act. See *Eldred v. Reno*, 74 F.Supp.2d 1 (D.D.C. 1999) (rejecting challenge).

[116] This provision could be useful in challenging overbroad intellectual property legislation that would defeat the constitutional purpose. See, e.g. Thomas B.

the Constitution as limiting the class of persons eligible to qualify for exclusive rights. The U.S. Supreme Court in *Graham v. John Deere Co.* construed the Constitution as enabling Congress to grant exclusive rights only to 'inventors' of new technologies, not to mere incremental innovators.[117] More recently, the Supreme Court in *Feist Pub., Inc. v. Rural Telephone Service Co.* stated that Congress did not have constitutional power to protect unoriginal works under copyright law.[118] This decision has fueled much of the ongoing debate about whether the U.S. Congress can constitutionally enact legislation to create a *sui generis* form of protection to databases akin to that adopted by the European Union in its 1996 directive on the legal protection of databases.[119]

When European authors' rights specialists ruminate on the Supreme Court's *Feist* opinion, they may view the decision as an affirmation of the Continental European standard of originality and as a repudiation of the utilitarian 'sweat of the brow' rationale that had long been used to justify copyright in

Richards, *The Value of the Copyright Clause in Construction of Copyright Law*, 2 Hastings Const. L.Q. 221, 226 (1975) (copyright statutes should be interpreted to effectuate constitutional purpose of promoting science and the useful arts); Malla Pollack, *Unconstitutional Incontestability? The Intersection Of The Intellectual Property And Commerce Clauses Of The Constitution: Beyond A Critique Of Shakespeare Co. v. Silstar Corp*, 18 Seattle U. L. Rev. 259, 280 (1995) ('[In *Feist*] [t]he Court's dicta on time limitations reflects its insistence that the Intellectual Property Clause be interpreted in harmony with the stated purpose of the clause ... [t]o promote the Progress of Science and useful Arts') (internal quotations omitted). But see Kenneth J. Burchfiel, *The Constitutional Intellectual Property Power: Progress of Useful Arts and the Legal Protection of Semiconductor Technology*, 28 Santa Clara L. Rev. 473, 518–24 (1988) (Congress is not limited by statements of purpose in the Constitution).

117 See *Graham v. John Deere*, 383 U.S. at 11. This may help to explain why the U.S. does not have an industrial design law as such. *Cf.* J.H. Reichman, *Design Protection and the New Technologies: The United States Experience in a Transnational Perspective*, 19 U. Balt. L. Rev. 6, 13 (1991) ('[T]he *Sears-Compco* decisions of 1964 had ruled that neither state nor federal laws appealing to the misappropriation rationale could protect unpatented, non-copyrightable industrial designs against slavish imitation') (internal citations omitted).

118 499 U.S. 340 (1991).

119 See, e.g. Mark Powell, *The European Union's Database Directive: An International Antidote to The Side Effects of Feist?*, 20 Fordham Int'l L.J. 1215 (1997); European Parliament and Council Directive 96/9/EC of 11 March 1996 on the Legal Protection of Databases, 1996 O.J. L077/20 [hereinafter 'Database Directive'].

fact-intensive works in the U.S. and U.K.[120] The Supreme Court did, of course, reject 'sweat of the brow' copyrights when deciding that the white pages listings of telephone directories lacked sufficient creativity and judgment to qualify for copyright protection, thereby endorsing a creativity-based standard of originality. However, there were both statutory and constitutional reasons for the Court's decision that distinguish this American ruling from Continental European authors' rights concepts.[121] Not just once, but thirteen times, did the Court invoke the U.S. Constitution as a grounding of its decision.[122] The Court regarded the Constitution as requiring a creativity-based standard for originality; that is, in order for a compilation to be considered a 'writing', and for its compiler to be considered an 'author', under the Constitution, that work must evidence a modicum of human creativity or judgment.[123]

The Court also invoked the constitutional purposes of copyright law in explaining its rationale for rejecting 'sweat of the brow' copyrights:

[120] Several European countries, such as the United Kingdom, Ireland and the Netherlands, traditionally applied the 'sweat of the brow' doctrine. For example, in *BBC v. Magill*, it was held that the BBC's weekly programming schedules could not be reproduced by Magill because the work, skill and judgment required to produce the schedules was sufficient to qualify them for copyright protection. See *BBC v. Magill* [1990] I.L.R.M. 534. However, this was before adoption of the European database directive that standardizes E.U. copyright/authors' rights law on an intellectual creation standard. See Database Directive, *supra* note 119, art. 3.1.

[121] Three provisions of U.S. copyright law influenced the Court's decision in *Feist*. First, the Copyright Act of 1976 had defined the term 'compilation' in such a way that the only sensible interpretation was that Congress had intended to require creativity in selection or arrangement of data before a compilation could qualify for copyright protection. See 17 U.S.C. sec. 101 (definition of 'compilation'). Thus, it is not fair to construe the *Feist* opinion as deriving a creativity-based originality standard from natural law or the influence of authors' rights law more generally. Second, the Court relied significantly on 17 U.S.C. 102(b)'s exclusion of 'discoveries' from the scope of copyright protection to justify its assertion that facts – even a compilation of many of them – could not be protected by copyright law. Facts, the Court opined, are not 'original' to authors; rather they are 'discovered' and hence fall within section 102(b)'s prohibition. However questionable the Court's epistemology, it is unquestionably true that there is a unique American strain to this analysis. Third, 17 U.S.C. 103(a) states that copyright protection for a compilation does not confer in the author of a compilation any rights in the preexisting data contained therein.

[122] See Paul Goldstein, *Copyright*, 55 Law & Contemp. Probs. 79 (Spring 1992).

[123] 499 U.S. at 345.

> It may seem unfair that much of the fruit of the compiler's labor may be used by others without compensation. As Justice Brennan has correctly observed, however, this is not 'some unforeseen byproduct of a statutory scheme.' [citation omitted] It is, rather, 'the essence of copyright,' ibid., and a constitutional requirement. The primary objective of copyright is not to reward the labor of authors, but to 'promote the Progress of Science and useful Arts.' Art. I, sec. 8, cl. 8. *** To this end, copyright assures authors the right to their original expression, but encourages others to build freely upon the ideas and information conveyed by a work.[124]

Although saying that 'raw facts can be copied at will',[125] the Court nevertheless opined that unfair competition law was an appropriate way to protect fact compilers against certain market-destructive appropriations. It cited approvingly an earlier unfair competition ruling in *International News Service v. Associated Press* that had enjoined INS's misappropriation of news from early editions of AP newspapers that INS republished in competing newspapers without permission or compensation.[126]

The implications of the constitutional analysis in *Feist* for *sui generis* legislation to protect the contents of databases are obvious.[127] If the U.S. Congress lacks power under Article I, section 8, clause 8, to extend copyright protection to 'sweat of the brow' compilations, it presumably cannot achieve essentially the same result by creating a *sui generis* intellectual property regime to protect these compilations under that clause.[128] The Constitution, after all, does not mention copyright as the kind of law Congress can enact. Rather, it speaks of giving Congress power to confer exclusive rights on 'authors', and *Feist* has made clear that this term does not include compilers of 'sweat of the brow' works. The century-old *Trademark Cases*, which the Supreme Court cited approvingly in *Feist*, suggest that if Congress lacks power under Article I, section 8, clause 8, to enact legislation creating an intellectual property right as to a subject matter that cannot meet the substantive criteria of Article I, section 8, clause 8, it

124 *Id.* at 349–50.

125 *Id.* at 350.

126 248 U.S. 215 (1918).

127 See, e.g. Yochai Benkler, *Constitutional Bounds of Database Protection: The Role of Judicial Review in the Creation and Definition of Private Rights in Information*, 14 Berkeley Tech L. J. (2000); Malla Pollack, *The Right To Know?: Delimiting Database Protection At The Juncture of The Commerce Clause, The Intellectual Property Clause, and The First Amendment*, 17 Cardozo Arts & Ent. L.J. 47 (1999); J.H. Reichman and Pamela Samuelson, *Intellectual Property Rights In Data?*, 50 Vand. L. Rev. 51 (1997).

128 See Benkler, *supra* note 127.

cannot circumvent the substantive restrictions of that clause simply by invoking a different clause of the Constitution, such as the commerce clause.[129] An unfair competition-based legal regime could easily be justified under the commerce clause. However, there is some disagreement among American scholars over whether the commerce clause enables Congress to enact an intellectual property statute.[130]

The constitutional analysis in *Feist* helps to explain why the U.S. has struggled so much over legislative proposals to provide a new form of legal protection for the contents of databases akin to the *sui generis* right of the European database directive.[131] Shortly after the E.U. adopted this directive in 1996, a bill closely modeled on the *sui generis* right in that directive, H.R. 3531, was introduced in the House.[132] This bill would have been vulnerable to constitutional challenge based not only on Article I, section 8, clause 8, but also on the First Amendment.[133] To grant an exclusive right in the data in databases raises, for some American commentators, free speech and free expression concerns.

In response to these constitutional concerns, subsequent legislative proposals, including the currently pending H.R. 354, have sought to characterize themselves as unfair competition bills.[134] H.R. 354 is, for instance, known as 'The Collections of Information Antipiracy Act'. Instead of setting forth a set of exclusive rights along with certain limitations or exceptions to these rights, as intellectual property statutes would do, H.R. 354 states two 'prohibitions'

[129] 100 U.S. 82 (1879).

[130] *Cf.* Benkler, *supra* note 127 (taking a narrow view of constitutional power); Jane C. Ginsburg, *No 'Sweat'? Copyright And Other Protection Of Works Of Information After Feist V. Rural Telephone*, 92 Colum. L. Rev. 338 (1992) (arguing that Congress does have power to enact database legislation).

[131] See, e.g. Jonathan Band & Laura F.H. McDonald, *The Proposed EC Database Directive: The 'Reversal' of Feist v. Rural Telephone*, 9 Computer Law. 19 (June 1992); William S. Strong, *Database Protection After Feist v. Rural Telephone Co.*, 42 J. Copyright Soc'y U.S.A. 39 (1994); Paul T. Sheils & Robert Penchina, *What's All The Fuss About Feist? The Sky Is Not Falling on The Intellectual Property Rights of Online Database Proprietors,* 17 U. Dayton L. Rev. 563 (1992).

[132] See Database Investment and Intellectual Property Antipiracy Act of 1996, H. R. 3531, 104th Cong., 2nd Sess.

[133] See, e.g. Reichman & Samuelson, *supra* note 127 at 56.

[134] See Collections of Information Antipiracy Act, 106th Cong., 1st Sess. [hereinafter H.R. 354]. There was also a bill with the same title put forward in the previous Congress. See Collections of Information Antipiracy Act, H. R. 2652, 105th Cong., 2nd Sess.

(extracting all or a substantial part of another's compilation and making extracted information available to others) along with certain 'permitted acts' (e.g. extracting information for news reporting purposes).[135] It is, however, simple to restate the basic prohibitions and permitted acts of H.R. 354 in intellectual property terms, that is, as a grant of two exclusive rights, one to control the extraction of all or a substantial part of a database and the other to control making publicly available all or a substantial part of another's compilation, plus certain exceptions to these rights, such as that for news reporting. For this and other reasons, some American scholars regard H.R. 354 as an intellectual property law masquerading as an unfair competition law.[136] The principal alternative bill, H.R. 1858, would outlaw only the duplication of another person's database that the duplicator then sold or distributed in competition with the person who initially compiled that database.[137] H.R. 1858 would more clearly be constitutional as a regulation of unfair competition because it more closely resembles the *INS* decision that the Supreme Court cited approvingly in *Feist*.[138]

Database protection is only one of a number of issues attracting constitutional analysis from American copyright scholars. Some years ago, when the Third Circuit's *Whelan v. Jaslow* decision was influential, a copyright scholar warned that the broad scope of copyright protection envisioned there would chill free expression in the field of computer programming.[139] A number of scholars have warned that a broad interpretation of the derivative work right in American copyright law would have deleterious effects on free expression and free speech interests embodied in both the First Amendment and in Article I, section 8, clause 8.[140]

In addition, some scholars offer a constitutionally based explanation for much of fair use law because it enables reuse of portions of copyrighted works

135 See H.R. 354, *supra* note 133, sections 1402 (prohibitions) and 1403 (permitted acts).

136 See Benkler, *supra* note 127.

137 Consumer and Investor Access to Information Act of 1999, H. R. 1858, 106th Cong., 1st Sess.

138 Benkler, *supra* note 127.

139 See Alfred C. Yen, *A First Amendment Perspective On The Idea/Expression Dichotomy And Copyright In A Work's 'Total Concept And Feel'*, 38 Emory L.J. 393 (1989).

140 See, e.g. Neil Weinstock Netanel, *Copyright And A Democratic Civil Society*, 106 Yale L.J. 283, 301–03 (1996); Peter Jaszi, *Toward A Theory Of Copyright: The Metamorphoses Of 'Authorship'*, 1991 Duke L.J. 455, 459–61 (1991).

to promote free speech and free expression values.[141] Subsequent authors, the theory goes, need to be able to reproduce portions of earlier works in order to engage in critical commentary on those works, sometimes even to poke fun at other authors. Free speech/free expression values also explain why the moral rights provision in American copyright law for certain 'works of visual art' is subject to a fair use limitation.[142] Some American copyright scholars worry that a broad moral rights law would interfere with free speech and free expression values.[143] Some American scholars believe that the First Amendment's strong policy against prior restraints on speech should be respected more frequently in copyright cases, particularly at the preliminary injunction stage.[144] Too often, these authors argue, courts assume irreparable harm in copyright cases when it should be proven. Some American scholars also view constitutionally based free speech/free expression values as grounds for overriding provisions of shrinkwrap or clickthrough licenses for digital information insofar as they purport to waive fair use rights, forbid disclosure of flaws in the product, or bind the user not to criticize the product or service.[145]

Free speech/free expression values were also significant in Congressional repudiation of the Clinton Administration's proposal to make online service providers strictly liable for user infringement.[146] Congress heeded these concerns in structuring a set of 'safe harbor' rules for OSPs in the Digital

[141] See, e.g. Kwall, *supra* note 18 at 65–66.

[142] See 17 U.S.C. sec. 106A.

[143] See, e.g. Lawrence Adam Beyer, *Intentionalism, Art, and The Suppression of Innovation: Film Colorization and The Philosophy of Moral Rights*, 82 Nw. U. L. Rev. 1011, 1070–71 (1988).

[144] See, e.g. Mark A. Lemley & Eugene Volokh, *Freedom of Speech and Injunctions In Intellectual Property Cases*, 48 Duke L.J. 147 (1998).

[145] See, e.g. Charles R. McManis, *The Privatization (Or 'Shrink-Wrapping') of American Copyright Law*, 87 Calif. L. Rev. 173 (1999).

[146] See White Paper, *supra* note 20 at 120–24 (proposing strict liability). See also *WIPO Copyright Treaties Implementation Act; and Online Copyright Liability Limitation Act: Hearing on H.R. 2281 and H.R. 2280 Before the Subcomm. on Courts and Intellectual Property of the House Comm. on the Judiciary*, 105th Cong. (1997); Niva Elkin-Koren, *Copyright Law and Social Dialogue on The Information Superhighway: The Case Against Copyright Liability of Bulletin Board Operators*, 13 Cardozo Arts & Ent. L.J. 345 (1995) (arguing that a strict liability rule for operators of online services would chill free speech on the Internet); Pamela Samuelson, *The Copyright Grab*, WIRED, Jan. 1996, at 134 (raising free speech concerns about strict liability for online service providers).

Millennium Copyright Act (DMCA).[147] To a lesser degree, it heeded expressions of concern about threats to First Amendment values arising from DMCA provisions that outlawed the circumvention of technical protection systems used by copyright owners to protect their works.[148] At least one American scholar believes that the DMCA's anti-circumvention regulations are constitutionally deficient.[149]

Constitutional analysis may also be important in establishing boundaries between copyright and patent protection. This boundary is particularly vexing and unclear in respect of computer program innovations.[150] Economic reasons certainly exist for finding separate roles for patents and copyrights in the protection of computer program innovations.[151] Given the substantial disparity in the costs and difficulty in obtaining patents as compared with copyrights, the higher standards and shorter term of patents as compared with copyrights, the disclosure that patent law requires that copyright does not, and economic reasons for these and other distinctions between the copyright and patent systems, it is reasonable to conclude that if a programmer decides not to seek a patent on, for example, a new algorithm or functional design for a program – either because he does not think it is inventive enough to qualify or he wants to keep it secret – he should not be able to get copyright protection for it merely by claiming it is part of the expressive structure of his program.

This principle was thoughtfully explored in the famous 19th century *Baker v. Selden* case that, as will become evident, has constitutional underpinnings.[152] Selden published a series of books about a new bookkeeping system he had devised. After Baker published a work containing very similar ledger sheets to

[147] 17 U.S.C. sec. 512.

[148] 17 U.S.C. sec. 1201(c)(4).

[149] See Yochai Benkler, *Free as The Air To Common Use: First Amendment Constraints on Enclosure of The Public Domain*, 74 N.Y.U. L. Rev. 354 (1999).

[150] See, e.g. Pamela Samuelson, *Survey on the Patent/Copyright Interface for Computer Programs*, 17 AIPLA Q. J. 256 (1989) (discussing divergent views); *Brief Amicus Curiae Of Copyright Law Professors In Lotus Development Corp. v. Borland International, Inc.*, 3 J. Intell. Prop. L. 103 (1995) (discussing the need for separate domains for patent and copyright protection for computer program innovations) available at http://www.lawsch.uga.edu/~jipl/vol3/brief.html [hereinafter Copyright Professors' Brief].

[151] See, e.g. Dennis S. Karjala & Peter S. Menell, *Brief Amicus Curiae Applying Fundamental Copyright Principles To* Lotus Development Corp. v. Borland International, Inc., 10 High Tech. L.J. 177, 182–86 (1995).

[152] 101 U.S. 99 (1879).

those in Selden's books, Selden sued for copyright infringement and won at the trial court level. Selden claimed that 'the ruled lines and headings, given to illustrate the system, are part of the book and, as such, are secured by the copyright; and that no one can make or use similar ruled lines and headings, or ruled lines and headings made and arranged on substantially the same system, without violating the copyright.'[153] The Court found this contention difficult to accept:

> There is no doubt that a work on the subject of book-keeping, though only explanatory of well-known systems, may be the subject of copyright; but then it is claimed only as a book. Such a book may be explanatory either of old systems, or of an entirely new system; and considered as a book, as the work of an author, conveying information on the subject of book-keeping, and containing detailed explanations of the art, it may be a very valuable acquisition to the practical knowledge of the community. But there is a clear distinction between the book, as such, and the art which it is intended to illustrate. *** A treatise on the composition and use of medicines, be they old or new; on the construction and use of ploughs, or watches, or churns; or on the mixture and application of colors for painting or dyeing; or on the mode of drawing lines to produce the effect of perspective, would be the subject of copyright; but no one would contend that the copyright of the treatise would give the exclusive right to the art or manufacture described therein. *** To give the author of the book an exclusive property in the art described therein, when no examination of its novelty has ever officially been made, would be a surprise and fraud upon the public. That is the province of letters-patent, not of copyright.[154]

The Court's concern about separate domains for patent and copyright law was apt in *Baker v. Selden* because Selden had, in fact, sought to patent his book-keeping system. Baker's lawyer argued that this demonstrated that the book-keeping system was a contribution to the 'useful arts', and hence was properly protected by patent law, not by copyright.[155] This argument evidently resonated with the Court.

The Supreme Court's decision in *Baker v. Selden* implicitly embodies a constitutionally based rationale for keeping the domains of copyright and patent separate. Recall that Article I, section 8, clause 8, empowers Congress to enact

[153] *Id.* at 101.

[154] *Id.* at 101–02. See also Pamela Samuelson, Baker v. Selden: Sharpening the Distinction Between Authorship and Invention in *Intellectual Property Stories* (Jane C. Ginsburg & Rochelle Cooper Dreyfuss, eds. 2006) (discussing Baker litigation and appeal).

[155] See John Shepard Wiley, Jr., *Copyright At The School of Patent*, 8 U. Chi. L. Rev. 119, 168 (1991).

laws 'to promote the progress of science and useful arts by securing for limited times to authors and inventors the exclusive right in their respective writings and discoveries'. One common interpretation of this clause holds that it conveniently embodies two separate rules: one granting Congress power to give exclusive rights to 'authors' in their 'writings' in order to promote 'science' (that is, knowledge), and the other giving Congress power to confer exclusive rights on 'inventors' as to their 'discoveries' in order to promote 'useful arts' (that is, technology).[156] The word 'respective' in the constitutional clause strongly supports the view that an author's writings and an inventor's useful discoveries are separate classes of innovations. This bifurcated understanding of the constitutional realms of patent and copyright law is evident in *Baker v. Selden*. Under the Supreme Court's analysis in *Baker v. Selden*, it is doubtful, for example, that Congress would have constitutional power to extend copyright protection to medicines, ploughs or bookkeeping systems, even if these innovations were embodied in writings, because the Court conceptualized them as 'useful arts' that the Constitution had consigned to the patent domain.[157]

Conflicts about the domain of patents and copyrights generally do not arise in the U.S. because the subject matter provisions of patent and copyright law are quite distinct. Mechanical devices, for example, do not qualify for copyright protection in the U.S. because even if original in a copyright sense, they have functions beyond the conveying of information or displaying of an appearance that render them ineligible for copyright protection as useful articles.[158] Consistent with *Baker v. Selden*, a special provision of U.S. copyright law makes clear that the copyright in a drawing of a useful article does not confer rights to control manufacture of the useful article depicted therein.[159] Mechanical devices do, however, qualify as 'machines' under the subject matter provision of U.S. patent law.[160]

If patent and copyright laws have separate domains in the legal protection of other innovations, it would seem they should also have separate domains in the protection of computer program innovations. The text of a computer program may be an 'original work of authorship' that qualifies for copyright protection.[161] However, algorithms and other functional designs embodied in program

[156] See, e.g. *Burrow-Giles Lithographic Co. v. Sarony*, 111 U.S. 53, 56 (1884).

[157] See *Taylor Instrument v. Fawley-Brost Co.*, 139 F.2d 98 (7th Cir. 1943) (rejecting copyright claim in chart because patent on it had expired).

[158] See 17 U.S.C. sec. 101 (definitions of 'pictorial, sculptural, and graphic works' and of 'useful article').

[159] 17 U.S.C. sec. 113(b).

[160] 35 U.S.C. sec. 101.

[161] 17 U.S.C. sec. 102(a).

texts should be protectable, if at all, through the patent system, even though they can be described as components of the structure, sequence and organization of programs.[162] Such a conclusion is especially appropriate under U.S. law because section 102(b) directs that courts exclude 'processes, procedures, systems, [and] methods of operation' from the scope of copyright protection'.[163] But even before this exclusion was made part of the U.S. copyright statute, the constitutional backdrop of the American copyright and patent traditions and the analysis in *Baker v. Selden* provided courts with ample reason to exclude processes and systems from the scope of copyright protection.[164]

Although the constitutional analysis discussed in this section may seem quite strange to Europeans, it is characteristic of American discourse on intellectual property matters. American scholars pay attention to the Constitution in part because they perceive the founders to have imposed certain limits on Congressional power – for example, limiting Article I, section 8, clause 8, to 'authors' and 'inventors' – to ward off possible repetition of historical experiences preceding the Constitution in which copyright and patent powers had been abused. At one time, monopolistic publishers claimed perpetual rights to control over the printing of ancient as well as new works, and monopolistic patent holders claimed exclusive rights to control the manufacture of well-known items. The Statute of Anne in 1710 repudiated the unwarranted copyright claims, conferring a short period of rights only on writers of new works,[165] just as the Statute of Monopolies in 1623 repudiated the unwarranted patent claims, limiting the power of the sovereign to confer patents only for inventions in the useful arts.[166] By speaking of 'authors' and 'inventors' in the Constitution, the founders wanted to ensure that the economic problems that had once beset the patent and copyright systems in England did not recur in the U.S. There is a strong resonance between the utilitarian tradition discussed in Section 2 of this essay and the constitutional tradition discussed in this section. This should

[162] See, e.g. Copyright Professors' Brief, *supra* note 150 (patentability of algorithms and other functional program designs may make copyright protection for them inappropriate).

[163] 17 U.S.C. sec. 102(b). See also Copyright Professors' Brief, *supra* note 150 (discussing *Baker v. Selden* and section 102(b)).

[164] See, e.g. *id.*

[165] See, e.g. Patterson, Free Speech, *supra* note 12 at 25.

[166] See, e.g. E. Wyndham Hulme, *The History of the Patent System Under the Prerogative and at Common Law*, 12 L.Q.R 141 (1896) *cited in* Robert Merges, *Patent Law & Policy*, 2nd edition, 6 (Michie, 1997).

not be surprising given that the U.S. Constitution is a profoundly economic document.[167]

4. CONCLUSION

European intellectual property specialists may perceive that American copyright law is moving towards convergence with European authors' rights laws in some significant respects. Formalities, such as requiring copyright notices on all published copies of protected works, although not entirely eradicated from U.S. copyright law, are nevertheless on the wane.[168] The U.S. Congress has amended copyright law in ways that conform to rules in authors' rights jurisdictions, for example restoring copyrights to foreign nationals who had lost their rights because of a failure to comply with U.S. formalities, extending copyright protection to architectural works, and adopting moral rights protection for works of visual art.[169] Certain judicial decisions, such as the U.S. Supreme Court's decision in *Feist*, have also reached conclusions in accord with European precepts.

However, it may be inaccurate to interpret these signs of convergence as presenting an unwavering trajectory towards authors' rights law. The utilitarian rationale for American copyright law remains strong in American copyright law, and manifests itself in many domains, such as the work for hire doctrine, the fair use doctrine and the narrow scope of moral rights law. Because they are grounded in economic thinking, these doctrines are among the features of American copyright law that are quite unlikely to change towards the European authors' rights model. Courts in the U.S. are also employing economic reasoning in interpreting the proper scope of copyright protection for computer programs. This may prefigure a wider use of economic reasoning in American copyright cases.

[167] See, e.g. Charles A. Beard, *An Economic Interpretation of the Constitution of the United States* (1935 ed.).

[168] Registration is no longer required for non-U.S. works, but failure to register affects the remedies available in an infringement suit. See 17 U.S.C. secs 411 (U.S. works must be registered to bring an infringement suit), 412 (only registered works qualify for attorney's fees and statutory damages).

[169] See, e.g. 17 U.S.C. secs 104A (restored copyrights); 101, 102(a)(8) (architectural works); 106A (moral rights for certain works).

In addition, the U.S. Constitution imposes an intellectual framework on the thinking of American intellectual property specialists that differs profoundly from the conceptual framework of authors' rights laws. The main constitutional provision that influences American copyright law is Article I, section 8, clause 8, which grants power to the U.S. Congress to enact legislation to give exclusive rights to authors and inventors. However, the First Amendment and certain other constitutional provisions affect copyright rulings in some circumstances. Because the Constitution is such a seminal document in the United States' legal tradition, constitutional influences on American copyright law seem likely to abide over time.

The principal goal of this essay has been to acquaint European intellectual property specialists with two interrelated influences – economics and the Constitution – that affect the formation and interpretation of American copyright law. Even if European readers do not agree or sympathize with American thinking, perhaps they will, after reading this essay, be somewhat less mystified about the American mindset about copyright law. If our laws do not converge completely, perhaps we can try to understand one another's perspectives better.

POSTSCRIPT

No better illustration of the substantial differences between American and European perspectives on copyright law can be found than the controversy that erupted after the initial writing of this essay over copyright term extensions in the U.S. From an authors' rights perspective, a legislative decision to extend the term of existing copyrights from fifty years after the death of the author to seventy years *post mortem* is unexceptional and unobjectionable.[170] To justify such a decision, it is not even necessary to invoke economic arguments, such as greater incentives for authors to produce new works based on legislative assurances that commercially valuable works will produce a longer revenue stream to support relatives whose life expectancies exceed the old Berne Convention norm.[171] In the EU, the 1993 decision to lengthen the copyright terms was principally justified on a principle of 'harmonizing up'.[172] Germany had adopted the longer term some years before, and rather than requiring German authors to give up

[170] See Council Directive 93/98/EEC of 29 October 1993 *Harmonizing the Term of Protection of Copyright and Certain Related Rights*, 1993 O.J L290/9 (extending EU copyright terms).

[171] But see Recital 5 (offering a partial economic justification).

[172] *Id.*, Recitals 6–11.

longer terms, the EU decided that the German term should become the EU standard.[173]

A parallel effort to lengthen copyright terms in the United States met with considerable resistance on both economic and constitutional grounds. Lengthening the term for works already in existence was unjustifiable, said economists, given that legal incentives to create these works had already achieved the desired objective.[174] For works yet to be created, economists theorized that an extra twenty year term, when discounted for present value, could not meaningfully contribute to incentives to engage in authorship.[175] Some scholars raised constitutional concerns to copyright term extensions, among them Peter Jaszi, who observed that in the late 20th century, Congress had repeatedly extended terms, raising the specter of 'perpetual copyrights on the installment plan'.[176] However, the U.S. Congress eventually extended copyright terms by twenty years under the Copyright Term Extension Act of 1998.[177]

Eric Eldred, an Internet-based publisher of public domain materials, challenged the constitutionality of the CTEA under Article I, section 8, clause 8, and under the First Amendment.[178] Eldred argued that the CTEA violated the Intellectual Property Clause because it conferred twenty years of exclusive rights upon owners of existing copyrights without the *quid pro quo* of a newly created work of authorship to justify it.[179] Eldred argued also that the CTEA violated the First Amendment because it abridged a very considerable amount of speech by those who wanted to republish and make derivatives of works that but for the

[173] See Dennis S. Karjala, *Judicial Review of Copyright Term Extension Legislation*, 36 Loyola L. Rev. 199, 207, n. 31 (2002) (discussing German law and harmonization).

[174] See, e.g. Brief Amicus Curiae of George Akerlof et al., to the U.S. Supreme Court in *Eldred v. Ashcroft*, available at http://eldred.cc/legal/supremecourt.html (cited hereinafter as Akerlof Amicus). See also Karjala, *supra* note 173, at 206–22 (reviewing testimony before Congress pertaining to CTEA); Richard A. Epstein, *The Dubious Constitutionality of the Copyright Term Extension Act*, 36 Loyola L. Rev. 123 157–58 (2002) (objecting to the CTEA as a Congressional 'giveaway').

[175] See *Eldred v. Ashcroft*, 123 S.Ct. at 807–08 (Breyer dissent, discussing Akerlof Amicus Brief).

[176] See Statement of Professor Peter Jaszi, Washington College of Law, American University, On S. 4839. The Copyright Term Extension Act of 1995, Before the Senate Judiciary Committee, Sept. 20, 1995.

[177] Pub. L. No. 105–298, 112 Stat. 2827 (1998).

[178] See *Eldred v. Reno*, 74 F. Supp.2d 1 (D.D.C. 1999), aff'd 239 F.3d 372 (D.C. Cir. 2001), aff'd sub nom. *Eldred v. Ashcroft*, 123 S.Ct. 769 (2003).

[179] *Id.* at 784–87 (discussing Eldred's *quid pro quo* theory).

CTEA would be in the public domain.[180] No important government purpose supported this law; nor was the law narrowly tailored.[181] Eldred's lawyer Lawrence Lessig wove together economic and constitutional arguments in support of these claims on the theory that the Framers intended to constrain Congressional power to grant limited monopolies to those that were economically justifiable.[182]

The U.S. Supreme Court created a flurry of speculation when it decided to hear Eldred's appeal of an appellate court ruling rejecting his constitutional arguments.[183] The Court received a large number of amicus curiae (friend of the court) briefs from a wide range of persons and organizations. Filing in support of Eldred were, among others, seventeen economists (including five Nobel Prize winners), five prominent First Amendment scholars, the National Writers Union and some of its individual members, the Computer & Communications Industry Association, the Internet Archive, a College Art Association, some individual historians and historical organizations, and a substantial number of intellectual property professors.[184] Copyright industry organizations, including the Motion Picture Association of America, the Recording Industry Association of America, the Association of American Publishers, AOL Time Warner, the estates of some deceased famous authors, Senator Hatch and Representative Sensenbrenner were among those who supported General Ashcroft.[185] European intellectual property professionals who wish to know more about American discourse on copyright law will find in the *Eldred* briefs a virtual treasure trove of constitutional analyses of intellectual property law.

Viewed from one angle, the *Eldred* case presents a narrow issue of very little significance because copyright term extensions are relatively rare and the extra costs the extensions impose on the public, while substantial in aggregate, are

[180] Brief for Petitioners to the U.S. Supreme Court in *Eldred v. Ashcroft*, available at http://eldred.cc/legal/supremecourt.html, at 35–47.

[181] *Id.* at 45–47. Eldred's First Amendment theory relied heavily on *Turner Broadcasting System, Inc. v. FCC*, 512 U.S. 622 (1994) as establishing the intermediate scrutiny standard under which content-neutral laws that abridge speech are typically judged. This standard requires the government to show that an important purpose underlies the law and that the law be narrowly tailored to accomplish this purpose. *Id.* at 675–76.

[182] Brief for Petitioners, *supra* note 180, at 9–10.

[183] See, e.g. Amy Harmon, *Case Could Shift the Balance in Debate Over Public Domain*, N.Y. Times, Feb. 20, 2002, at C7; Steven Levy, *Glitterati v. Geeks*, Newsweek, Oct. 14, 2002.

[184] These briefs are available at http://eldred.cc/legal/supremecourt.html.

[185] These briefs too are available at http://eldred.cc/legal/supremecourt.html.

nevertheless diffuse and relatively invisible.[186] Viewed from another angle, the *Eldred* case could not be more significant. The government argued in *Eldred* that Congress has virtually unfettered power to enact intellectual property legislation under the Intellectual Property Clause, whereas Eldred argued that the Clause imposes significant limitations on Congressional power.[187] Whether the CTEA should be subject to rational basis review or to some form of heightened scrutiny was squarely presented in the *Eldred* case.[188] The Court's answer to the standard of review question was certain to have significant implications for other potential constitutional challenges to intellectual property rules.

Among the other important questions discussed in the *Eldred* briefs were these: If Congress does not have power to enact a particular intellectual property law under the Intellectual Property Clause, can it invoke its Commerce Clause powers instead?[189] Or does Congress' power to regulate foreign commerce allow it to enact legislation that could not be justified under the Intellectual Property Clause?[190] Are Congressional judgments under the Intellectual Property Clause categorically immune from First Amendment challenges, as the D.C. Circuit opined?[191] If not, must Congressional judgments about intellectual property rules be subject to strict scrutiny analysis insofar as they favor one set of speakers (e.g. Walt Disney and other major content industry firms) to the detriment of others (e.g. Eric Eldred and his fellow plaintiffs)?[192] Or should intermediate First Amendment scrutiny be applied to the CTEA, given that this law, although content-neutral (i.e. all existing terms were extended), restricts the free speech/press rights of Eldred and his fellow plaintiffs who want to make public

[186] See *Eldred v. Ashcroft*, 123 S.Ct. at 804 (citing a study estimating that the CTEA would result in a transfer of 'several billion extra royalty dollars' to copyright owners) (Breyer dissent).

[187] See Brief for Respondents to the U.S. Supreme Court in *Eldred v. Ashcroft*, available at http://eldred.cc/legal/supremecourt.html.

[188] See Reply Brief of Petitioners to the U.S. Supreme Court in *Eldred v. Ashcroft*, available at http://eldred.cc/legal/supremecourt.html (discussing heightened scrutiny standards). See also Epstein, *supra* note 174 (discussing rationale for heightened scrutiny rules).

[189] See, e.g. Brief Amicus Curiae of Intellectual Property Owners to the U.S. Supreme Court in *Eldred v. Ashcroft*, available at http://eldred.cc/legal/supremecourt.html. This issue is of particular significance for EU-style database legislation in the U.S.

[190] See, e.g. Brief Amicus Curiae of International Coalition for Copyright Protection to the U.S. Supreme Court in *Eldred v. Ashcroft*, available at http://eldred.cc/legal/supremecourt.html.

[191] See *Eldred v. Reno*, 239 F.3d at 375.

[192] See Reply Brief, supra note 187, at 15.

domain works available to the public or create new works from existing ones (as Disney has so imaginatively done as to public domain fairytales)?[193]

The Supreme Court issued its decision in *Eldred* in January 2003, addressing some, but not all, of the constitutional questions posed in the briefs. The Court held that enactment of the CTEA was within the broad powers of Congress under Article I and did not run afoul of the First Amendment.[194] Speaking for a seven Justice majority, Justice Ginsburg observed that '[t]o comprehend the scope of Congress' power under the Copyright Clause, "a page of history is worth a volume of logic"'.[195] Congress had extended the terms of existing copyrights, as well as of patents, numerous times in the past two centuries, including in 1790.[196] 'Thus, history reveals an unbroken congressional practice of granting to authors of works with existing copyrights the benefit of term extensions so that all under copyright protection will be governed evenhandedly under the same regime.'[197] Moreover, the new terms established by the CTEA – life of the author plus seventy years or ninety-five years from first publication for corporate-authored works – were, literally speaking, for 'limited Times',[198] and there was, the Court concluded, 'no cause to suspect that a purpose to evade the "limited Times" prescription prompted Congress to adopt the CTEA'.[199] Calibrating economic impacts of copyright legislation was, in the Court's view, a task the Constitution assigned to Congress.[200] Courts are 'not at liberty to second-guess congressional determinations and policy judgments ... however debatable or arguably unwise they may be'.[201] As for the First Amendment claim, the Court viewed copyright's fair use defense as 'generally adequate' to resolve tensions between copyright and free speech interests, including those posed by people such as Eldred who wished to republish other people's speech.[202]

193 *Id.* at 16 (pointing to Disney's use of public domain works).

194 *Eldred v. Ashcroft*, 123 S.Ct. 769, 777–78 (2003). Justices Stevens and Breyer dissented and wrote separate opinions expressing their views, the former offering an alternative historical and constitutional analysis than the majority, and the latter mainly focusing on the economic effects of the CTEA. See *id.* 790–801 (Stevens dissent) and 801–15 (Breyer dissent).

195 *Id.* at 778, quoting *New York Trust Co. v. Eisner*, 256 U.S. 345, 349 (1921).

196 *Eldred v. Ashcroft*, 123 S.Ct. at 775–76 (discussing copyright extensions), 779–80 (discussing patent extensions).

197 *Id.* at 778.

198 *Id.*

199 *Id.*

200 *Id.* at 782–83.

201 *Id.* at 783.

202 *Id.* at 789–90.

American intellectual property and constitutional law scholars will undoubtedly be debating the *Eldred* decision and its implications for many years. Already in the litigation pipeline is a constitutional challenge to the 'restoration' of foreign copyrights for works that were in the public domain for many years for failure to comply with statutory formalities.[203] This challenge stands a better chance than Eldred's challenge to the CTEA for two reasons: first, there is no historical precedent for this action, and second, the Supreme Court has repeatedly stated that the Constitution forbids grants of exclusive rights to that which is in the public domain.[204] Also challenged on constitutional grounds are the Digital Millennium Copyright Act's anti-circumvention provisions[205] because these rules grant exclusive rights of unlimited duration, without requiring either a showing of originality or invention, and without fair use-like limitations to accommodate First Amendment interests.[206] If Congress or one or more states enact EU-style database legislation, this will almost certainly be challenged on constitutional grounds as well.[207] Whether courts rebuff or embrace these challenges, American discourse on copyright law and policy will almost certainly continue to be influenced, even if somewhat erratically, by economic and constitutional learning. Thus, convergence of American copyright law with European authors' rights conceptions is still a long way off.

[203] *Luck's Music Library v. Gonzales*, 407 F. 3d 1262 (D.C. Cir. 2005) (rejecting constitutional challenges to restoration of foreign copyrights).

[204] See, e.g. *Graham v. John Deere Co.*, 383 U.S. 1, 5–6 (1966).

[205] See 17 U.S.C. sec. 1201. Among the many articles questioning the constitutionality of the DMCA anti-circumvention provisions are: Craig Allan Nard, *The DMCA's Anti-Device Provisions: Impeding the Progress of the Useful Arts*, 8 Wash. U. J. L. & Pol'y 19, 34–35 (2002); L. Ray Patterson, *The DMCA: A Modern Version of the Licensing Act of 1662*, 10 J. Intell. Prop. L. 33, 57 (2002); Eugene R. Quinn, *An Unconstitutional Patent in Disguise: Did Congress Overstep Its Constitutional Authority in Adopting the Circumvention Prevention Provisions of the Digital Millennium Copyright Act?*, 41 Brandeis L.J. 33, 37 (2002). See also Benkler, *supra* note 149; Glynn S. Lunney, *The Death of Copyright: Digital Technology, Private Copying, and the DMCA*, 87 Va. L. Rev. 813, 910–11 (2001). One judge has, however, rejected an Article I, sec. 8, cl. 8, challenge to the DMCA. See *United States v. Elcom, Ltd.*, 203 F. Supp.2d 1111, 1127–42 (N.D. Cal. 2002).

[206] See, e.g. Brief Amicus Curiae of Intellectual Property Professors, 321 Studios, available at http://www.law.georgetown.edu/faculty/jec/2600ipprofsamicus.htm.

[207] See *supra* notes 131–38 and accompanying text for a discussion of the U.S. debate over the constitutionality of EU-style database legislation.

Index